New Castle New Hampshire

Vital Records

1891–1997

Richard P. Roberts

HERITAGE BOOKS
2015

HERITAGE BOOKS

AN IMPRINT OF HERITAGE BOOKS, INC.

Books, CDs, and more—Worldwide

For our listing of thousands of titles see our website
at
www.HeritageBooks.com

Published 2015 by
HERITAGE BOOKS, INC.
Publishing Division
5810 Ruatan Street
Berwyn Heights, Md. 20740

International Standard Book Numbers
Paperbound: 978-0-7884-1454-1
Clothbound: 978-0-7884-6171-2

TABLE OF CONTENTS

BIRTHS

INTRODUCTION

Early vital records of many New Hampshire towns can be located either through the State's Vital Records Department or on microfilms made available through LDS Family History Centers. Some, however, have been lost or are inaccessible for various reasons. A valuable, but time-consuming, source of information for events occurring after 1886 is the vital statistics which are provided in a section of the Annual Town Reports of many New Hampshire towns. Many of these town reports have been collected at the New Hampshire State Library in Concord, as well as more local repositories.

The amount of information published in these Annual Town Reports varies tremendously over time. Early records are far more detailed and comprehensive. Recent records are rather cursory, but issues of confidentiality and sensitivity to the privacy of those residents still living offsets the lack of information of genealogical value.

While the information provided is often very helpful, one must remember that it is not fool-proof or universally accurate, nor is it the primary source or the actual vital record itself. The fact that much of the data is self-reported suggests that it is reliable. However, errors in transcription, spelling, and printing often are obvious. In addition, there may be, for example, two children listed as the third child of a particular couple, or the mother's maiden name, age or place of birth differs or is inconsistent from one entry to another. It is also important to note that a birth, marriage or death may have been reported in another town although the subject resided in New Castle, or the entry may not have been made in the first place.

Despite these shortcomings, the information contained in the Annual Town Reports can be a valuable tool for the genealogist. Marriage and death records from the late 1800's often identify parents who were married nearly a century before. In addition, due to the presence of numerous naval and military personnel during the period covered, many transient or temporary residents are covered by these records. Finally, those families that have remained in New Castle for several generations can be traced and connected to the present.

Births - To the extent the information is available, the entries in the list of births are given as follows: child's name; date of birth; place of birth (New Castle, unless otherwise indicated); the number of children in the family; father's name, place of birth, age and occupation; and the mother's maiden name, age and place of birth. The residence of the parents is sometimes given when it is shown as other than New Castle. As noted above, the amount of information in earlier records is substantially greater.

At times, the given names of many children are missing from the early reports. In this case, the sex of the child is given and they are listed chronologically at the beginning of the surname heading. On occasion, the child's name can be determined from marriage or death records, as well as secondary sources. These names are shown in brackets where available. The records for 1910 have not been located and are not included.

Marriages - To the extent the information is available, the entries in the list of marriages follow this format: groom's name; groom's residence; bride's name; brides residence; date of marriage; place of marriage (New Castle, unless otherwise indicated); H, signifying husband's information, and W, signifying wife's information, each in the following order - age, occupation, number of the marriage (if other than first), father's name, father's place of birth, father's occupation, mother's name, mother's place of birth, and mother's occupation. The name of the official conducting the marriage has been omitted but is generally provided in the original document. The records for 1910 have not been located and are not included.

Because of the presence of military installations, it is noteworthy that an exceptionally large number of marriages occurred during the early 1940's. Just as an example, 1940 and 1941 records show three

2

marriages each. In contrast, 1942 and 1943 reflect the marriages of 28 and 29 couples, respectively. The vast majority of these later couples were not permanent residents of New Castle.

Deaths - To the extent available, the entries in the list of deaths contain the following information: name of decedent; place of death; date of death; age at death; cause of death; marital status; birthplace; father's name; father's place of birth; mother's name; and mother's place of birth. Later entries give the residence of the individual. Some data has been taken from the Social Security Death Benefit database to supplement later records. These are indicated with an asterisk. The records for 1910 have not been located and are not included.

Most of the entries listing a cause of death are self-explanatory. In older entries, the phrase "senectus" is sometimes used and is essentially equivalent to "old age", and "phthisis" is similar to "consumption" and "tuberculosis". As one would expect, the death records often contain somber entries for young mothers and small children, as well as tragic instances of individuals passing before their time due to accidents or suicide.

The death records taken from the Annual Town Reports in some cases varies from the information shown on an individual's tombstone. There is an excellent compilation of cemetery inscriptions which has been done by Dr. John E. Frost which would be a valuable complement to the information contained in this book, particularly for earlier families.

ADAMS,

Haley McCarthy, b. 12/25/1988 in Portsmouth; Douglass S. Adams and Sue M. McCarthy

Tyler Scott, b. 2/23/1990 in Portsmouth; Douglass Scott Adams and Sue McCarthy

ADDAMS,

Peter M., b. 9/6/1956 in Kittery, ME; second; John F. Addams (USN, KY) and Mary Ellen Waugh (VT)

AHRENS,

Meghan Anne, b. 11/16/1964 in Portsmouth; first; Michael C. Ahrens (IL) and Ellen A. McGarr (NY)

ALLEN,

Charles Lincoln, b. 5/4/1985 in Portsmouth; Robert Bruce Allen and Carol Jo Lamereaux

Robert Jeffrey, b. 1/24/1980; Robert Bruce Allen, Jr. and Carol Conlin L'Amoreaux

ALLEY,

Joseph S., Jr., b. 4/6/1930 in New Castle; third; Joseph S. Alley (coast guardsman, Jonesport, ME) and Eulala B. Alley (Jonesport, ME)

ALMGREN,

George Bertil, III, b. 1/4/1969 in Portsmouth; George B. Almgren, Jr. (MA) and Margaret M. Nay (MA)

Kristen Lea, b. 8/21/1970 in Portsmouth; George B. Almgren, Jr. (MA) and Margaret J. Nay (MA)

AMAZEEN,

Charles B., Jr., b. 9/19/1903 in New Castle; first; Charles B. Amazeen (heatersmith, 48, New Castle) and Margie Hutchins (22, Ogunquit, ME)

Eleanor Jessie, b. 5/16/1944 in Portsmouth; fourth; Gerald B.
Amazeen (rigger, N. Yard, Portsmouth) and Elsie L. Jones (W.
Kennebunk, ME)

Gerard Berton, b. 4/21/1909 in New Castle; second; Luther M.
Amazeen (iceman, New Castle) and Marian ----- (England)

James, b. 10/27/1893 in New Castle; sixth; Granville Amazeen
(laborer, 32, New Castle) and Hattie K. Baker (28, New Castle)

Nancy, b. 5/9/1940 in Portsmouth; second; Gerard B. Amazeen
(laborer, Portsmouth) and Elsie L. Jones (W. Kennebunk, ME)

Paul G., b. 3/24/1939 in Portsmouth; first; Gerard B. Amazeen (mech.
engr., Portsmouth) and Elsie Louise Jones (W. Kennebunk, ME)

Raymond, b. 6/23/1901 in New Castle; first; Luther Amazeen
(merchant, 31, New Castle) and Mollie Gleavy (31, Lancaster,
England)

Regina Jessie, b. 7/13/1962 in East Derry; first; Paul G. Amazeen
(NH) and Caroline J. Ells (MA)

Tania Elsie, b. 1/3/1942 in Portsmouth; third; Gerard B. Amazeen
(rigger, NY, Portsmouth) and Elsie L. Jones (W. Kennebunk,
ME)

William G., b. 11/5/1891 in New Castle; Granville A. Amazeen
(farmer, New Castle) and Hattie K. Baker (New Castle)

ANDERSON,
Cheryl Lee, b. 7/25/1958; first; Elton R. Anderson (Portsmouth) and
Nancy D. Poole (Portsmouth)

ANDREWS,
James F., b. 4/22/1950 in Portsmouth; first; Robert F. Andrews (test
man, ME) and Annette Fowler (ME)

Jeffrey R., b. 4/18/1957 in Portsmouth; fourth; Robert F. Andrews
(N.E. Tel. & Tel., ME) and Annette S. Fowler (ME)

Nancy, b. 12/31/1952 in Portsmouth; third; Robert F. Andrews (test
man, ME) and Annette S. Fowler (ME)

ARMITAGE,
Nicole Marie, b. 10/16/1964 in Portsmouth; first; Michael L.
Armitage (ME) and Joanne S. Brunelle (NH)
Peter W., b. 12/26/1951 in Portsmouth; first; Perley W. Armitage, Jr.
(US Navy, ME) and Margaret A. Willard (VT)
Rebecca Elizabeth, b. 2/18/1966 in Portsmouth; second; Michael L.
Armitage (ME) and Joanne S. Brunelle (NH)

ARNOLD,
son, b. 11/28/1952 in Kittery, ME; second; Thomas S. Arnold (US
Navy, OH) and Agnes J. Allanson (NY)
Wendy J., b. 11/18/1951 in Portsmouth; first; Thomas S. Arnold (US
Navy, OH) and Agnes J. Allanson (NY)

ARSENAULT,
Haley Elizabeth, b. 4/8/1987 in Portsmouth; Edmund Joseph
Arsenault, III and Cathleen Ann Russo
Ryan Liberty, b. 6/1/1987 in Portsmouth; Ernest Lamb Arsenault and
Karen Ann Liberty

ASPEN,
Cassandra Nicole, b. 3/7/1990 in Portsmouth; Kenneth Aspen and
Stacy Ann Shea
Derek Svend, b. 9/18/1992 in Portsmouth; Kenneth Aspen and Stacy
A. Shea-Aspen
Erik C., b. 7/4/1950 in Portsmouth; first; Erik S. Aspen (taxi driver,
NY) and Besse M. McKenzie (GA)
Karen, b. 6/4/1952 in Portsmouth; second; Erik S. Aspen (taxi prop.,
NY) and Betsy M. MacKenzie (GA)
Kenneth, b. 3/16/1956 in Portsmouth; fifth; Eric Svend Aspen
(carpenter, NY) and Bessie Mae McKenzie (GA)
Kirt, b. 12/2/1954 in Portsmouth; fourth; Erik S. Aspen (carpenter,
NY) and Bessie McKenzie (GA)
Pamela S., b. 10/4/1953 in Portsmouth; third; Erik S. Aspen (taxi
prop., NY) and Bessie M. McKenzie (GA)

BAGLEY,

Jeffrey Alan, b. 4/25/1968 in Portsmouth; Harvey A. Bagley (NH) and Karen E. Barry (NJ)

BAILEY,

William Mason, III, b. 11/11/1961 in Exeter; second; William M. Bailey, Jr. (NY) and Mary A. Williford (IL)

BAKER,

David L., Jr., b. 9/14/1955 in Exeter; first; David L. Baker (automotive elec., NH) and Sandra Moore (MA)

Herman, Jr., b. 6/20/1920 in New Castle; third; Herman Baker (New Castle) and Bridget Kelley (PEI)

James Alexander, b. 9/26/1974 in Portsmouth; Peter J. S. Baker (England) and Anne Kellas (England)

John Philip, b. 8/13/1967 in Portsmouth; first; Philip G. Baker (MA) and Carolyn Atwell (MA)

Stephanie Ann, b. 4/9/1978; Christopher Baker and Katherine Wilcox

Stephen Gordon, b. 8/2/1968 in Portsmouth; Philip G. Baker (MA) and Carolyn Atwell (MA)

BANJANIN,

Dora Marie, b. 4/1/1978; Milan Banjanin and Claire Gvozdenovic

Lara Ana, b. 1/4/1981; Milan Banjanin and Claire Gvozdenovic

BANKS,

Sally Barbara, b. 7/25/1932 in Portsmouth; second; William F. Banks (sergeant, US Army, Arson, TX) and Mary MacLean (Portland, ME)

BARKER,

William Haywood, b. 9/30/1914 in Washington, DC; second; Quentin J. Barker (Sgt., 1st Class HC, Canada) and Gladys Haywood (New Castle); residence - Washington, DC

BARRY,
Mark Lawrence, b. 9/4/1960 in Portsmouth; fourth; Daniel A. Barry, Jr. (MA) and Janet Tinkham (MA)

BARTER,
Richard Edwin, b. 12/1/1935 in New Castle; fourth; Gordon E. Barter (electrician's helper, Beverly, MA) and Myrtle R. Phillips (Broadway, VA)

BASTELIER,
Christine Anne, b. 3/23/1964 in Portsmouth; first; Ian A. Bastelier (NY) and Carol M. Forbes (MA)
Peter Forbes, b. 4/9/1966 in Portsmouth; second; Ian A. Bastelier (NY) and Carol M. Forbes (MA)

BATCHELDER,
David Soper, b. 7/26/1958; second; John P. Batchelder (Exeter) and Sylvia M. Soper (PEI)
John Payson, Jr., b. 5/27/1956 in Portsmouth; first; John P. Batchelder (beautician, NH) and Sylvia Marlene Soper (Canada)
Peter Clark, b. 9/25/1959 in Portsmouth; third; John P. Batchelder (NH) and Sylvia M. Soper (PEI)

BATSON,
Virginia Amy, b. 10/19/1921 in New Castle; first; Wallace A. Batson (electrician helper, E. Candia) and Eleanor F. Dixon (Gloucester, MA)

BAUER,
Jean Patricia, b. 5/28/1965 in Portsmouth; third; Edward G. Bauer (NH) and Estelle A. Misiaszek (NY)
Suzanne Marie, b. 4/27/1961 in Portsmouth; second; Edward G. Bauer (NH) and Estelle Misiaszek (NY)

BEARCE,
Brian Christopher, b. 3/25/1970 in Kittery, ME; Charles R. Bearce (MO) and Jean E. Andreasen (CA)

BEARD,
Elizabeth Caroline, b. 3/23/1961 in Portsmouth; second; Jack B. Beard (TN) and Alice R. Cummings (TN)

BEBBINGTON,
Hannah Emily, b. 3/23/1992 in Portsmouth; Andrew C. Bebbington and Rachel M. Bebbington
Jonathan William, b. 9/26/1993 in Portsmouth; A. C. Bebbington and R. M. Sherred

BECKER,
son, b. 1/23/1898 in New Castle; third; Charles H. Becker (laborer, 39, Kittery, ME) and Leona Ricker (housewife, 31, New Castle)
Anthony, b. 7/12/1959 in Portsmouth; third; Peter C. Becker (NH) and Sylvia M. Paradis (ME)
Barbara Susan, b. 4/14/1936 in Newburyport, MA; first; Henry Becker (quarter-master, New Castle) and Dorothy M. Schafner (Newburyport, MA)
Dorothy E., b. 1/29/1905 in New Castle; second; Chester Becker (engineer, 27, New Castle) and Martha B. Amazeen (22, New Castle)
Floyd O., b. 11/24/1902 in New Castle; first; Chester A. Becker (engineer, 24, New Castle) and Martha B. Amazeen (20, New Castle)
Henry, 3d, b. 1/8/1907 in New Castle; third; Chester A. Becker (engineer, 28, New Castle) and Martha B. Amazeen (24, New Castle)
Peter C., b. 8/10/1937 in Portsmouth; first; Walter M. Becker (clerk, New Castle) and Dorothy Lawrence (St. Johnsbury, VT)
Shari Ann, b. 7/9/1968 in Portsmouth; Charles J. Becker (PA) and Betty A. LaRose (NH)

Walter Miller, b. 8/5/1915 in New Castle; first; Forrest L. Becker (steamfitter, New Castle) and Anne L. Miller (Riverside, ME)

BEEBE,
Cynthia Frances, b. 10/4/1965 in Portsmouth; second; Irving K. Beebe (NH) and Nancy M. Parisi (NH)
Kathryn Marie, b. 5/9/1967 in Portsmouth; third; Irving R. Beebe (NH) and Nancy M. Parisi (NH)

BEEDE,
son, b. 7/19/1938 in Portsmouth; eighth; Ralph E. Beede (mill wright, Surry, ME) and Della Cousins (Brooksville, ME)

BEEVERS,
Geraldine Martha, b. 2/16/1934 in New Castle; second; Harry A. Beevers (chauffeur, Lawrence, MA) and Phyllis M. Gilman (New Castle)
Walter Harry, b. 7/4/1935 in New Castle; third; Harry A. Beevers (laborer, Lawrence, MA) and Phyllis M. Gilman (New Castle)

BENNETT,
Saige Elizabeth, b. 11/13/1995 in Portsmouth; Philip H. Bennett and Brenda L. Doubleday

BENSLEY,
James Scott, b. 8/15/1960 in Exeter; first; Loren B. Bensley, Jr. (MI) and Joan P. Cowell (MI)

BERG,
Richard Ryan, b. 3/13/1980; Richard Cecil Berg and Polly Jacalyn MacDonald

BERGH,
Hadley Jardine, b. 11/16/1990 in Portsmouth; Peter Davis Bergh and Janet Ellen Prince

BERRY,
Arlington Albert, b. 6/4/1899 in New Castle; first; Gardner L. Berry (shoemaker, 19, Portsmouth) and Helen M. Hawes (15, New Castle)

BETHEA,
David McLeod, b. 5/12/1948 in Kittery, ME; third; James S. Bethea (US Navy, Latta, SC) and Dorothy Thomas (Swampscott, MA)

BISCHOFF,
Robert C., b. 3/8/1947 in Portsmouth; second; Jean A.R. Bischoff (op. Mgr., Airw's, New York, NY) and Dorothy G. Spiller (Arlington, MA)

BLACK,
Constance, b. 7/28/1941 in Portsmouth; first; George Fulton Black (store owner, Malden, MA) and Vivian Barstow (Malden, MA)

BLAISDELL,
Irving Claude, b. 6/2/1926 in New Castle; third; Clyde V. Blaisdell (machinist, Belmont) and Florence M. Batson (Haverhill, MA)

BOLAN,
Cassandra Jane, b. 11/8/1963 in Portsmouth; first; John F. Bolan III (NJ) and Joanne Pettonovich (MA)

BOSWORTH,
John Warren, b. 4/29/1961 in Portsmouth; second; Warren M. Bosworth, Jr. (RI) and Barbara A. Bedard (RI)

BOUGHTON,
Emily Christine, b. 3/27/1983; George W. Boughton and Roberta Mae Zengerle

BOWDOIN,

Colleen Marie, b. 7/1/1959 in Biddeford, ME; first; James A. Bowdoin (ME) and Colleen M. Sullivan (ME)

BRACKETT,

Anne Virginia, b. 10/31/1931 in Portsmouth; third; Eugene Brackett (merchant, Anson, ME) and Erma Gilmore (Industry, ME)

Donald Burton, b. 6/25/1926 in New Castle; Burton Brackett (sheet metal worker, Providence, RI) and Rachel Brinklander (Valentine, NE)

Harvey Ray, b. 8/1/1918 in New Castle; third; Burton Brackett (sheet metal worker, Providence, RI) and Rachel M. Breicklander (Valentine, NE)

Helen May, b. 5/25/1924 in New Castle; fourth; Burton Brackett (sheet metal worker, Providence, RI) and Rachel Brenkland (Valentine, NE)

BRADLEY-LEWIS,

Thaddeus Marc, b. 10/24/1989 in Portsmouth; Michael A. Lewis and Lorinda A. Bradley

BRANCH,

Jonathan Winslow. II, b. 12/8/1968 in Kittery, ME; Jonathan W. Branch (NH) and Donna G. Albro (MA)

BRIDGES,

Robert Wentworth, b. 12/5/1942 in Portsmouth; second; Herbert G. Bridges (mgr. fin. co., Winchester, MA) and Annette W. French (Nantucket, MA)

Stephen, b. 7/21/1941 in Portsmouth; first; Herbert G. Bridges (office manager, Winchester, MA) and Annette W. French (Nantucket, MA)

BRIMFIELD,

daughter, b. 11/9/1899 in New Castle; first; John A. Brimfield (laborer, 26, England) and Lavina A. Yeaton (25, New Castle)

BRODIE,
Robert, IV, b. 3/1/1956 in Kittery, ME; first; Robert Brodie, III (USN, RI) and Marjory Gordon Oakey (NC)

BROOKS,
Barbara E., b. 2/17/1945 in Portsmouth; second; Holman M. Brooks (Sgt., US Army, Stewartstown) and Eleanor R. Cates (Dover)

BROWN,
stillborn daughter, b. 5/1/1904 in New Castle; third; Frank A. Brown (watchman, 33, Somerville, MA) and Lucy Hubley (25, Pleasantville, NS)
Charles Laurel, b. 3/8/1899 in New Castle; first; Frank A. Brown (shoe cutter, 28, Somerville, MA) and Lucy M. Hubley (20, Pleasantville, NS)
Geralyn Ann, b. 8/4/1956 in Kittery, ME; first; John Patrick Brown (USAF, MA) and Dorothy Hynes White (Canada)

BRYSON,
Gregory Lance, b. 8/9/1972 in Kittery, ME; Joseph L. Bryson (RI) and Cynthia L. Rowley (NB)

BULLARD,
Roy James, b. 1/7/1915 in New Castle; first; Abraham L. Bullard (elec. sgt., CAC, US Army, MO) and Margaret O'Rella Carlson (TN)

BURKE,
Stephanie Creal, b. 10/26/1960 in Portsmouth; third; Daniel F. Burke (KY) and Nancy B. Creal (NY)

BURNS,
Brenda K., b. 6/10/1940 in Portsmouth; second; Homer W. Burns (truck driver, Waterbury, VT) and Anna C. Harris (New Castle)

BUTLER,
Ernest P., b. 7/1/1901 in New Castle; second; Leon Butler (laborer, 31, DC) and Mary E. Reed (20, DC)
Frederick C., b. 10/7/1903 in New Castle; third; Leon P. Butler (laborer, 32, VA) and Mary Reed (23, Washington, DC)

CAHILL,
Mary M., b. 4/24/1891 in New Castle; Thomas Cahill (soldier, Ireland) and ----- (Plattsburg, NY); residence - Fort Constitution

CALL,
Mark Thomas, b. 9/18/1958; second; Thomas E. Call, Jr. (Portsmouth) and Margaret E. Jacques (Exeter)
Michael Robert, b. 12/4/1959 in Exeter; third; Thomas E. Call, Jr. (NH) and Margaret E. Jacques (NH)

CALLAHAN,
Brennan Kevin, b. 3/26/1991 in Exeter; Kevin J. Callahan and Deborah Anne Carrier
Emily Adele, b. 4/5/1989 in Exeter; Kevin J. Callahan and Deborah A. Carrier

CAMACK,
Eleanor Vincent, b. 1/13/1914 in New Castle; first; Clarence T. Camack (soldier, E. Beanstead, KY) and Lula Rundles (Chillicote, OH)

CAMERON,
Ashley Dawn, b. 7/29/1983; Richard M. Cameron and Catherine S. Atrock

CAMMETT,
daughter, b. 6/18/1945 in Portsmouth; fifth; Elizabeth Cammett
Lena A., b. 3/13/1940 in Portsmouth; sixth; Charles H. Cammett, Jr. (laborer, Portsmouth) and Elizabeth F. Lowe (Portsmouth)

Pauline Frances, b. 12/5/1934 in Portsmouth; fourth; Charles Cammett, Jr. (laborer, Portsmouth) and Elizabeth Lowe (Portsmouth)

CAMPBELL,

Charles Rose, b. 2/10/1900 in New Castle; second; Henry E. Campbell (shoemaker, 38, New Castle) and Rose L. McCerron (28, Ireland)

Charles Wentworth, b. 6/8/1935 in Portsmouth; second; Wentworth Campbell (truck driver, New Castle) and Katherine E. Strachan (Auld's Cove, NS)

Charlotte, b. 4/17/1914 in New Castle; seventh; Henry E. Campbell (engineer, New Castle) and Rose McCarron (Ireland)

Henry S., b. 7/6/1902 in Portsmouth; third; Henry E. Campbell (shoemaker, 39, New Castle) and Rose McCasson (30, Ireland)

James, b. 9/27/1941 in Portsmouth; fourth; Wentworth Campbell (machinist, Portsmouth) and Katherine E. Strachan (Mulgrave, NS)

James Wentworth, b. 8/3/1933 in New Castle; Wentworth Campbell (truck driver, New Castle) and Catherine Strachan (Mulgrave, NS)

Julie Ann, b. 4/28/1961 in Portsmouth; first; James H. Campbell (NH) and Cheryl L. Brissette (NY)

Katherine, b. 7/4/1938 in Portsmouth; third; Wentworth Campbell (mach. helper, New Castle) and Katherine E. Strachan (NS)

Kevin Charles, b. 2/12/1958; second; Charles W. Campbell (Portsmouth) and Virginia A. Sims (NJ)

Kevin John, b. 10/18/1946 in Portsmouth; fifth; Wentworth Campbell (lead. mach., New Castle) and Katherine E. Strachan (NS)

Mary Alice, b. 7/17/1907 in New Castle; fifth; Henry E. Campbell (engineer, 45, New Castle) and Rose J. McCarron (35, Ireland)

Richard Joseph, b. 3/18/1943 in Portsmouth; third; Wentworth Campbell (machinist, New Castle) and Katherine E. Strachan (Auldcove, NS)

Sarah Jane, b. 3/20/1897 in New Castle; first; Henry E. Campbell (New Castle) and Rose E. McCerron (Ireland)

Walter L., b. 10/22/1904 in New Castle; fourth; Henry E. Campbell
(watchman, 41, New Castle) and Rose I. McCerron (32, Ireland)
Wentworth, b. 10/27/1909 in New Castle; sixth; Henry E. Campbell
(watchman, New Castle) and Rose McCarron (Ireland)
Wentworth R., b. 12/2/1964 in Portsmouth; third; Richard J.
Campbell (NH) and Gussie L. Cregger (WY)

CANNON,
Katherine Douglas, b. 9/30/1944 in Kittery, ME; first; Albert Cannon
(Lt., USNR, SC) and Mary J. Ferrell (Boston, MA)

CARPENTER,
Theodore Raymond, b. 9/27/1934 in Portsmouth; first; Raymond L.
Carpenter (USCG, Detroit, MI) and Rhoda Vane (Machias, ME)

CARSON,
Charles Duncan, b. 10/1/1917 in New Castle; third; Charles W.
Carson (private, USA, Mystic, CT) and Edna Brewster (Medford,
MA)

CARTER,
son, b. 7/18/1899 in New Castle; second; William A. Carter (soldier,
USA, 27, Ruffin, NC) and Lulu Hatton (20, Prince George Co.,
MD)
daughter, b. 10/6/1900 in New Castle; second; William A. Carter
(laborer, 29, Ruffin, NC) and Lulu C. Hatton (22, MD)

CARTON,
Christopher Paul, b. 12/20/1958; third; Harold M. Carton, Jr.
(Norwood, MA) and Jane K. Foss (Portsmouth)

CHACE,
Peter Hanson, b. 5/23/1966 in Portsmouth; second; Robert M. Chace
(RI) and Linda J. Hanson (MA)

CHASE,

Clara Crystine, b. 5/13/1993 in Portsmouth; Samuel H. Chase and Lea Anne Golter

CHICHESTER,

Mehera Amber, b. 1/13/1987 in Portsmouth; Ben Joseph Chichester and Christina Lynn Jordan

Travis Meyer, b. 1/13/1987 in Portsmouth; Ben Joseph Chichester and Christina Lynn Jordan

CLARK,

Cheryl Lynn, b. 9/28/1970 in Portsmouth; Paul L. Clark (NH) and Connie D. Varney (NH)

Kim Marie, b. 4/12/1966 in Portsmouth; first; Paul L. Clark (NH) and Connie D. Varney (NH)

COCHRAN[E],

Ira Dwight, b. 1/2/1917 in New Castle; second; Ira L. Cochran (soldier, E. Calais, VT) and Lillian G. Kezer (Quebec)

Lillian Beryl, b. 1/24/1914 in New Castle; first; Ira L. Cochrane (US Army, Calais, VT) and Lillian G. Kezar (N. Hatley, PQ)

COHEN,

Margaret Elizabeth, b. 10/9/1996 in Portsmouth; Burton J. Cohen and Patricia L. Scholz

COLE,

Andrew James, b. 3/28/1964 in Portsmouth; third; Arthur P. Cole (NH) and Carol Seybolt (NH)

David Arthur, b. 3/18/1959 in Portsmouth; second; Arthur Parker Cole (NH) and Carol Seybolt (NH)

Jason Michael, b. 5/8/1972 in Portsmouth; Thomas G. Cole (NH) and Jane F. Pendergast (NH)

John Parker, b. 7/11/1956 in Portsmouth; first; Arthur Parker Cole (ass't mgr. Seybolt Motors, MA) and Carol Seybolt (NH)

COLLIN[G]S,

son, b. 10/23/1900 in New Castle; fifth; Luther P. Collins (laborer, 40, Kittery, ME) and Addie A. Simpson (33, New Castle)

Addie, b. 6/25/1892 in New Castle; Luther P. Collings (laborer, Kittery, ME) and Addie Simpson (New Castle)

Cora Mertis, b. 7/29/1893 in New Castle; second; Luther P. Collins (laborer, 33, Kittery Point, ME) and Addie Simpson (26, New Castle)

Gertrude M., b. 3/4/1904 in New Castle; sixth; Luther P. Collins (laborer, 43, Kittery, ME) and Addie Simpson (35, New Castle)

Rance Gilmore Collins, b. 1/26/1936 in Portsmouth; second; Clifford A. Collins (foreman, New Castle) and Margaret I. Brackett (Anson, ME)

COLLITON,

Frank Leo, b. 12/2/1931 in Holyoke, MA; Frank Leo Colliton (electrician, Boston, MA) and Alice L. Gilligan (Holyoke, MA)

Justine, b. 5/21/1930 in Portsmouth; third; Frank Colliton (electrician, Boston, MA) and Alice Gilligan (Holyoke, MA)

Katherine Edna, b. 8/26/1934 in Holyoke, MA; Frank L. Colliton (electrician, Malden, MA) and Alice Gilligan (Holyoke, MA)

Rosamary, b. 1/12/1923 in New Castle; first; Frank Colliton (electrician, Faulkner, MA) and Alice Gilligan (Holyoke, MA)

CONDRAN,

William E., b. 10/10/1950 in Kittery, ME; first; Benjamin C. Condran (US Navy, AR) and Florence A. Sullivan (NH)

COOK,

Marilyn Genevieve, b. 4/19/1944 in Kittery, ME; first; Harry M. Cook (Lt., USNR, Denver, CO) and Edna G. Reed (New York, NY)

COPLEY,

Ann Theresa, b. 9/21/1931 in Portsmouth; fifth; James R. Copley (soldier, KY) and Theresa Joyce (Ireland)

CORTINA,

Aaron Charles, b. 10/3/1961 in Kittery, ME; first; Arturo F. Cortina (Mexico) and Carol A. Langley (MA)

Enrique Manuel, b. 11/22/1962 in Kittery, ME; second; Arturo F. Cortina (Mexico) and Carol A. Langley (MA)

COYLE,

Barbara A., b. 3/6/1955 in Portsmouth; third; Charles F. Coyle (superv'r nav'l b., MA) and Virginia L. White (NH)

Frederick Michael, Jr., b. 5/13/1967 in Kittery, ME; first; Frederick M. Coyle (NH) and Sue E. Desmond (RI)

CROMPTON,

Neal Thomas, b. 11/9/1963 in Portsmouth; second; Thomas W. Crompton (NH) and June M. Elliott (NH)

CROTHERS,

Isaac Randolph, b. 12/2/1989 in Portsmouth; Edgar R. Crothers and Anne M. Signorello

CROUSE,

Timothy Paul, b. 7/27/1967 in Kittery, ME; sixth; Lawrence F. Crouse (MD) and Theresa A. Reardon (MA)

CROWELL,

Jo Nancy, b. 1/6/1942 in Portsmouth; second; Samuel Crowell, 3d (ensign, USNR, Boston, MA) and Lillian R. Herrick (Stockton Springs, ME)

Stacey Jean, b. 10/11/1969 in Portsmouth; Cedric L. Crowell (ME) and Jean M. Trenholm (MA)

CULLEN,

Jeffrey Wayne, b. 4/27/1971 in Portsmouth; Paul E. Cullen (MA) and Pamela E. Pitts (ME)

Laura Anne, b. 8/11/1976 in Portsmouth; Paul E. Cullen (MA) and Pamela E. Pitts (ME)

CULP,

Kristin Anne, b. 11/23/1970 in Kittery, ME; William G. Culp (NY) and Ruth P. Kunstadt (CT)

CUMMINS,

Anna, b. 4/2/1920 in New Castle; first; Irving Cummins (laborer, NJ) and Anna Connie (Ireland)

CURTIN,

Kate Coffin, b. 11/19/1945 in Kittery, ME; third; Neale W. Curtin (c'md'r, USNR, Haverhill, MA) and Caroline M. Neilson (Vallejo, CA)

Mary E., b. 10/17/1939 in Portsmouth; second; Neale W. Curtin (insurance mgr., Haverhill, MA) and Caroline M. Neilson (Vallejo, CA)

CURTIS,

Ballard D., b. 8/8/1902 in New Castle; second; Alvah H.M. Curtis (teacher, 31, New Castle) and Mary E. Dana (31, Chelsea, MA); residence - Portsmouth

Herman D., b. 8/8/1902 in New Castle; first; Alvah H.M. Curtis (teacher, 31, New Castle) and Mary E. Dana (31, Chelsea, MA); residence - Portsmouth

CUSHMAN,

Jeffrey William, b. 7/2/1974 in Dover; William E. Cushman (IL) and Mary M. Dawson (NH)

Sarah Mary, b. 12/6/1976 in Dover; William E. Cushman (IL) and Mary M. Dawson (NH)

D'ALFONSO,

Rose Marie, b. 4/22/1944 in Portsmouth; first; Michael D'Alfonso (Pfc, USA, Philadelphia, PA) and Anna M.C. Miller (Philadelphia, PA); residence - Fort Dearborn

D'ANTONIO,
Mary E., b. 7/30/1953 in Portsmouth; second; Albert M. D'Antonio
(dispatcher, MA) and Patricia A. Barr (NJ)
Michael, b. 5/11/1955 in Portsmouth; third; Albert M. D'Antonio
(dispatcher, MA) and Patricia A. Barr (NJ)
Patrick, b. 7/22/1956 in Portsmouth; fourth; Albert M. D'Antonio
(disp., Iafolla Co., MA) and Patricia Anne Barr (NJ)

DARRACQ,
Nicole Andrea, b. 5/19/1961 in Kittery; second; Dal J. Darracq (CA)
and Pamela J. Bush (CA)

DAVIDSON,
son, b. 6/13/1893 in New Castle; first; George H. Davidson
(carpenter, 30, New Castle) and Josephine Ordi (29, Digby, NS)
son, b. 1/21/1900 in New Castle; second; George H. Davidson
(carpenter, 36, New Castle) and Josephine Ord (34, NS)
Claire, b. 4/13/1927 in Portsmouth; second; Reginald O. Davidson
(Coast Guard, New Castle) and Hazel E. Ricker (New Castle)

DAVIS,
Alice Hazel, b. 12/5/1913 in New Castle; first; Henry A. Davis
(fireman, Worcester, MA) and Mary B. Moody (Portsmouth)
Bertrum Wellington, b. 8/11/1930 in Portsmouth; second; Bertrum W.
Davis (laborer, Jonesport, ME) and Orrie Crowley (Jonesport,
ME)
Nathalie Elaine, b. 12/26/1928 in Portsmouth; first; Bertram Davis
(laborer, Beals, ME) and Orrie Crowley (Jonesport, ME)

DAY,
Betty Joan, b. 6/23/1930 in Portsmouth; second; Gordon A. Day
(driver, Essex, MA) and Doris J. Davis (Jonesport, ME)
Gordon Warren, b. 4/5/1929 in Portsmouth; first; Gordon A. Day
(carpenter, Essex, MA) and Doris Davis (Jonesport, ME)
Harold Arthur, b. 3/8/1932 in Portsmouth; third; Gordon A. Day
(caretaker, Essex, MA) and Doris Davis (Jonesport, ME)

DEARBORN,

Frank K., Jr., b. 1/14/1921 in New Castle; first; Frank K. Dearborn (electrician, No. Hampton) and Evelyn Tarlton (New Castle)

DECOFF,

Barbara, b. 3/26/1928 in Portsmouth; fifth; Raymond DeCoff (carpenter, Fitchburg, MA) and Blanche Whitcomb (Lunenburg, MA)

DECOURCEY,

Katherine D., b. 8/13/1951 in Portsmouth; second; John H. DeCourcey (ins., real est., NH) and Ruth Hassett (NH)

DECOURSEY,

John H., Jr., b. 12/15/1943 in Kittery, ME; first; John H. DeCoursey (Lt., USNR, Manchester) and Ruth Hassett (Portsmouth)

DELABRUERE,

Mathew James, b. 7/23/1988 in Portsmouth; Louis J. deLaBruere and Patricia A. Klann

DEVANEY,

Thomas Mitchell, b. 11/2/1984 in Portsmouth; Thomas M. Devaney and Leslie Young

DEVANNA,

Neil Alex, b. 9/17/1980; Michael Victor Devanna and Dawn Marie Foster

DEWHIRST,

Jeanne Louise, b. 7/19/1974 in Portsmouth; Gary L. Dewhirst (CA) and Kathleen E. Shea (NH)

DICHARD,

Peter C., b. 2/13/1956 in Kittery, ME; third; Charles J. Dichard (USN, ME) and Eva May Eaton (MA)

DONALDSON,

Robert Scott, Jr., b. 2/28/1944 in Portsmouth; first; Robert S. Donaldson (2d Lt., USA, Freeport, LI) and Shirley V. Barbour (Manchester)

DOODA,

Kimberly Ann, b. 2/21/1970 in Portsmouth; Richard Dooda (NH) and Diane C. Barry (NH)

DOROW,

Donald Scott, b. 10/4/1961 in Portsmouth; first; David A. Dorow (MI) and Patricia A. Thompson (NH)

DOW,

Frances E., b. 7/8/1892 in New Castle; John Dow (shoemaker, Portsmouth) and Dorothy M. Yeaton (New Castle)

Guy Alvin, Jr., b. 7/27/1921 in New Castle; second; Guy A. Dow (auto mechanic, The Weirs) and Edna Poole (Lynn, MA)

Harold Leroy, b. 6/3/1894 in New Castle; John T. Dow (shoemaker, Portsmouth) and Dorothy Yeaton (New Castle)

Lawrence Taylor, b. 7/8/1896 in New Castle; John T. Dow and Dorothy M. Yeaton

DUGAS,

Adele Marie, b. 3/9/1992 in Portsmouth; Normand P. Dugas and Merriel Dugas

Julia Louise, b. 10/15/1990 in Portsmouth; Norman Paul Dugas and Merriel Rohrer

DURWARD,

Linda Loletta, b. 4/17/1942 in Claremont; first; David W. Durward (sign painter, Claremont) and Georgia W. Cochrane (Portland, ME); residence - Claremont

EARL,
Donald Carrol, b. 1/18/1947 in Portsmouth; second; Nellis C. Earl
(mason, New Milford, CT) and Phyllis A. McKenney (Quincy,
MA)

EDGEMOND,
William Stuart, b. 9/5/1963 in Kittery, ME; first; William R.
Edgemond (WV) and Betty J. Wright (England)

EDWARDS,
John Raymond, b. 1/1/1934 in New Castle; first; John C. Edwards
(joiner, Kittery, ME) and Alma C. Allen (No. Berwick, ME);
residence - Kittery, ME

ELDERS,
daughter, b. 12/23/1911 in New Castle; second; John H. Elders
(sergeant, USA, 38, Atlanta, GA) and ----- Ramsdell (24,
Greenland)

EMERICK,
R. J., b. 8/13/1949 in Kittery, ME; first; Robert W. Emerick (US
Army, Renovo, PA) and Carmen R. Borden (Trieste, Italy)

EPSTEIN,
Jeremy Robert, b. 2/20/1995 in Portsmouth; Roger M. Epstein and
Susan A. Johnson

ERICKSON,
daughter, b. 5/28/1908 in New Castle; third; George B. Erickson
(soldier, 31, Sweden) and S. H. Anderson (27, Sweden)

ERNEST,
stillborn daughter, b. 4/19/1909 in New Castle; first; Jetta W. Ernest
(engineer, OH) and Alice ----- (New Castle)

ESTEY,
Michael Quentin, b. 11/21/1972 in Portsmouth; Michael Q. Estey (IL) and Cheryl Ann Chisholm (NH)

FARNSWORTH,
John Timothy, b. 11/26/1965 in Kittery, ME; seventh; Elwood V. Farnsworth (CA) and Virginia Wakefield (CA)

FARRINGTON,
Mary Jean, b. 2/15/1934 in New Castle; second; William I. Farrington (machine operator, Kittery, ME) and Elsie S. Sylvester (New Castle)
Priscilla Mae, b. 8/9/1932 in Kittery, ME; first; William I. Farrington (machine operator, Kittery, ME) and Elsie S. Sylvester (New Castle); residence - Kittery, ME

FAULKINGHAM,
Janice, b. 8/28/1940 in Portsmouth; fourth; Cleo R. Faulkingham (Coast Guard, Jonesport, ME) and Hazel B. Courtney (Littleton, MA)

FAY,
stillborn child, b. 10/1/1892 in New Castle; W. S. Fay (laborer, MA) and Sadie E. Straw (New Castle)

FELLOWS,
Lydia, b. 8/4/1953 in Portsmouth; third; Charles F. Fellows (self-employed, NH) and Martha E. Wilcox (MA)

FERNALD,
Cara Marcia, b. 4/8/1975 in Portsmouth; Michael E. Fernald (NH) and Christina J. Pridham (ME)

FETYKO,
David Andrew, b. 10/15/1967 in Kittery, ME; first; Michael D. Fetyko (PA) and Wanda R. Charwell (TN)

FIELDS,
William Glenn, b. 1/3/1960 in Kittery, ME; third; Ronald J. Fields
(NY) and Dorothy J. Shaver (NY)

FINN,
John Marshall, b. 10/16/1959 in Kittery, ME; fourth; Philip P. Finn
(MA) and Ann J.E. Theiler (OH)
Michael Paul, b. 1/16/1962 in Kittery, ME; fifth; Philip P. Finn (MA)
and Ann J.E. Theiler (OH)

FISK,
Austin Charles, b. 2/23/1992 in Portsmouth; Eugene C. Fisk and Betty
A. Fisk

FLAHIVE,
Erik Jon, b. 11/9/1968 in Portsmouth; William J. Flahive (MA) and
Jane F. Wareing (NH)

FLETCHER,
Andrew Richard, b. 9/20/1988 in Portsmouth; Darel R. Fletcher and
Barbara B. Crosby
Christopher Tyler, b. 5/30/1986 in Portsmouth; Darel Richard
Fletcher and Barbara Barclay Crosby

FOLEY,
Anne Jacqueline, b. 8/4/1975 in Portsmouth; Dennis J. Foley (NH)
and Colette T.M. Garnier (France)
Elizabeth Marie Monique, b. 10/1/1973 in Portsmouth; D. John Foley
(NH) and Colette T.M. Garnier (France)
Emily Erin, b. 9/3/1977 in Portsmouth; D. John Foley (NH) and
Collette T.M. Garnier (France)

FOSTER,
Deborah Ann, b. 11/5/1958; first; Richard E. Foster (Glendale, CA)
and Penelope A. Lowe (Glendale, CA)

FOWLER,
Myrtle Snowden, b. 1/20/1917 in New Castle; first; Thomas C.
Fowler (soldier, NC) and Phoebe S. Thistle (NS); residence - Ft.
Constitution

FRAMPTON,
Emma Katherine, b. 6/14/1993 in Portsmouth; D. H. Frampton and T.
M. Christman
Molly Ahlene, b. 9/27/1995 in Portsmouth; Damon H. Frampton and
Theresa M. Christman
Sophia Eleanor, b. 5/27/1997 in Portsmouth; D. H. Frampton and T.
M. Frampton

FRAZIER,
John Arthur, b. 3/30/1959 in Kittery, ME; fourth; Arthur C. Frazier
(MO) and Ruth R. Morrison (LA)

FREE,
stillborn son, b. 4/6/1916 in New Castle; second; Vern Free (soldier,
Williamsport, PA) and Cora M. Collins (New Castle)
Harry Verne, b. 1/1/1915 in New Castle; first; Verne Free (soldier,
PA) and Cora M. Collins (New Castle)
Verne, Jr., b. 8/25/1917 in New Castle; third; Verne Free (sergeant,
USA, Williamsport, PA) and Cora M. Collins (New Castle)

FRENCH,
Cheryl Irene, b. 10/23/1947 in Portsmouth; first; Jack French (store
prop., Lincoln, NE) and Sonja A. Aspen (Brooklyn, NY)
Jack, Jr., b. 6/21/1949 in Portsmouth; second; Jack French (store
manager, Lincoln, NE) and Sonja A. Aspen (Brooklyn, NY)
Stuart P., Jr., b. 9/14/1945 in Portsmouth; first; Stuart P. French
(ensign, USN, Chelsea, MA) and Bernice M. Rand (Portsmouth)
Wayne A., b. 7/5/1945 in Portsmouth; eighth; William F. French
(sheetmetal smith, Columbia, ME) and Isabel I. Bunker (Gaze,
VT)

FRIES,
Michael Kurt, b. 1/6/1959 in Kittery, ME; third; Robert G. Fries (NY) and Vernice I. Christensen (UT)
Teresa Marie, b. 2/2/1960 in Kittery, ME; fourth; Robert G. Fries (NY) and Vernice I. Christensen (UT)

FUQUA,
Steven Levi, b. 1/30/1959 in Portsmouth; first; Lloyd L. Fuqua (MO) and Judith E. Littlefield (NH)

GALLANT,
Linda S., b. 8/12/1955 in Portsmouth; third; Joseph E. Gallant (gen. helper, MA) and Azelia M. Lavoie (MA)

GARRETT,
Alexander Allison Taylor, b. 2/1/1982; William E. Garrett and Heidi M. Allison

GARRISON,
Stephen, b. 5/10/1940 in Portsmouth; first; Malcolm E. Garrison (LT, USN, Keyport, NJ) and Dorothea L. Brooks (Clarendon, TX)

GAUDETTE,
Joseph Stephen, b. 11/9/1973 in Kittery, ME; Barry S. Gaudette (MA) and Patricia Ann Nemeth (NJ)

GELB,
Mark Edward, b. 1/30/1959 in Exeter; first; Robert M. Gelb (NY) and Joanna F. Gough (RI)

GELINAS,
David Gerald, b. 8/23/1963 in Portsmouth; first; Gerald G. Gelinas (MA) and Nancy R. Evans (Newfoundland)

GERLACH,
Russell Willis, b. 11/6/1942 in Portsmouth; first; Charles H. Gerlach
(Lieut, USN, Marietta, OH) and Ione Capel Grimes
(Washington)

GETMAN,
Margaret Jensen, b. 7/5/1997 in Portsmouth; F. W. Getman and I. M.
Getman

GILBERT,
Charles Franklin, b. 11/3/1942 in Portsmouth; first; Charles F. Gilbert
(auto mechanic, Ayer, MA) and Ruth B. Fletcher (Stark, ME)

GILES,
Michael Aron, b. 11/21/1958; second; Gerald F. Giles (Concord) and
Carmen A. Demers (Gardiner, ME)

GILLIAM,
Janet Elaine, b. 7/5/1931 in Portsmouth; first; Phyllis Gilliam (New
Castle)
Phyllis Mildred, b. 11/1/1913 in New Castle; third; Claud C. Gilliam
(machinist, Yale, VA) and Mildred Batson (Haverhill, MA)

GLIDDEN,
Cindy Lee, b. 2/4/1964 in Portsmouth; second; Walter W. Glidden
(NH) and Sandra L. Keen (ME)
Jacquelin M., b. 1/20/1947 in Portsmouth; stillborn; third; Earl W.
Glidden (laborer, Augusta, ME) and Norma M. Reed (Palermo,
ME)

GOLDEN,
Connor James, b. 9/8/1993 in Portsmouth; E. K. Golden and Karen E.
Passon

GOLDSMITH,
Joachim Eric L., b. 9/28/1942 in Portsmouth; first; Charles F. Gilbert (physician-surgeon, Mayener, Germany) and Edith Irma Pistora (Budapest, Austria)

GOLTER,
Amy Christine, b. 8/30/1968 in Portsmouth; Thomas W. Golter (NH) and Theresa Anne Clark (ME)
Lea Anne, b. 6/6/1965 in Portsmouth; third; Thomas W. Golter (NH) and Theresa A. Clark (NH)
Susan Jean, b. 11/5/1961 in Portsmouth; second; Thomas W. Golter (NH) and Theresa A. Clark (ME)

GOODMAN,
Thomas Patterson, b. 2/17/1909 in Ft. Constitution; second; Samuel W. Goodman (post qm. Sgt., Hungary) and Louise ----- (Maderson, NC); residence - Fort Constitution

GOODRICH,
Marion Bell, b. 8/24/1921 in New Castle; third; William E. Goodrich (painter, E. Haven, CT) and Marguerite F. Renfield (Killingworth, CT)

GORDON,
Kathleen Ellen, b. 2/27/1948 in Portsmouth; second; James J. Gordon (truck driver, Portsmouth) and Helen R. Berner (Boston, MA)

GOTTWALD,
Paul Charles, b. 2/18/1945 in Portsmouth; first; Charles Gottwald (Capt., US Army, New York, NY) and Bernice M. Heady (Carmel, NY)

GOUCHER,
Caroline L., b. 11/2/1952 in Portsmouth; fourth; Harold J. Goucher (shipfitter, ME) and Evangeline B. Voyer (ME)

GRANACKI,

Sara Anne, b. 6/21/1980; Robert Jan Granacki and Cheryl Susan Kantor

GRANT,

Betheny J., b. 7/8/1950 in Rochester; second; David F. Grant (custodian, ME) and Jeanine C. Fontaine (MA)

GRAY,

McKenzie Bowden, b. 10/21/1987 in Portsmouth; Norman Gerald Gray and Leanne Powell

Whitney Elizabeth, b. 2/20/1986 in Portsmouth; Lawrence Neal Gray and Ruth Helen Soper

GREELEY,

Jennifer Mae, b. 8/26/1958; second; Arthur W. Greeley (Oakland, ME) and Patricia L. Batting (NY)

Linda Diane, b. 2/8/1956 in Portsmouth; first; Arthur W. Greeley (minister, ME) and Patricia Lucy Batting (NY)

GREELY,

Ellen Constance, b. 6/24/1968 in Portsmouth; George R. Greely (MA) and Mary L. Pence (ME)

GRIFFIN,

Gail Drew, b. 10/6/1943 in Portsmouth; second; Arnold H. Griffin (machinist, Portsmouth) and Dorothea G. Drew (Kittery Pt., ME)

Kenneth Leary, Jr., b. 1/12/1962 in Portsmouth; first; Kenneth L. Griffin (FL) and Joanne R. Skidmore (NH)

Richard A., b. 9/24/1941 in Portsmouth; first; Arnold Henry Griffin (mach. opr., Portsmouth) and Dorothea G. Drew (Kittery Pt., ME)

GRIMES,

Darlene Anne, b. 11/13/1960 in Kittery, ME; first; Gerald A. Grimes (NH) and Shirley A. Thorp (ME)

31

GROTON,
Janet Elaine, b. 7/2/1931 in Portsmouth; first; John W. Groton
(Portsmouth) and Phyllis Gilliam (New Castle)
Pamela Jane, b. 4/19/1948 in Portsmouth; second; Richard W. Groton
(student, Portsmouth) and Miriam E. Herrick (Springfield, MA)
Ruth Joan, b. 2/20/1930 in Portsmouth; sixth; Robert E. Groton
(trainman, B&M RR, Augusta, ME) and Ruth E. Gray
(Portsmouth)

GUPTILL,
Laura Mary, b. 5/12/1932 in Portsmouth; second; William B. Guptill
(clerk, Charlestown, MA) and Ellen C. Hoitt (Durham)

GUZY,
April Sandra, b. 4/7/1975 at Pease AFB; Gary E. Guzy (OH) and
Sandra S. Devost (VT)

HALE,
Ashleigh Brook, b. 10/30/1992 in Portsmouth; Shawn E. Hale and
Lucero P. Hale

HANSCOM,
Justin M., b. 3/5/1893 in New Castle; second; Justin F. Hanscom
(clerk, 25, New Castle) and Martha E. Marvin (29, Boston, MA)

HARDIGAN,
Andrew Alexander, b. 7/3/1986 in Portsmouth; Kenneth Russell
Hardigan and Lori Ann Alexander
Ross Alexander, b. 3/30/1989 in Portsmouth; Kenneth R. Hardigan
and Lori A. Alexander
Trevor Alexander, b. 7/3/1986 in Portsmouth; Kenneth Russell
Hardigan and Lori Ann Alexander

HARLFINGER,
Dorothy, b. 6/29/1942 in Portsmouth; first; Frederick J. Harlfinger (Lt. JG, USN, Albany, NY) and Frances Clark Blance (Baltic, CT)

HARRINGTON,
Anne H., b. 8/12/1953 in Portsmouth; third; William F. Harrington, Jr. (lawyer, NH) and Margaret Hemingway (NY)

HARRIS,
Anna Katherine, b. 11/9/1913 in New Castle; third; Joseph T. Harris (fireman, Springfield, MO) and Katherine Nugent (St. Johns, NF)

Bevuel J., b. 4/15/1918 in New Castle; fifth; Joseph T. Harris (machinist's helper, Springfield, MO) and Katherine Nugent (St. Johns, NF)

Clinton Bryzeal, b. 5/1/1921 in New Castle; seventh; Joseph Harris (machinist helper, Springfield, MO) and Katherine Nugent (St. Johns, NF)

Ernest Joseph, b. 1/8/1911 in New Castle; second; Joseph Harris (soldier. 27, Springfield, MO) and Katherine Nugent (25, St. Johns, NF)

Evelyn Nugent, b. 2/25/1916 in New Castle; fourth; Joseph T. Harris (general helper, Springfield, MO) and Katherine Nugent (St. Johns, NF)

Myrtle Marie, b. 12/16/1926 in New Castle; ninth; Joseph Harris (machinist helper, Springfield, MO) and Catherine Nugent (St. John, NF)

Nora Arville Nugent, b. 6/28/1909 in New Castle; first; Joseph L. Harris (soldier, Springfield, MO) and Katherine Nugent (Newfoundland)

Priscilla G., b. 5/27/1941 in Portsmouth; second; Bevuel J. Harris (fireman, New Castle) and Pauline D. Stenzel (Manchester)

Sidney William, b. 11/11/1923 in New Castle; eighth; Joseph T. Harris (machinist helper, Springfield, MO) and Katie J. Nugent (St. Johns, NF)

Suzanne D., b. 7/3/1939 in Portsmouth; first; James B. Harris
(engineer, yacht, New Castle) and Pauline D. Stenzel
(Manchester)
Woodrow Wilson, b. 10/1/1919 in New Castle; sixth; Joseph Harris
(machinist's helper, Springfield, MO) and Katherine Nugent (St.
Johns, NF)

HARTSHORNE,

Benjamin M., III, b. 8/23/1950 in Melrose, MA; first; Benjamin M.
Hartshorne (bank clerk, MA) and Louise M. Newhouse (MA);
residence - MA

HARVEY,

Lois Mae, b. 6/14/1939 in Exeter; second; John L. Harvey (caretaker,
Nottingham) and Delia M. Whitney (New Ipswich)

HASSETT,

Stephen Michael, b. 1/13/1959 in Portsmouth; third; John J. Hassett
(NH) and Marjorie E. Thomas (SC)

HATCHER,

Dorothy, b. 5/6/1937 in Portsmouth; second; Joel H. Hatcher
(quartermaster, GA) and Sally B. McDonald (E. Deering, ME)
Sally Ann, b. 12/30/1932 in Portsmouth; first; Joel H. Hatcher
(sergeant, CAC, Macon, GA) and Sally B. McDonald (East
Deering, ME)

HAWKINS,

Jennifer Lynn, b. 1/10/1978; Robert T. Hawkins and Mary L. Bussell

HAY,

Arline J., b. 9/8/1904 in New Castle; first; Thomas H. Hay (soldier,
26, NJ) and Lizzie Meloon (19, New Castle)

HAYNES,
Patricia Ann, b. 11/21/1947 in Portsmouth; first; Laurence G. Haynes (chauffeur, Northeast Harbor, ME) and Muriel C. Burgess (Bath, ME)

HEINDEL,
Annaliese Alexandria, b. 8/5/1995 in Portsmouth; Clifford C. Heindel and Margaret A. Braun

HENDRICKSON,
Erin Chelsea, b. 6/4/1991 in Portsmouth; Jon D. Hendrickson and Karen Pauline Smith

HENLEY,
stillborn son, b. 4/30/1902 in New Castle; first; C. D. Henley (laborer, 30, Washington, DC) and Bertha Manson (20, Washington, DC)

HERMENEAU,
Bruce Philip, b. 11/22/1962 in Portsmouth; second; Waldemar Hermeneau, Jr. (CA) and Carol A. Bainbridge (MA)
Kevin Andrew, b. 3/12/1965 in Portsmouth; third; Waldemar Hermenau (sic) (CA) and Carol A. Bainbridge (IL)

HILDEBRANDT,
Justin John, b. 10/16/1972 in Kittery, ME; Richard C. Hildebrandt (NY) and Beverly A. Irona (NY)

HITCHENS,
Loretta Ann, b. 1/1/1934 in Portsmouth; first; Floyd Hitchens (USCG, Norfolk, VA) and Agnes Doyle (Erie, PA)

HODGDON,
Janice Elaine, b. 2/18/1947 in Portsmouth; first; John F. Hodgdon (laborer, Augusta, ME) and Greta B. Beal (Jonesport, ME)
John F., Jr., b. 9/19/1952 in Portsmouth; second; John F. Hodgdon (clerk, navy yard, ME) and Greta B. Beal (ME)

HOFFMAN,

Stephanie Diane, b. 9/19/1974 in Portsmouth; Elliott W. Hoffman (MA) and Diane C. Mavros (TX)

Tana Isabeth, b. 2/27/1986 in Portsmouth; Walter Erben Hoffman, Jr. and Gail Marie Mooz

HOGAN,

Richard Henry, b. 10/25/1944 in Portsmouth; first; George R. Hogan (USA, T/4, Southbridge, MA) and Janet G. Smith (Portsmouth)

HOLT,

Christopher David, b. 1/14/1964 in Portsmouth; fourth; Shirley H. Holt, 3d (NH) and Constance Pendergast (NH)

Melissa Jane, b. 9/20/1965 in Portsmouth; fifth; Shirley H. Holt III (NH) and Constance Pendergast (NH)

HOLZAEPFEL,

Peter Frederick, b. 11/19/1982; Jonathan L. Holzaepfel and Etoile Heifner

HORNING,

Anna L., b. 7/28/1902 in New Castle; second; Andrew J. Horning (laborer, 23, OH) and Ivalean W. Emery (22, New Castle)

Arnold E., b. 7/14/1904 in New Castle; third; Andrew J. Horning (fireman, 25, Richmond, IN) and Ivalean Emery (24, New Castle)

Elise Florence, b. 7/7/1909 in New Castle; seventh; Andrew J. Horning (engineer, Melville, OH) and Ivalean Emery (New Castle)

George Edwin, b. 8/13/1905 in New Castle; fourth; Andrew J. Horning (laborer, 26, Hamilton, OH) and Ivalean Emery (25, New Castle)

Harrold, b. 4/19/1901 in New Castle; first; Andrew J. Horning (soldier, 22, Hamilton, OH) and Ivalean W. Emery (20, New Castle)

Harry Gilmore, b. 7/11/1908 in New Castle; sixth; Andrew J. Horning
(engineer, 29, Hamilton, OH) and Ivalean W. Emery (28, New
Castle)
Rufus Jonathan, b. 1/11/1912 in New Castle; ninth; Andrew J.
Horning (engineer, Melville, OH) and Ivalean Emery (New
Castle)
Sarah Angeline, b. 1/12/1907 in New Castle; fifth; Andrew J. Horning
(fireman, 28, Hamiton, OH) and Ivalean W. Emery (27, New
Castle)

HOYT,
Althea Gertrude, b. 8/9/1934 in Portsmouth; first; Milton E. Hoyt
(blacksmith, Kittery, ME) and Dorothy Foss (Northwood)

HUBBARD,
Cherylyn Ann, b. 10/28/1948 in Portsmouth; first; Lloyd F. Hubbard
(melter, Wells, ME) and Beatrice A. Sibson (Rugbey, England)

HUBLEY,
Charles Swan, b. 5/20/1894 in New Castle; Louis H. Hubley
(fisherman, New Castle) and Sophia Hanson (Guttenberg,
Sweden)

HUFF,
David Brian, b. 12/2/1957 in Portsmouth; second; Donald C. Huff
(USAF, MI) and Ruth F. Beck (MO)
Mark Douglas, b. 12/26/1958; third; Donald C. Huff (MI) and Ruth F.
Beck (St. Louis, MO)

HUFFMAN,
Chelsea, b. 4/1/1988 in Portsmouth; Robert A. Huffman, Jr. and
Melissa J. Holt

HUMPHREYS,
Louise, b. 10/18/1950 in Kittery, ME; George C. Humphreys (US
Navy, MA) and Josephine L. Lutes (WI)

HURLEY,

son, b. 3/7/1920 in New Castle; tenth; Fred Hurley (riveter, Livermore Falls, ME) and Blanche S. Lewis (Kittery Point, ME)

Josephine Grace, b. 9/10/1918 in New Castle; ninth; Fred Hurley (riveter, Livermore Falls, ME) and Blanche Lewis (Kittery, ME)

Justine Blanche, b. 1/4/1917 in New Castle; eighth; Fred Hurley (laborer, Livermore Falls, ME) and Blanche Lewis (Kittery, ME)

HUSSEY,

Charles William, Jr., b. 7/27/1920 in New Castle; fourth; Charles W. Hussey, Sr. (draftsman, Cambridge, MA) and Mildred M. Smith (Hingham, MA)

Katherine Elizabeth, b. 9/5/1918 in New Castle; third; Charles W. Hussey (draftsman, Cambridge, MA) and Mildred M. Smith (Hingham, MA)

HUTCHINGS,

Grace Ellen, b. 8/26/1898 in New Castle; third; Elmer J. Hutchings (seaman, 33, ME) and Mary T. Simpson (housewife, 28, New Castle)

Mertie M., b. 12/3/1901 in New Castle; fourth; Elmer J. Hutchings (sailor, 30, Wells, ME) and Mary Simpson (35, New Castle)

Ralph Alden, b. 8/20/1896 in New Castle; Elmer J. Hutchings and Mary T. Simpson

Raymond J., b. 5/29/1905 in New Castle; fifth; Elmer J. Hutchins (captain, 38, Wells, ME) and Mary F. Simpson (33, New Castle)

HUTCHINSON,

Albert Warren, b. 8/12/1942 in Portsmouth; first; Arthur W. Hutchinson (soldier, USA, Portsmouth) and Ruth E. Mori (Portsmouth)

Deborah Ann, b. 10/4/1947 in Portsmouth; second; Arthur W. Hutchinson (apprentice, Portsmouth) and Ruth E. Mori (Portsmouth)

Ruth Elizabeth, b. 3/31/1966 in Portsmouth; third; Albert W. Hutchinson (NH) and Sharon A. Colpritt (ME)

ICHILLING,

stillborn son, b. 11/17/1906 in New Castle; first; H. G. Ichilling (soldier, 26, NJ) and P. Hussey (28, St.John, NJ)

INGLIS,

Brittany Paige, b. 4/10/1992 in Portsmouth; David L. Inglis and Robin L. Inglis

IRELAND,

Jessica Leigh, b. 12/28/1976 in Portsmouth; John Ireland (NH) and Joanne Petlick (MI)

JACKSON,

Bessie Louise, b. 5/6/1913 in New Castle; fourth; Thomas G. Jackson (machinist's helper, Hazelville, DE) and Eva Amazeen (New Castle)

Granville A., b. 11/7/1921 in New Castle; fifth; Thomas Jackson (machinist, Hazelville, DE) and Era Amazeen (New Castle)

Herbert W., b. 7/27/1902 in New Castle; first; Thomas Jakcosn (laborer, 26, Hazelville, DE) and Eva Amazeen (22, New Castle)

Katherine Baker, b. 5/19/1908 in New Castle; second; Thomas G. Jackson (laborer, 32, Hazelville, DE) and Eva Amazeen (28, New Castle)

JAMES,

Osary, Jr., b. 4/15/1946 in Portsmouth; second; Osary James (US Army, Pensacola, FL) and Rita Massa (Lowell, MA)

JANUSZ,

Lucie Mika, b. 6/20/1969 in Portsmouth; Kenneth C. Janusz (IN) and Diane L. Cole (GA)

JEFFCO,

Heather Ann, b. 9/21/1978; Stephen T. Jeffco and Marjory Learmonth

Scott Robinson, b. 3/2/1977 in Dover; Stephen T. Jeffco (PA) and Marjory E. ----- (NH)

JENNESS,
Vivian M., b. 4/22/1903 in New Castle; first; Willard M. Jenness
(laborer, 31, Rye) and Emily Warton (25, Worcester, MA)

JENNINGS,
Kimberly Joy, b. 4/1/1966 in Portsmouth; third; Peter D. Jennings
(VT) and Gloria F. Epperson (TX)
Kristy Leigh, b. 8/18/1970 in Portsmouth; Peter D. Jennings (VT) and
Gloria F. Epperson (TX)
Lindsay Edward, b. 9/20/1965 in Portsmouth; second; Granville E.
Jennings (CT) and Jane L. Butterworth (NH)
Ruth I., b. 10/27/1904 in New Castle; second; William J. Jennings
(laborer, 23, Bermuda) and Blanche J. Gage (28, Dover)

JERVIS,
David Richard, b. 1/14/1964 in Portsmouth; first; Robert C. Jervis
(OH) and Cynthia Rodimon (CT)

JOHNSON,
daughter, b. 3/2/1921 in New Castle; fourth; Olgia Johnson (soldier,
KY) and ----- Walsh (Ireland)
Alden Goodwin, b. 12/21/1933 in Portsmouth; fourth; Haven W.
Johnson (truck driver, York, ME) and Annie G. Goodwin
(Boston, MA)
Brian Mathew, b. 9/1/1979; Donald K. Johnson and Karen Aspen
John, b. 9/26/1915 in New Castle; first; Olgio Johnson (soldier,
Brownsfield, KY) and Margaret Walsh (Galway, Ireland)
Lawrence, b. 1/23/1917 in New Castle; second; Olgia Johnson
(soldier, Brownville, KY) and Margaret Walch (Galway, Ireland)
Michael Allen, b. 6/23/1974 in Portsmouth; Robert F. Johnson (MA)
and Harriet L. Willey (MD)
Miriam Corrinth, b. 2/14/1925 in New Castle; second; Haven W.
Johnson (bus operator, York, ME) and Annie Grace Goodwin
(Boston, MA)
Patricia Jean, b. 4/30/1966 in Portsmouth; second; Walter H. Johnson
(NH) and Fredah F. Lindsey (CA)

Rosaline, b. 1/29/1919 in New Castle; third; Olgia Johnson (soldier, USA, Brownsfield, KY) and Margaret Walsh (Galaway, Ireland)

JONES,
daughter, 9/17/1920 in New Castle; Warner Edrick Jones (ensign, USN, Franklin) and Mary Hite (Huntington, WV)
son, b. 12/26/1945 in Portsmouth; second; Ernest E. Jones (deceased, Tulsa, OK) and Miriam C. Johnson (New Castle)
David Becker, b. 7/18/1928 in Portsmouth; first; Harold L. Jones (chauffeur, Langdon) and Dorothy E. Becker (New Castle)
Foster Tarleton, b. 3/16/1942 in Portsmouth; first; Robert S. Jones (boatswain, CG, So. Portland, ME) and Beverly J. Tarleton (Springfield, MA)
Henry Warren, b. 1/2/1930 in Portsmouth; second; Harold L. Jones (machinist, Langdon) and Dorothy E. Becker (New Castle)
Jacquelyn Grace, b. 2/17/1944 in Kittery, ME; first; Ernest E. Jones (F.1/c, USN, Tulsa, OK) and Marian C. Johnson (New Castle)
Jeffrey Robert, b. 2/29/1948 in Portsmouth; second; Robert S. Jones (carpenter, Portland, ME) and Beverly J. Tarlton (Springfield, MA)
Niel C., b. 1/20/1940 in Portsmouth; third; Harold Louis Jones (pipe fitter, Langdon) and Dorothy E. Becker (New Castle)
Roxanne, b. 9/28/1950 in Portsmouth; third; Robert S. Jones (carpenter, ME) and Beverly J. Tarlton (MA)

JOYCE,
Cheryl Elaine, b. 6/10/1948 in Portsmouth; first; Clarence E. Joyce (mechanic, Coal City, IN) and Georgette L. Lyons (Portsmouth)

KAROSIS,
Alexandra, b. 5/25/1988 in Portsmouth; Robert J. Karosis and Lauren A. Erlandson

KAZILIONIS,
John Joseph, Jr., b. 3/23/1946 in Portsmouth; first; Joseph J.
Kazilionis (laborer, Portland, ME) and Adeline Pinto
(Portsmouth)

KEENE,
Larry Robert, Jr., b. 4/2/1970 in Portsmouth; Larry R. Keene (NH)
and Marion E. Rogers (NH)

KELLENBECK,
Shirley Irene, b. 6/7/1929 in Portsmouth; second; William R.
Kellenbeck (machinist, Portsmouth) and Lavinia Ruth Morrill
(Portsmouth)
William Raymond, Jr., b. 5/25/1930 in Portsmouth; second; William
R. Kellenbeck (laborer, Portsmouth) and Levina Ruth Morrill
(Portsmouth)

KELLY,
Arthur W., III, b. 12/13/1957 in Portsmouth; first; Arthur W. Kelly,
Jr. (USCG, RI) and Verna E. Kumpulainen (MA)
Robert Francis, b. 11/22/1982; William G. Kelly and Mary E. Dalton

KENNEDY,
Christopher David, b. 10/3/1967 in Portsmouth; first; Brooks S.
Kennedy (MA) and Mary P. Alfriend (TN)
Elizabeth, b. 6/12/1949 in Portsmouth; second; Robert G. Kennedy
(reporter, Lowell, MA) and Carol C. Brooks (Unionville, CT)
Mary Kathryn, b. 9/22/1969 in Portsmouth; Brooks S. Kennedy (MA)
and Mary Alfriend (TN)

KEYES,
Linda Yvonne, b. 5/23/1943 in Portsmouth; third; Ralph Keyes (Pfc,
USA, Ft. Cobb, OK) and Juanita McPherson (Ft. Cobb, OK)

KIELING,

Karl Alfred, b. 4/21/1898 in New Castle; first; John Kieling
(shoemaker, 22, Germany) and Fanny H. Yeaton (housewife, 23,
New Castle)

KIMBALL,

Charles M., b. 6/8/1903 in New Castle; fourth; Charles M. Kimball
(engineer, 23, Chelsea, MA) and Florence E. Luery (21,
Rockland, ME)

Jon A., b. 3/18/1952 in Portsmouth; first; Ivory G. Kimball (cert.
officer, NH) and Margaret E. Anderson (ME)

Karoline Laura, b. 10/29/1959 in Portsmouth; second; Ivory G.
Kimball (NH) and Margaret E. Anderson (ME)

KING,

Charles Douglas, b. 6/9/1912 in New Castle; eighth; Humphrey King
(soldier, IN) and Delia Eblin (OH)

Dennis C., b. 1/7/1949 in Portsmouth; third; Linn A. King
(draughtsman, Methuen, MA) and Mary A. Little (Kittery, ME)

Frederick Gilbert, b. 7/25/1917 in New Castle; second; Frederick King
(corporal, USA, Whitinsville, MA) and Grace Trefethen
(Portsmouth)

John Marlin, Jr., b. 3/19/1961 in Portsmouth; first; John M. King
(NH) and Jacqueline D. DeSilva (HA)

KLOTZ,

Jennifer Virginia, b. 7/13/1970 in Portsmouth; Louis H. Klotz (NJ)
and Virginia H. Roll (OH)

KOVAL,

Franklin John, b. 12/24/1960 in Kittery, ME; first; Franklin N. Koval
(OH) and Barbara A. Paczosa (NH)

Jonathan Paul, b. 8/9/1962 in Kittery, ME; second; Franklin N. Koval
(OH) and Barbara N. Paczosa (NH)

43

KUCHTEY,
John Gregory, b. 12/4/1961 in Portsmouth; second; Michael A.
Kuchtey (NH) and Barbara A. Gray (NH)
Michael Alexander, Jr., b. 3/27/1968 in Portsmouth; Michael A.
Kuchtey (NH) and Barbara A. Gray (NH)

KUHN,
Margaret, b. 7/9/1914 in New Castle; first; Peter V. Kuhn (soldier,
Schoharie, NY) and Edith Mary Tolton (Leicester, England);
residence - Ft. Constitution

L'ESPERANCE,
Ruth Estelle Margaret, b. 11/23/1919 in New Castle; first; Philip
L'Esperance (electrician, Lynn, MA) and ----- (Brockton, MA);
residence - Lynn, MA

LAHAN,
John Henry, b. 9/27/1914 in New Castle; fourth; John Lahan (1st
Sergt., NHC Art., Troy, NY) and Emily A. Linsman (Boston,
MA)

LALONDE,
Carol Ann, b. 9/26/1956 in Kittery, ME; first; Carroll Joseph Lalonde
(USAF, LA) and Paula Ann Lagrange (LA)

LAMBERT,
Abigail Eliza, b. 6/10/1976 in Portsmouth; Thomas N. Lambert (WV)
and Mary Beth Norwood (OH)
Nicholas Brooks, b. 2/19/1974 in Portsmouth; Thomas D. Lambert
(WV) and Mary Beth Norwood (OH)
Zachary Thomas, b. 3/2/1980; Thomas Douglas Lambert and Mary
Beth Norwood

LANDRY,
Robert Michael, b. 1/26/1943 in Portsmouth; fourth; Clifford J.
Landry (dynamiter, Benedicta, ME) and Charlotte K. Hart
(Everett, MA)

LANTZ,
Katherine Mary, b. 1/9/1960 in Kittery, ME; first; Richard M. Lantz
(MN) and Margaret J. Driscoll (NH)

LAPINSKI,
Helen Elizabeth, b. 2/17/1919 in New Castle; first; Iznor Lapinski
(wood and iron merch., Austria) and Anna Susan Frankow
(Austria)

LAROSE,
Betty Ann, b. 9/16/1948 in Portsmouth; third; Harold J. LaRose
(carpenter, New Castle) and Stella Karokostas (Lowell, MA)
Elsie Mary, b. 4/24/1942 in Portsmouth; first; Harold J. LaRose
(laborer, NY, New Castle) and Stella Karakostas (Lowell, MA)
Harold Joseph, b. 8/24/1916 in New Castle; first; Harry R. LaRose
(soldier, NY) and Elsie Viola Norton (ME); residence - Ft.
Constitution
John Harold, b. 1/12/1947 in Portsmouth; second; Harold J. LaRose
(carpenter, New Castle) and Stella Karokostas (Lowell, MA)
Judith Annette, b. 1/15/1947 in Portsmouth; second; Loring P. Larose
(plumber, New Castle) and Lucille E. Lacey (S. Portland, ME)
Loring Paul, b. 9/24/1918 in New Castle; second; Harry Raymond
LaRose (sergeant, USA, Warwick, NY) and Elsie Viola Norton
(York, ME)
Michael John, b. 4/11/1967 in Portsmouth; first; John H. LaRose
(NH) and Linda C. Schultz (ME)
Nancy C., b. 6/23/1952 in Portsmouth; fourth; Harold J. LaRose
(carpenter, NH) and Stella Karadostas (NH)
Sean Michael, b. 1/23/1974 in Portsmouth; Michael P. LaRose (NH)
and Ann C. Parnham (NH)

LASKA,

Sonya Ruth, b. 12/5/1972 in Portsmouth; Paul F. Laska (NY) and
Patricia Kaminski (WI)

LAWRENCE,

Walter Shepard, b. 5/15/1920 in New Castle; second; Charles
Lawrence (laborer, Nashua) and Dorothy Mead (Manchester)

LEACH,

Douglas Edward, b. 11/1/1963 in Portsmouth; second; Donald B.
Leach (MA) and Vivian D. Williams (FL)

LEARY,

Kenneth Almond, b. 11/10/1914 in New Castle; fifth; Thomas Leary
(surfman, Boston, MA) and Josephine McKenna (Ireland)

Margaret Louise, b. 4/4/1926 in New Castle; first; Arthur T. Leary
(apprentice machinist, Boston, MA) and Helen G. McKay (Sandy
Cove, NS)

LEGARE,

Gina Rose, b. 12/3/1968 in Kittery, ME; Armand F. Legare (MA) and
Virginia G. Trujillo (CO)

James Justin, b. 2/10/1966 in Kittery, ME; first; Armand F. Legare
(MA) and Virginia C. Trujillo (CO)

Sherry Anne, b. 12/3/1968 in Kittery, ME; Armand F. Legare (MA)
and Virginia G. Trujillo (CO)

LEHAN,

Cornelius Richard, b. 10/16/1915 in New Castle; fifth; John R. Lehan
(1st Sgt., US Army, Troy, NY) and Emily A. Linsmon (So.
Boston, MA)

LEVENSON,

Amy Suzanne, b. 4/28/1994 in Portsmouth; Stuart Levenson and
Donna Knowles

Brian Kyle, b. 3/30/1996 in Portsmouth; Stuart M. Levenson and
Donna K. Knowles

LEVESQUE,
Donald Ernest, II, b. 6/5/1967 in Portsmouth; first; Donald E.
Levesque (NH) and Barbara J. Sheehe (NH)
Sue-Ann, b. 4/15/1968 in Portsmouth; Donald E. Levesque (NH) and
Barbara J. Sheehe (NH)

LIBBY,
Carrie M., b. 10/6/1902 in New Castle; sixth; William Libby
(carpenter, 38, Bristol, RI) and Emelia Gardener (30, Beluham,
MA)

LINDEN,
Robert Royal, b. 8/4/1915 in New Castle; first; Robert Royal Linden
(sgt., 1st C, Hosp. Cor., US Army, New York, NY) and Rose
Anna Perry (Hollister, CA)

LIPE,
Bradley A., b. 10/25/1953 in Kittery, ME; first; John V.S. Lipe (USN,
NY) and Iris M. Livingston (NY)

LITTLEFIELD,
son, b. 4/19/1900 in New Castle; seventh; Oliver C. Littlefield
(seaman, 35, Ogunquit, ME) and Susie C. Trussell (31, New
Castle)
Katie A., b. 11/1/1893 in New Castle; fourth; Oliver C. Littlefield
(laborer, 28, Wells, ME) and Susie F. Trussell (25, New Castle)
Ray Curtis, b. 5/30/1895 in New Castle; fifth; Oliver C. Littlefield
(seaman, 30) and Susie Trussel (26, New Castle)
Sidney Harland, b. 8/19/1897 in New Castle; sixth; Oliver C.
Littlefield (Wells, ME) and Susie F. Trussell (New Castle)

LLOYD,

Thelma Elizabeth, b. 6/4/1920 in Ft. Constitution; first; Ira F. Lloyd (electrician, Jessup, IA) and Beatrice Jones (Fall River, MA); residence - Ft. Constitution

Viola Agnes, b. 6/7/1921 in Ft. Constitution; second; Ira J. Lloyd (soldier, US) and Beatrice Jones (MA); residence - Ft. Constitution

LOCKE,

Elias Ernest, b. 4/27/1945 in Portsmouth; first; Wallace W. Locke (Sgt., US Army, Barnstead) and Winifred M. Pollard (Marlboro)

Rebecca Ann, b. 4/25/1944 in Portsmouth; first; Wallace W. Locke (Sgt, USA, Barnstead) and Winifred M. Pollard (Marlow)

LOCKHART,

Abigail Herrick, b. 10/12/1990 in Portsmouth; Richard Spence Lockhart and Caroline Olson Dorman

Elizabeth Dorman, b. 5/14/1992 in Portsmouth; Richard S. Lockhart and Caroline O. Lockhart

Richard Spencer, Jr., b. 11/7/1958; second; Richard S. Lockhart (Belmont, MA) and Penelope A. Lowe (Gardiner, ME)

LUNT,

Ann L., b. 9/21/1951 in Portsmouth; second; Daniel E. Lunt, Jr. (mechanic, ME) and June F. Averill (NH)

Daniel Edward, b. 7/29/1944 in Kittery, ME; first; Daniel E. Lunt, Jr. (USN, Portland, ME) and June F. Averill (Portsmouth)

MACBRIDE,

Benjamin Thayer, b. 12/14/1984 in Portsmouth; Harold E. MacBride and Joanna L. Trulson

MACDONALD,

Catherine Susan, b. 8/4/1984 in Portsmouth; Roderick M. MacDonald and Susan O. Eldredge

Margaret R., b. 12/9/1952 in Portsmouth; first; Roy J. MacDonald
(FBI, MN) and Carolyn V. Nelson (NC)
Polly, b. 6/18/1954 in Exeter; third; D. S. MacDonald (draftsman
Navy Yard, FL) and Margaret S. Snyder (NH)
R. M., b. 9/3/1949 in Exeter; first; D. S. MacDonald (draughtsman,
Jacksonville, FL) and Margaret S. Snyder (Portsmouth)

MACINTIRE,
Vicki Maxine, b. 5/18/1944 in Portsmouth; second; Donald K.
MacIntire (USA, Painesville, OH) and Johanna Obradovie
(Lorain, OH); residence - Fort Constitution

MAGOWAN,
David James, Jr., b. 10/5/1958; fourth; David J. Magowan
(Newburyport) and Norma G. Russell (Newburyport)

MAGUIRE,
Melissa Anne, b. 3/12/1960 in Kittery, ME; first; James P. Maguire
(NY) and Patricia A. While (CA)

MAN,
Madeline Adams, b. 1/2/1994 in Portsmouth; Adam Man and Beth
Disbrow

MARCOUS,
Neil Phillip, b. 1/13/1948 in Portsmouth; third; Joseph E. Marcous
(painter, Portsmouth) and Shirley M. Chandler (Lowell, MA)

MARGESON,
Jennifer Ann, b. 9/29/1966 in Portsmouth; third; Robert K. Margeson
(NH) and Joanne M. Adams (ME)

MARKEY,
Suzanne Nyhan, b. 10/12/1965 in Kittery, ME; first; William L.
Markey (MA) and Marilyn Hook (NH)

MARPLE,

son, b. 8/2/1971 in Portsmouth; Jeffrey H. Marple (NJ) and Sylvia E. Hoffman (SC)

Jeffrey Hoffman, b. 8/22/1972 in Portsmouth; Jeffrey H. Marple (SC) and Sylvia E. Hoffman (NJ)

William Edward, b. 5/4/1976 in Portsmouth; Jeffrey H. Marple (NJ) and Sylvia E. Hoffman (SC)

MARSHALL,

Sarah Elizabeth, b. 9/18/1971 in Portsmouth; Grover E. Marshall (ME) and Linda K. Curtis (ME)

MARVIN,

Edward Gerald, b. 6/6/1962 in Portsmouth; first; William E. Marvin (MA) and Helen E. Brett (NH)

Julie Elizabeth, b. 9/25/1964 in Portsmouth; second; William E. Marvin (MA) and Helen E. Brett (NH)

Oliver L., b. 4/1/1900 in New Castle; first; Oliver B. Marvin (clerk, 20, New Castle) and Cora Idella Wheeler (22, Lynn, MA)

Philip E., b. 6/30/1902 in New Castle; second; Oliver B. Marvin (merchant, 22, Portsmouth) and Cora I. Wheeler (25, Lynn, MA)

Sarah, b. 4/23/1899 in New Castle; second; William E. Marvin (lawyer, 27, Portsmouth) and Susan R. Bent (26, Wayland, MA)

William Bent, b. 3/23/1897 in New Castle; first; William E. Marvin (Portsmouth) and Susan R. Bent (Cochituate, MA)

MATTHEWS,

Darlene, b. 3/31/1957 in Portsmouth; fourth; Frederick Matthews (sign painter, NH) and Beverly I. White (ME)

MATTISON,

Byron Duane, b. 5/4/1899 in New Castle; first; William H. Mattison (soldier, USA, 27, Detroit, MI) and Frances Hughes (18, Wilmington, DE)

MAXAM,
Stephen Eugene, b. 1/13/1946 in Portsmouth; second; Kenneth E.
Maxam (contractor, Springfield, MA) and Grace V. Bohannon
(W. Newton, MA)

McAFEE,
Marilyn, b. 1/23/1940 in Portsmouth; second; Jesse Stuart McAfee
(Lt., USN, Heflin, LA) and Mary E. Nolen (St. Louis, MO)
Robert, b. 9/14/1938 in Portsmouth; first; Jesse S. McAfee (Sr. Lt., N.
Yd., Hefflin, LA) and Mary E. Nolen (St. Louis, MO)

McCARTHY,
Erin A., b. 9/26/1957 in Kittery, ME; fourth; John J. McCarthy, Jr.
(USN, MA) and Nancy J. Tabbutt (NH)
John C., b. 3/22/1952 in Kittery, ME; second; John J. McCarthy, Jr.
(US Navy, MA) and Nancy J. Tabbott (NH)
Nancy A., b. 6/27/1955 in Kittery, ME; third; John J. McCarthy (US
Navy, MA) and Nancy J. Tabbutt (NH)
Thomas, b. 11/14/1952 in Kittery, ME; sixth; Robert J. McCarthy
(US Navy, PA) and Helen E. Jackson (NY)

McCORMACK,
Benjamin James Varner, b. 3/21/1992 in Portsmouth; Thomas M.
McCormack and Rebecca A. Varner
Jennifer May Varner, b. 10/8/1985 in Portsmouth; Thomas Martin
McCormack and Rebecca Anne Varner
Simon Thomas Karmen, b. 10/10/1988 in Portsmouth; Thomas M.
McCormack and Rebecca A. Varner

McDONALD,
A.T. Michael, b. 2/2/1953 in Portsmouth; third; Arthur T. McDonald
(cable splic., NH) and Ruth V. Kanada (ME)
Bonnie, b. 11/20/1952 in Exeter; second; Douglas S. McDonald (eng.
drafts., FL) and Margaret S. Snyder (NH)

McDONOUGH,

Amanda Ruth, b. 6/29/1969 in Portsmouth; Michael J. McDonough (CA) and Deborah T. Marvin (MA)

Perry Ann, b. 11/28/1997 in Portsmouth; J. C. McDonough and S. C. McDonough

McGEE,

Hiram Blaine, b. 5/12/1976 in Exeter; James B. McGee III (MO) and Bonnie R. Daugherty (AL)

McGRAW,

David Dion, b. 3/18/1947 in Portsmouth; third; Kenneth D. McGraw (US Army, Eureka, MO) and Miriam C. Johnson (New Castle)

McINTYRE,

Amy Bridget, b. 5/16/1982; Hugh D. McIntyre and Nancy A. McCarthy

Heather Nancy, b. 12/5/1977 in Portsmouth; Hugh D. McIntyre (Scotland) and Nancy A. McCarthy (ME)

McLEAN,

Allyn B., b. 5/13/1939 in Brentwood; third; Edwin B. McLean (physician, Plymouth, MA) and Ruth E. Moffatt (Brookings, SD)

McTIGUE,

Mary A., b. 2/19/1954 in Kittery, ME; first; John W. McTigue (USN, WV) and Georgene A. Davis (FL)

MEERER,

George Henry, 3d, b. 12/10/1944 in Exeter; first; George H. Meerer, Jr. (Major, USA, Binghamton, NY) and Maude A. Wood (Altoona, PA)

MELOON,

Alfred, b. 9/9/1904 in New Castle; first; George B. Meloon (teamster, 24, New Castle) and Julia Healey (23, Ireland)

Alice E., b. 5/11/1906 in New Castle; second; George B. Meloon
(teamster, 26, New Castle) and Julia Healy (24, Ireland)

Arleane Leighton, b. 6/7/1897 in New Castle; ninth; Amory J. Meloon
(New Castle) and Sarah E. Yeaton (New Castle)

Charles L., b. 1/26/1900 in New Castle; tenth; Amory J. Meloon
(carpenter, 43, New Castle) and Sarah S. Yeaton (39, New
Castle)

Everett S., b. 1/22/1893 in New Castle; seventh; Amory J. Meloon
(carpenter, 36, New Castle) and Sarah S. Yeaton (33, New
Castle)

Henry, b. 3/10/1895 in New Castle; eighth; Amory J. Meloon
(carpenter, 37, New Castle) and Sarah Yeaton (35, New Castle)

William D., b. 5/21/1908 in New Castle; third; George B. Meloon
(teamster, 28, New Castle) and Julia Healey (26, Ireland)

MENEELY,

John K., Jr., b. 2/5/1917 in New Castle; first; John K. Meneely
(lieutenant, USA, Coeymans, NY) and Sarah Suderley (Waterlist,
NY)

METHOT,

Casey Rene, b. 8/29/1994 in Portsmouth; Gary Methot and Sueann
Brennan

MEYERS,

Virginia Violette, b. 8/30/1914 in New Castle; first; Rollie Meyers
(USA, Columbus, OH) and Anna Mabel Hartley (Waterford, NJ)

MILES,

James Robert, b. 5/11/1968 in Portsmouth; Philip G. Miles (NH) and
Priscilla R. Greene (ME)

Tracy Lee, b. 5/3/1965 in Portsmouth; first; Arthur L. Miles (NH) and
Shirley L. Owsley (NH)

MILLER,
Adelbert F., b. 3/15/1903 in New Castle; first; Daniel F. Miller
(laborer, 23, England) and Arta Manson (17, Merrimac, MA)
Ann, b. 7/3/1939 in Exeter; first; Norman O. Miller (machine op.,
Peabody, MA) and Dorothy M. Broadway (Montgomery, AL)
Elizabeth Frances, b. 10/1/1944 in Portsmouth; second; Norman O.
Miller (machinist, Peabody, MA) and Dorothy M. Broadway
(Montgomery, AL)
Ivery Bell, b. 11/26/1904 in New Castle; second; Daniel F. Miller
(laborer, 26, England) and Arta Manson (18, Merrimack)

MOEBUS,
Robin R., b. 11/17/1953 in Portsmouth; first; Robert A. Moebus
(engineer, NY) and Ruth M. Boyan (MA)

MOORE,
James Augustus, b. 2/27/1928 in New Castle; third; Eugene M. Moore
(soldier, US Army, New Haven, CT) and Josephine A. Eagen
(NF)

MORAN,
Sean Spence-Patrick, b. 3/11/1969 in Portsmouth; Geoffrey P. Moran
(MA) and Judith A. Flagg (MA)

MORI,
Bette Lynette, b. 9/25/1944 in Portsmouth; third; Albert Mori
(machinist, Arezzo, Italy) and Hilda G. Ricker (New Castle)
Charles Albert, b. 3/28/1931 in Portsmouth; second; Albert Mori
(toolmaker, Springfield, MA) and Hilda Ricker (New Castle)
Ruth E., b. 5/1/1925 in Portsmouth; first; Albert Mori (US Army,
Springfield, MA) and Hilda Ricker (New Castle)

MORRILL,
Andrea J., b. 5/14/1951 in Portsmouth; second; Eugene W. Morrill
(postal clerk, NH) and Nella N. Foss (ME)

Arthur E., b. 1/21/1957 in Portsmouth; third; Eugene W. Morrill
(postal clerk, NH) and Nella M. Foss (ME)
Brent Wesley, b. 1/3/1971 in Kittery, ME; Richard T. Morrill (NH)
and Deborah L. Hodgdon (NH)
Corey Sage, b. 6/7/1974 in Exeter; Richard T. Morrill (NH) and
Deborah L. Hodgdon (NH)
Richard Irvin, b. 5/14/1929 in New Castle; second; Harris W. Morrill
(machinist, navy yard, Portsmouth) and Doris Poole Maxam
(Springfield, MA)
Richard Tristram, b. 11/2/1948 in Portsmouth; first; Eugene W.
Morrill (gen'l helper, Portsmouth) and Nella M. Foss (Jonesport,
ME)

MORRISSY,
Robert E., b. 9/27/1908 in New Castle; third; Thomas Morrissy
(soldier, 42, Ireland) and Catherine Quill (41, Portsmouth)

MOUNTFORD,
Elizabeth Marie, b. 9/6/1991 in Portsmouth; Walter J. Mountford and
Deborah J. Mountford

MOURO, (see Munroe)
Winnifred Kay, b. 7/2/1933 in Portsmouth; second; Oscar Carl Mouro
(USCG, Halifax, NS) and Essie Francis Ricker (New Castle)

MUIR,
Diana H., b. 6/11/1949 in Portsmouth; first; William C. Muir (student,
Clinton, MA) and Barbara H. Hayden (Portsmouth)

MULLIN,
Francis Robert, b. 7/11/1994 in Portsmouth; Christopher Mullin and
Stephanie Higgins
Olivia Rose, b. 11/23/1987 in Portsmouth; Christopher Francis Mullin
and Stephanie Higgins
William Joseph, b. 11/23/1987 in Portsmouth; Christopher Francis
Mullin and Stephanie Higgins

MUNIZ,
Kevin Patrick, b. 6/25/1978; Luis A. Muniz and Josephine A. Wood

MUNRO[E],
Bert White, b. 2/23/1935 in New Castle; third; Oscar C. Munro
(USCG, Halifax, NS) and Essie F. Ricker (New Castle)
Carl George, b. 2/3/1932 in Portsmouth; first; Oscar C. Munroe
(USCG, Halifax, NS) and Essie F. Ricker (New Castle)

MURRAY,
stillborn son, b. 6/1/1904 in New Castle; William E. Murray (army
officer, Allen, TX) and Anna E. Calhone (SC)
Floyd Calhoun, b. 8/15/1905 in New Castle; second; William Elmer
Murray (lieut, USA, 28, Gatesville, TX) and Ann Eliza Cahoun
(29, Barnwell, SC)

NEWTON,
Karen Louise, b. 12/25/1958; fifth; Ray B. Newton (Portsmouth) and
Ethel M. Hurd (Derry)
Kevin Duane, b. 2/8/1958; fourth; Ray B. Newton (Portsmouth) and
Ethel M. Hurd (Derry)

NICHOLS,
Carrie D., d. 5/10/1972 in Kittery, ME; John P. Nichols (ME) and
Patricia H. Lincoln (MA)

NORDIE,
Bartholomus Horatio, b. 8/28/1918 in New Castle; third; Lewis
Nordie (carpenter, Norway) and Anna O'Donnell (Manchester);
residence - Manchester

NOSEWORTHY,
Norman Lloyd, b. 11/30/1935 in Kittery, ME; second; Randall
Noseworthy (laborer, St. Jacques, NF) and Elsie C. Littlefield
(Portsmouth)

Randell Wilfred, b. 9/19/1934 in Kittery, ME; first; Randell
Noseworthy (laborer, Fortune Bay, NF) and Elsie K. Littlefield
(New Castle)

NOYES,
David Chandler, b. 9/4/1923 in New Castle; fourth; Fred R. Noyes
(painter, Windsor, ME) and Alice M. Robinson (New Castle)
Lois Mildred, b. 7/26/1912 in New Castle; third; Fred R. Noyes
(porter, Windsor, ME) and Alice Robinson (New Castle)

O'BRIEN,
Virginia, b. 8/29/1938 in Portsmouth; first; Kenneth O'Brien (laborer,
Cape Breton) and Dorothy A. Davis (Buffalo, NY)

O'CONNOR,
Margaret Helen, b. 6/14/1965 in Portsmouth; fourth; William J.
O'Connor (NY) and Margaret Chandler (NH)
Patricia Anne, b. 12/7/1967 in Portsmouth; fifth; William J. O'Connor
(NY) and Margaret Chandler (NH)

O'NEILL,
Neal, b. 6/13/1922 in New Castle; first; Vincent T. O'Neill (US
Army, White River Jct., VT) and Ann F. Coye (Malden, MA)
Vincent Coye, b. 6/13/1923 in New Castle; second; Vincent T.
O'Neill (soldier, White River Jct., VT) and Anna F. Coye
(Malden, MA)

ODIORNE,
son, b. 12/19/1893 in New Castle; fourth; Frank P. Odiorne
(carpenter, 39, Rye) and Lavinia Murray (37, New Castle)
Ellen Louise, b. 12/14/1931 in Portsmouth; second; John M. Odiorne
(caretaker, Rye) and Ouida Alley (Jonesport, ME)
Frank A., b. 1/26/1892 in New Castle; Frank P. Odiorn (carpenter,
Rye) and Lavinia Murray (New Castle)

OGLES,

Helen Marion, b. 12/15/1924 in New Castle; first; Lucian G. Ogles (US Army, Bowling Green, KY) and Edith M. Rand (Portsmouth)

OLIVER,

William, b. 2/17/1906 in New Castle; first; Robert L. Oliver (laborer, 62, New Castle) and Ellen Costello (37, Ireland)

ORR,

William Jordan, b. 12/28/1934 in Portsmouth; first; Jordan Orr (USCG, Manchester) and Helen Lyon (Hancock, MA)

OSGOOD,

Vincent S., b. 9/27/1954 in Portsmouth; second; Roland L. Osgood (welfare worker, NH) and Elinor D. Sawyer (NH)

OTT,

Paul, b. 10/15/1943 in Portsmouth; first; Raymond H. Ott (serg., USA, Wawsaw, WI) and Rosemary C. Gendron (Wawsaw, WI)

OWSLEY,

Raymond James, b. 3/2/1943 in Portsmouth; second; Raymond J. Owsley (serg., USA, John's R., KY) and Mary E. Homing (Portsmouth)

Shirley L., b. 7/2/1941 in Portsmouth; first; Raymond J. Owsley (sgt, USA, Johns Run, KY) and Mary Earline Horning (Portsmouth)

PACE,

Lisa Marie, b. 5/22/1967 in Portsmouth; first; Brandt P. Pace (NH) and Sandra L. Harris (NH)

PADGETT,

Kevin Westmore, b. 6/10/1969 in Portsmouth; Gerald Padgett (FL) and Nancy D. Poole (NH)

Kimberly Ann, b. 9/17/1966 in Portsmouth; fourth; Gerald Padgett (FL) and Nancy D. Poole (NH)

Vincent Wadsworth, b. 4/25/1971 in Portsmouth; Gerald Padgett (FL) and Nancy D. Poole (NH)

PAFFORD,

Corey Stephen, b. 12/21/1972 in Portsmouth; Robert B. Pafford (NH) and Barbara A. Pavlidis (NH)

James E., b. 9/26/1941 in Portsmouth; first; Ernest H. Pafford (sgt, USA, Eva, TN) and Sarah H. Hutchinson (Kittery, ME)

PAGE,

Nancy, b. 5/8/1946 in Portsmouth; first; Frederick G. Page (lineman, Portsmouth) and Lucille Dore (Portsmouth)

PAINE,

Isabelle, b. 9/9/1966 in Portsmouth; second; Lincoln D. Paine (MA) and Caroline Wogan (LA)

Sarah M., b. 7/25/1903 in New Castle; first; Joseph S. Paine (baker, 25, Mt. Vernon, KY) and Edith Simpson (16, New Castle)

PARKER,

Herman Wendell, b. 8/28/1913 in New Castle; fourth; Charles A. Parker (secretary, YMCA, Neponset, MA) and Mildred Rankin (Malden, MA)

Jonathan, b. 11/29/1986 in Portsmouth; Anthony Parker and Margaret Mary Brown

Samuel, b. 9/1/1989 in Portsmouth; Anthony Parker and Margaret M. Brown

PARRISH,

Hugh R., b. 11/14/1957 in Kittery, ME; fourth; Hugh M. Parrish (USAF, MD) and Therese P. Sellers (PA)

PARSONS,

Brett Kelly, b. 4/23/1989 in Portsmouth; Ronald R. Parsons and Joan Kelly

John Jennings, b. 12/2/1960 in Kittery, ME; second; Frederic J. Parsons (Rumania) and Wananda J. Wimberley (MS)

PASSON,

Alexander Hill, b. 6/29/1990 in Portsmouth; Kurt Douglas Passon and Melanie Ruth Hill

PATCH,

George S., b. 3/23/1904 in New Castle; second; Leon S. Patch (engineer, Kittery, ME) and M. Gertrude Patch (York, ME)

PATTEN,

Peggy B., b. 9/29/1954 in Portsmouth; third; George A. Patten (dentist, NH) and Mildred E. Cook (RI)

PAULMANN,

Katherine Lindsay, b. 12/10/1986 in Portsmouth; Oswald Sven Paulmann and Valerie Margaret Hartman

PAYNE,

Harry M., b. 3/4/1914 in New Castle; second; Joseph S. Payne (laborer, Mt. Vernon, KY) and Edith Simpson (New Castle); residence - Columbus, OH

PELLETIER,

Jodi Anne, b. 8/23/1964 in Portsmouth; third; Adrian R. Pelletier (NH) and Judith K. Lyman (NH)

PERKINS,

Wilbur Sheldon, b. 9/7/1925 in New Castle; ninth; Charles N. Perkins (fisherman) and Emeline Wakeham (Boston, MA)

PERRAULT,

Kristen Daniel, b. 11/23/1968 in Portsmouth; John P. Perrault (ME)
and Anita H. Hages (NH)

Tracie Elizabeth, b. 11/23/1968 in Portsmouth; John P. Perrault (ME)
and Anita H. Hages (NH)

PERRY,

Isabel G., b. 6/9/1904 in New Castle; first; Lewis K. Perry (soldier,
USA, 21, KY) and Mabel Meloon (23, New Castle)

Jessie Ione, b. 9/5/1906 in New Castle; third; Louis K. Perry (soldier,
24, KY) and Mabel L. Meloon (25, New Castle)

Nellie Elizabeth, b. 7/10/1905 in New Castle; second; Lewis K. Perry
(sergeant, USA, 22, KY) and Mable L. Meloon (24, New Castle)

Paul Donald, b. 4/29/1961 in Portsmouth; third; Paul F. Perry (NH)
and Mary E. MacLeod (ME)

PETLICK,

Charles Arnold, b. 12/13/1944 in Portsmouth; first; Casimir J. Petlick
(Corp., USA, B. Har., MI) and Marion E. White (Portsmouth)

Michael Arnold, b. 6/24/1977 in Portsmouth; Charles A. Petlick (NH)
and Charlene M. McKie (GA)

Sandra Elizabeth, b. 12/9/1980; Charles Arnold Petlick and Charlene
Mary McKie

PHILIP,

Stephanie Elizabeth, b. 2/19/1981; Stephen G. Philip and Sheila Ann
Noonis

PIADER,

Edward Joseph, b. 6/30/1913 in New Castle; second; John E. Piader
(soldier, USA, Austria) and Ruth E. Peltis (Dover)

PIERCE,

Robert E., b. 6/2/1941 in Portsmouth; third; Elmer William Pierce
(electrician, Kittery, ME) and Blanche Edna Dailey (Hallowell,
ME)

William Elmer, Jr., b. 1/31/1948 in Portsmouth; first; William E.
Pierce (machinist, Portsmouth) and Barbara C. Dunbar
(Stoneham, MA)

PINGREE,
Sarah E., b. 10/14/1955 in Portsmouth; first; Stanley C. Pingree
(supply dept. NB, NH) and Elinor C. Hanscom (NH)

PIO,
Agnes May, b. 11/13/1927 in New Castle; second; Harry L. Pio
(roofer, Ellsworth, ME) and Agnes M. Williams (Exeter)

PIPER,
Charles Alonzo, b. 7/31/1921 in New Castle; second; Alonzo C. Piper
(mechanic, E. Hingham, NH) and Marguerite Tuttle (Epping)

PITTS,
Andrea Denice, b. 6/21/1959 in Kittery, ME; second; Frederick P.
Pitts (NH) and Greselda N. Strasner (AR)

POOLE,
David Wayne, b. 11/1/1972 in Portsmouth; Robert W. Poole (NH) and
Pamela S. Aspen (NH)
Kendrick G., b. 5/23/1945 in Portsmouth; first; Kendrick W. Poole
(USCG, New Castle) and Roberta E. Groton (Portsmouth)
Kendrick Wadsworth, b. 8/2/1912 in New Castle; second; Wayne D.
Poole (New Castle) and Alice G. Winnn (Augusta, ME)
Nancy D., b. 3/26/1940 in Portsmouth; first; Vincent W. Poole
(manager, New Castle) and Nancy D. Holden (New Castle)
Sarah Elizabeth, b. 9/8/1976 at Pease AFB; Robert W. Poole (NH)
and Pamela S. Aspen (NH)

POULIN,
Victor T., b. 4/1/1954 in Portsmouth; third; Joseph R. Poulin
(unemployed, Canada) and June T. Amazeen (ME)

William P., b. 3/9/1949 in Portsmouth; third; Joseph R. Poulin (student, Dorchester, Canada) and Ruth T. Amazeen (Kittery, ME)

PRAIL,
Anne Mary, b. 9/11/1918 in New Castle; second; Myer Prail (post tailor, Russia) and Rosie Trailer (Russia)

PRESTI,
Adriene Louise, b. 10/27/1966 in Portsmouth; second; Louis J. Presti (CT) and Cynthia M. Wick (NY)

PRICE,
Jacqueline Frances, b. 7/21/1960 in Kittery, ME; second; Herbert J. Price (OH) and Lorraine M. Paradis (MA)
Ronald Lee, b. 5/30/1958; second; Roger Lee Price (Minneapolis, MN) and Irene K. Bott (Lauger, Germany)

PRIDHAM,
stillborn son, b. 9/24/1946 in Portsmouth; Stanley W. Pridham (USCG, New Castle) and Jeanne Cochrane (Boston, MA)
Beryl Elaine, b. 6/6/1948 in Portsmouth; fourth; Stanley W. Pridham (USCG, New Castle) and Jeanne Cochrane (Boston, MA)
Clinton D., b. 1/11/1906 in New Castle; first; Elmer S. Pridham (27, New Castle) and Ethel Poole (27, New Castle)
Cynthia Alice, b. 12/13/1933 in Portsmouth; fourth; Gordon L. Pridham (chauffeur, New Castle) and Viola Noyes (Cooper's Mills, ME)
D. Cavanaugh, b. 9/5/1948 in Portsmouth; first; Douglas C. Pridham (policeman, New Castle) and Arline M. Cousins (Portsmouth)
Debora, b. 7/11/1950 in Portsmouth; second; Douglas C. Pridham (file clerk, NH) and Arline Cousins (NH)
Denise Marie, b. 3/8/1958; third; Frederick J. Pridham (Portsmouth) and Mary T. Moran (Newburyport, MA)
Donald, b. 11/3/1951 in Portsmouth; third; Douglas C. Pridham (clk, n. base, NH) and Arline M. Cousins (NH)

Douglas Cavanaugh, b. 7/14/1913 in New Castle; third; Elmer S.
Pridham (laborer, New Castle) and Ethel Poole (New Castle)
Douglas Willard, b. 6/26/1936 in Portsmouth; second; Stanley W.
Pridham (coast guard, New Castle) and Jeanne L. Cochran
(Boston, MA)
Frederic John, b. 3/26/1931 in Portsmouth; third; Gordon L. Pridham
(chauffeur, New Castle) and Niola Noyes (Coopers Mills, ME)
Gorden L., b. 2/18/1903 in New Castle; first; John W. Pridham
(surfman, 29, New Castle) and Anna F. Bates (29, Boston, MA)
Gordon, b. 12/3/1937 in Portsmouth; fifth; Gordon L. Pridham
(chauffeur, New Castle) and Niola W. Noyes (Coopers M., ME)
Isadore Elizabeth, b. 9/29/1915 in New Castle; fourth; Elmer S.
Pridham (shoemaker, New Castle) and Ethel Poole (New Castle)
Julie Arline, b. 11/14/1987 in Portsmouth; Donald Francis Pridham
and Karen Lee Sorensen
Laura Ann, b. 11/5/1983; Donald F. Pridham and Karen L. Sorensen
Morris Bates, b. 4/9/1905 in New Castle; second; John W. Pridham
(surfman, 32, New Castle) and Anna F. Bates (32, Boston, MA)
Nancy Claire, b. 6/14/1930 in New Castle; second; Gordon L.
Pridham (chauffeur, New Castle) and Viola Watson Noyes
(Coopers Mills, ME)
Stanley Merle, b. 3/1/1932 in Portsmouth; first; Stanley W. Pridham
(laborer, New Castle) and Jeanne Cochrane (Boston, MA)
Stanley Wentworth, b. 7/19/1911 in New Castle; second; Elmer S.
Pridham (laborer, 32, New Castle) and Ethel Poole (32, New
Castle)
Timothy Martin, b. 2/8/1967 in Kittery, ME; fourth; Stanley M.
Pridham (NH) and Gloria M. Sawyer (ME)

PRIEST,
Wanda J., b. 5/10/1957 in New Castle; first; Daniel W. Priest (USN,
FL) and Catherine J. Campbell (NH)

PRIESTLEY,
Donna E., b. 9/5/1945 in Portsmouth; second; William Priestley
(stereotypist, Barre, MA) and Isadore E. Pridham (New Castle)

William Richard, b. 2/9/1936 in Portsmouth; first; William Priestley (chauffeur, Barre, MA) and Elizabeth Pridham (New Castle)

PROHASKA,
Bradley Jackson, b. 11/14/1914 in New Castle; third; Charles F. Prohaska, Jr. (carpenter, Chelsea, MA) and Ida Murray (Newfoundland)
Ira Francis, b. 4/21/1923 in New Castle; third; Roy Prohaska (prop. grocery, Hull, MA) and Maud E. Metcalf (Danville, VT)
Izola Mauray, b. 9/12/1912 in New Castle; second; C. F. Prohaska, Jr. (carpenter, Boston, MA) and Ida Murray (Newfoundland)

RANDALL,
Ruth Mary, b. 4/19/1912 in New Castle; first; Hazen C. Randall (carpenter, New Castle) and Abbie DeLancey (Hampton)

REED,
Clifford W., b. 11/14/1941 in Portsmouth; third; Walter Burton Reed (sgt, USA, Winthrop, MA) and Martha J. Branham (Waltz, KY)

REMICK,
Stanton G., Jr., b. 8/27/1937 in Portsmouth; first; Stanton G. Remick (foreman, Rye) and Elizabeth Prohaska (Portsmouth)

REYNOLDS,
John Thomas, b. 1/29/1942 in Portsmouth; second; Richard Reynolds (DMD, USA, Quincy, MA) and Perle E. Thomas (Statesboro, PA)

RICHARDS,
Karen Ruth, b. 3/21/1943 in Portsmouth; first; William E. Richards (soldier, USA, Ipswich, MA) and June T. Amazeen (Kittery, ME)

RICKER,
Annette Muriel, b. 7/24/1918 in New Castle; eighth; George B. Ricker (Captain, USCG, New Castle) and Sadie E. Whitye (New Castle)

Arline R., b. 2/7/1908 in New Castle; fourth; George B. Ricker (US Life Saving Service, 33, New Castle) and Sadie E. White (35, New Castle)

Charles H., b. 3/4/1903 in New Castle; second; George B. Ricker (surfman, 28, New Castle) and Sadie E. White (30, New Castle)

Essie Frances, b. 4/8/1913 in New Castle; seventh; George B. Ricker (USLSS, New Castle) and Sadie E. White (New Castle)

George B., II, b. 8/29/1945 in Portsmouth; Lyndon H. Ricker (carpenter, New Castle) and Louise E. Gardreault (So. Berwick, ME)

Hazel E., b. 2/1/1902 in New Castle; first; George B. Ricker (surfman, 25, New Castle) and Sadie E. White (27, New Castle)

Hilda Graham, b. 9/6/1905 in New Castle; third; George B. Ricker (Life Sav. Service, 28, New Castle) and Sadie E. White (32, New Castle)

Leona Madeline, b. 11/14/1915 in New Castle; seventh; George B. Ricker (USCG, New Castle) and Sadie E. White (New Castle)

Linda Diane, b. 5/6/1942 in Portsmouth; first; Lyndon H. Ricker (joiner, NY, New Castle) and Louise E. Gaudreault (Berwick, ME)

L[yndon]., Jr., b. 6/6/1949 in Portsmouth; L[yndon]. H. Ricker, Jr. (carpenter, New Castle) and Louise Saudreault (So. Berwick, ME)

RIDDIOUGH,
Dennis, b. 6/8/1957 in Portsmouth; first; LeRoy F. Riddiough (laborer, WI) and Donna M. DeWitt (WI)

RIFFE,
Christopher Robert, b. 8/17/1962 in Kittery ME; third; Michael C. Riffe (IN) and Margaret Legnard (PA)

Jennifer Ellen, b. 9/29/1964 in Kittery, ME; fifth; Michael C. Riffe (IN) and Margaret Legnard (PA)

Michael Kevin, b. 10/12/1960 in Kittery, ME; third; Michael C. Riffe (IN) and Margaret Legnard (PA)

ROBBINS,
Bonnie Ann, b. 2/19/1966 in Portsmouth; first; Theodore F. Robbins
(MA) and Mary A. Skruta (CT)
Todd Franklin, b. 9/1/1977 in Portsmouth; Theodore F. Robbins
(MA) and Mary Anne Skruta (CT)

ROBINSON,
Christine, b. 3/24/1949 in Portsmouth; second; Edward G. Robinson
(secretary, Milford, MA) and D. A. Pendleton (Franklin, MA)
Deborah, b. 12/10/1964 in Portsmouth; second; Peter G. Robinson
(NH) and Carol L. Green (MA)
Diane, b. 12/10/1964 in Portsmouth; third; Peter G. Robinson (NH)
and Carol L. Green (MA)
Douglas P., b. 10/11/1904 in New Castle; first; J. Blake Robinson
(physician, 55, ME) and L. Gertrude Palmer (33, ME)
Leland Basil, b. 5/25/1895 in New Castle; first; Fred A. Robinson
(shoe cutter, 23) and Minnie Poole (22)

ROGERS,
William, b. 9/23/1937 in New Castle; first; Angelo Landoni (mill
hand, Norwich, CT) and Lily I. Rogers (Ledyard, CT); residence -
Norwich, CT

ROPER,
stillborn son, b. 9/14/1912 in New Castle; first; Robert Roper (soldier,
Belleville, IL) and Jennie Lenard (Boston, MA)

ROTHENBERG,
William Von Hindenberg, b. 2/26/1915 in Ft. Constitution; fourth;
Marton Rothenberg (elec. Sgt., 1st C., CAC, Austria) and Esther
Weiss (Austria)

ROWLAND,
Rodney Douglas, b. 3/26/1966 in Lawrence, MA; second; Benjamin
A. Rowland (PA) and Barbara Bearse (NH)

ROWLEY,

Dana P., b. 6/5/1952 in Portsmouth; first; Donald W. Rowley (clergyman, NY) and Norma D. Philbrick (RI)

Joseph Edward, b. 12/26/1984 in Portsmouth; Mark E. Rowley and Kathleen M. Smith

Samantha Colleen, b. 12/18/1986 in Portsmouth; Mark Edward Rowley and Kathleen Marie Smith

ROY,

Kathleen Anne, b. 8/1/1963 in Portsmouth; tenth; Thomas L. Roy (MA) and Patricia M. Tergesen (NH)

RUGG,

Cheri Ruth, b. 3/18/1970 in Exeter; Douglass W. Rugg (NH) and Shelley A. Wiggin (NH)

RUMPH,

Meghan Alexandra, b. 7/13/1995 in Portsmouth; Gary J. Rumph and Jennifer L. Morin

Meredith Ashley, b. 6/9/1993 in Portsmouth; Gary G. Rumph and J. L. Morin

RUSSELL,

Amy Elizabeth, b. 9/17/1973 in Portsmouth; Bayard Russell (MA) and Pamela M. Strohm (IN)

RUTH,

Leo John, II, b. 9/8/1966 in Portsmouth; first; Leo John Ruth (PA) and Margaret E. Reid (England)

RYLANDER,

Karen J., b. 7/11/1957 in Portsmouth; fourth; Ralph T.N. Rylander (off. mgr. Chev., MA) and Betty J. Harwood (NY)

William H., b. 6/22/1952 in Portsmouth; third; Ralph N. Rylander (bookkeeper, MA) and Betty J. Harwood (NY)

SABINS,

Virginia, b. 6/7/1937 in Portsmouth; fourth; William T. Sabins (laborer, Portsmouth) and Doris Davis (Jonesport, ME)

SALTER,

Joshua Orr, b. 1/17/1972 in Portsmouth; John O. Salter (IL) and Patricia L. Herman (MI)

SAMMARTINO,

Benning Wentworth, b. 8/19/1918 in New Castle; second; Pasquale Sammartino (tailor, Italy) and Erminia Mancini (Italy)

SAMUELS,

Joseph Goodman, b. 7/1/1982; George F. Samuels and Joanne Goodman

Julie, b. 6/4/1985 in Portsmouth; George Frederick Samuels and Joanne Goodman

SARTORELLI,

Nina Marie, b. 8/19/1993 in Portsmouth; M. Sartorelli and L. M. Anderson

SAWYER,

Ida May, b. 5/26/1907 in New Castle; tenth; Daniel Sawyer (surfman, 42, Jonesport, ME) and Carrie Smith (36, St. John, NB)

Patrick James, b. 11/12/1971 in Portsmouth; Stephen D. Sawyer (NH) and Judith A. LaRose (NH)

Thomas Paul, b. 2/3/1966 in Portsmouth; first; Stephen D. Sawyer (NH) and Judith A. LaRose (NH)

SCHLIEPER,

Arthur William, Jr., b. 5/11/1944 in Portsmouth; first; Arthur W. Schlieper (Lt, USA, Brooklyn, NY) and Doris M. Campbell (Beachmont, MA)

SCHMIDT,
Amber Renae, b. 11/26/1979; Robert S. Schmidt and Crystal D. Hunt

SCHWARTZ,
Rachel Conant, b. 5/23/1987 in Portsmouth; Ira Sanford Schwartz and Jennifer Law Conant

Rebecca Ostrander, b. 5/23/1987 in Portsmouth; Ira Sanford Schwartz and Jennifer Law Conant

SEMPRINI,
Brian Paul, b. 4/30/1979; Wayne P. Semprini and Paulette Darcy

Jeffrey Charles, b. 5/2/1983; Wayne P. Semprini and Paulette W. Darcy

SHAW,
Richard Everett, b. 12/9/1935 in Portsmouth; first; Everett Samuel Shaw (electrician, Portland, ME) and Amy Margaret Snell (Starks, ME)

SHEA,
Karen E., b. 5/30/1956 in Portsmouth; third; Leo Francis Shea (allowance insp., NH) and Ellen Louise Robbins (MA)

Lorrie Ellen, b. 4/6/1965 in Portsmouth; fourth; Leo F. Shea (NH) and Ellen L. Robbins (MA)

SHEAR,
Larry J., b. 1/14/1952 in Kittery, ME; first; Donald A. Shear (US Navy, NY) and Cathleen D. Gerard (NJ)

SHEEHAN,
Jane Elizabeth, b. 10/9/1947 in Portsmouth; second; Thomas L. Sheehan (metallurgist, Lowell, MA) and Julia M. Bubelis (Philadelphia, PA)

SHERBONEAU,
James E., b. 11/22/1953 in Portsmouth; second; Richard T.
Sherboneau (take-off man, NY) and Dorothy L. Trefethen (NH)

SHUTER,
daughter, b. 10/26/1912 in New Castle; second; Charles O.
Shuter (plumber, Vance, NC) and Catherine O'Malley (Boston, MA)

SIBSON,
Elizabeth Jane, b. 2/22/1962 in Kittery, ME; first; Donald A. Sibson
(NH) and Virginia L. Wiley (NH)

SICHERI,
Peter Lyndon, b. 11/2/1959 in Kittery, ME; first; Peter M. Sicheri
(England) and Linda D. Ricker (NH)

SIMPSON,
Jessica Linn, b. 7/17/1982; Robert W. Simpson and Lorraine M.
Bridges

SIMSON,
Benjamin C., b. 3/7/1953 in Portsmouth; second; Alfred H. Simson,
Jr. (oiler, MA) and Carol M. Lindsay (MA)

SKIDMORE,
Joanne, b. 3/28/1940 in Portsmouth; second; Harry T. Skidmore
(power plant, Jane Lew) and Mary A. Dwyer (Portsmouth)
Michael Thomas, b. 4/21/1960 in Portsmouth; third; Sheridan N.
Skidmore (NH) and Shirley E. Lankford (VA)

SKIPPER,
Yvonne D., b. 7/12/1954 in Portsmouth; first; Robert E. Skipper
(USCG, NC) and Mary L. Cabana (RI)

SMITH,

son, b. 8/10/1923 in New Castle; third; Luella Collins Smith (New Castle)

Ashley Tanner, b. 6/7/1974 in Portsmouth; James B. Smith II (TX) and Brenda Stroupe (NC)

Daniel Wesley, b. 9/18/1974 in Portsmouth; Thomas W. Smith (MA) and Karen L. Tarvers (ME)

Harry W., b. 1/24/1916 in New Castle; second; Francis L. Smith (farmer, Sabine, NE) and Luella A. Collins (New Castle); residence - New Castle and Nebraska

Heather Lyn, b. 12/29/1964 in Portsmouth; second; Richard A. Smith (PA) and Marie A. Wood (PA)

Hilda May, b. 8/17/1917 in New Castle; first; Arthur C. Smith (painter, Portsmouth) and Nellie M. Grace (Rochester)

James Barker, III, b. 5/20/1969 in Portsmouth; James B. Smith II (TX) and Sandra M. Gleason (MA)

Jean, b. 12/13/1925 in New Castle; first; Clarence H. Smith (salesman, Dover) and Mildred Roach (Brigham, ME)

Scott Michael, b. 11/19/1973 in Portsmouth; Paul A. Smith (MA) and Beatrice F. McCole (MA)

Terrence LeRoy, b. 2/6/1912 in New Castle; first; Francis L. Smith (soldier, Sabine, NE) and Luella A. Collins (New Castle)

SNODGRASS,

Britt Elaine, b. 5/1/1970 in Portsmouth; LeRoy Snodgrass (HA) and Linda S. Wade (NH)

SNYDER,

Heidi Jo, b. 12/28/1956 in Portsmouth; third; William L. Snyder (part. mgr. gas sta., NH) and Jean Phyllis Wojciak (MA)

Karl Meloon, b. 2/6/1962 in Portsmouth; fourth; William L. Snyder (NH) and Jean P. Wojciak (NH)

William Lewis, b. 3/2/1924 in New Castle; second; Harold S. Snyder (US Army, Centralia, IL) and Alice E. Meloon (New Castle)

SPEAR,
Susan Beth, b. 4/12/1971 in Portsmouth; Charles G. Spear (ME) and
Kay F. Pecunies (NH)

SPRAGGINS,
Jeffrey Wayne, b. 8/2/1960 in Kittery, ME; first; Cecil W. Spraggins
(FL) and Elsie M. LaRose (NH)

SPRINGER,
Catherine Ann, b. 1/10/1945 in Portsmouth; first; Herbert J. Springer
(Lt., US Army, Brooklyn, NY) and Betty L. Welterden
(Edgewood, IA)

STAC[E]Y,
Kenneth Russell, b. 8/30/1936 in New Castle; second; Russell Stacey
(bell boy, Cambridge, MA) and Mildred J. Leary (Portsmouth)
Louise Alice, b. 4/19/1933 in New Castle; first; Russell James Stacy
(Belmont, MA) and Mildred J. Leary (Portsmouth)

STANDISH,
Myles, Jr., b. 5/17/1928 in Portsmouth; first; Myles Standish
(machine operator, ME) and Mary McArthur (Manchester)

STANLEY,
Louise Bainbridge, b. 6/15/1914 in New Castle; second; William P.
Stanley (minister, Concord) and Marina E. Pattison (Rochester,
NY); residence - Portsmouth

STANWOOD,
Aaron Taylor, b. 6/6/1988 in Portsmouth; Richard J. Stanwood and
Linda E. McNeil

STEARNS,
Guy Beckley, III, b. 9/18/1995 in Portsmouth; Guy B. Stearns and
Pamela J. Fessenden

Kaitlin Anne, b. 8/25/1994 in Portsmouth; Guy Stearns and Pamela Fessenden

STEVENSON,
Jane, b. 7/14/1942 in Portsmouth; first; Henry B. Stevenson (officer, USA, Chicago, IL) and May E. Wehner (Aspinwall, PA)
Jean, b. 7/14/1942 in Portsmouth; second; Henry B. Stevenson (officer, USA, Chicago, IL) and May E. Wehner (Aspinwall, PA)

STEWART,
John R., b. 8/3/1952 in Kittery, ME; first; Hugh R. Stewart (USAF, MS) and Jacquelibe H. Kitchen (NY)

STRAUS,
Elise C., b. 4/14/1952 in Portsmouth; second; David A. Straus (physician, PA) and Clotilde T. Magnant (France)

STRAW,
Joanne G., b. 5/8/1957 in Portsmouth; fourth; Eldred V. Straw (salesman, MA) and Joy Eldredge (MA)
Lawrence Andrew, b. 1/31/1959 in Portsmouth; fifth; Eldred V. Straw (MA) and Joy Eldredge (MA)
Marilyn Elizabeth, b. 4/28/1961 in Portsmouth; sixth; Eldred V. Straw (MA) and Joy Eldredge (MA)

STRINGHAM,
Corey Francis, b. 6/28/1993 in Portsmouth; P. S. Stringham and C. A. Fitzgerald
Michael Edward, b. 4/2/1997 in Portsmouth; P. S. Stringham and C. A. Stringham

STUART,
Donald Alastair, b. 6/22/1915 in New Castle; first; Kenneth A. Stuart (clerk, Huntington, NY) and Ethel P. Urch (New Castle)

Eleanore Urch, b. 5/27/1917 in New Castle; second; Kenneth A. Stuart (accountant, Charleston, NY) and Ethel P. Urch (New Castle)

SUPRI,
Glen Carl, b. 1/17/1958; second; Willis L. Supri (Durand, WI) and Claire A. Werner (NY)

SWEENEY,
Sean Patrick, b. 6/1/1969 in Portsmouth; Thomas F. Sweeney (MA) and Margaret F. McAvoy (ME)

SYLVESTER,
Elsie S., b. 4/27/1909 in New Castle; fourth; James E. Sylvester (ship fitter, Quincy, MA) and Elsie ----- (Kittery, ME)

TABBUTT,
Jeanne Estelle, b. 8/19/1962 in Portsmouth; second; Richard C. Tabbutt (NH) and Sylvia M. Harrison (VA)
Judith E., b. 7/13/1940 in Portsmouth; third; Clifford C. Tabbutt (machinist, Addison, ME) and Arlene R. Ricker (New Castle)
Richard Colon, b. 4/13/1935 in New Castle; second; Clifford C. Tabbutt (USCG, Jonesport, ME) and Arlene R. Ricker (New Castle)
Stephen Richard, b. 9/12/1960 in Portsmouth; first; Richard C. Tabbutt (NH) and Sylvia M. Harrison (VA)
Susan Kay, b. 8/14/1946 in Portsmouth; fourth; Clifford C. Tabbutt (USCG, Addison, ME) and Arlene R. Ricker (New Castle)

TAPLEY,
Alison Marie, b. 10/9/1964 in Kittery, ME; fourth; Philip H. Tapley (ME) and Janice E. Williams (ME)

TARBELL,
Charles Arnold, b. 6/10/1960 in Portsmouth; first; Daniel Badger Tarbell (MA) and Anne V. Marshall (MA)

Daniel W.B., b. 3/14/1932 in Boston, MA; Edmund A. Tarbell (New Castle) and Margery Badger (Newington)

Elizabeth Souther, b. 7/11/1964 in Portsmouth; third; Daniel B. Tarbell (MA) and Anne V. Marshall (MA)

Frances Elizabeth, b. 10/19/1994 in Portsmouth; Charles Tarbell and Barbara Knight

Julia Penrose, b. 9/13/1968 in Portsmouth; Edmund C. Tarbell (MA) and Barbara Penrose (PA)

Mark Alan, b. 10/30/1962 in Portsmouth; second; Daniel B. Tarbell (MA) and Anne V. Marshall (MA)

Thomas, b. 11/10/1959 in Portsmouth; third; Edmond C. Tarbell (MA) and Barbara Penrose (PA)

TARLTON,

Cecil, b. 5/2/1893 in New Castle; second; Elias Tarlton, Jr. (lighthouse keeper, 36, New Castle) and Carrie E. Poole (32, Isles of Shoals)

TAUTE,

Sedonie Emma, b. 1/14/1912 in Lawrence, MA; first; Carl M. Taute (soldier, USA, Germany) and Anna S. Glasser (Germany)

THAYER,

James Edward, b. 8/25/1960 in Portsmouth; third; Charles L. Thayer (NH) and Elizabeth A. Winn (NH)

Jeremy Lawrence, b. 8/25/1960 in Portsmouth; second; Charles L. Thayer (NH) and Elizabeth A. Winn (NH)

Katherine Winn, b. 4/24/1962 in Portsmouth; fourth; Charles L. Thayer (NH) and Elizabeth A. Winn (NH)

THOMITS,

Albert Raymond, b. 10/10/1947 in Portsmouth; first; Albert R. Thomits (mechanic, Portsmouth) and Myrtle M. Harris (New Castle)

Diane M., b. 10/4/1950 in Portsmouth; second; Albert R. Thomits (student, NH) and Myrtle M. Harris (NH)

THOMPSON,

Ryan Eugene, b. 7/28/1991 in Portsmouth; Donald B. Thompson and
Mary Ann Kreimer

THWAITES,

Nina Marie, b. 12/9/1970 in Kittery, ME; Thomas H. Thwaites (NC)
and Judith M. Graliano (WA)

THYNG,

James Nelson, b. 10/23/1969 in Portsmouth; Arthur L. Thyng (ME)
and Verna A. Foss (NH)

John Stephen, b. 4/15/1971 in Portsmouth; Alan R. Thyng (ME) and
Bonnie S. Hart (ME)

TIBBETTS,

Millard, b. 3/8/1902 in New Castle; first; Fred Tibbetts (surfman, 28,
Bath Bay, ME) and Fannie White (26, New Castle)

Verna, b. 3/14/1903 in New Castle; second; Fred Tibbetts (surfman,
29, ME) and Fannie White (28, New Castle)

TILLMAN,

Edward Jon, b. 8/16/1963 in Kittery, ME; first; Frederick J. Tillman
(OH) and Cecilia N. Briod (NJ)

Nicole Elizabeth, b. 9/2/1965 in Kittery, ME; second; Frederick J.
Tillman (OH) and Cecilia N. Briod (NJ)

TONER,

Kathleen, b. 10/18/1961 in Portsmouth; first; John W. Toner (NH)
and Claire R. McGovern (CT)

TOOMEY,

Richard Andrew, b. 10/21/1944 in Portsmouth; first; Richard A.
Toomey (Lt., USA, Danvers, MA) and Elizabeth N. Rylander
(Newton, MA)

TOUSIGNANT,

Jean M., b. 9/27/1955 in Portsmouth; second; Leo A. Tousignant (civil engin. AB, MA) and Gertrude M. Roberts (MA)

TOWNSEND,

Dorothy Lida, b. 12/18/1911 in New Castle; first; Lloyd W. Townsend (Lieutenant, USN, 29, Camden, NJ) and ----- Baldwin (22, San Francisco, CA)

TREDICK,

Mary, b. 8/16/1892 in New Castle; John L. Tredick (laborer, New Castle) and Julia A. Ford (Ireland)

TREFETHEN,

Ordway H., b. 6/14/1894 in New Castle; Judson Trefethen (shoemaker, New Castle) and Apelomia Oezko (Glacia, Austria)

Sean Michael, b. 1/13/1968 in Portsmouth; Ralph P. Trefethen (NH) and Jean M. Gaffney (NH)

Stephanie Dawn, b. 3/20/1980; Donald P. Trefethen and Patricia Elizabeth Noyes

TRIPP,

Mark L., b. 12/30/1949 in Portsmouth; second; Leslie R. Tripp (electrician, MA) and Emily L. Newman (ME)

TROCCOLI,

Joseph Anthony, b. 3/7/1962 in Portsmouth; first; Vincent P. Troccoli (NY) and Anne M. Lorello (NY)

TROUSDELL,

Kenneth, b. 5/16/1901 in New Castle; first; Jack Trousdell (soldier, 20, Scotland) and Celia F. Pridham (19, New Castle)

TROMBLY,

Bryant James, b. 10/25/1985 in Portsmouth; Jeffrey Bryant Trombly and Judith Remington Johnston

TURNER,
Andrew A., b. 1/1/1904 in New Castle; first; John J. Turner (soldier, 22, Mandan, ND) and Ethel Manson (19, Merrimac, MA)

URQUHART,
Matthew Jon, b. 1/27/1972 in Kittery, ME; Harvard W. Urquhart (NJ) and Nancy Lee Conley (ME)

VANELLI,
Barbara Jean, b. 2/1/1961 in Portsmouth; first; Alfred W. Vanelli (MA) and Dorothy E. Lovelace (MA)

WARGO,
Anna, b. 10/6/1914 in New Castle; third; Stephen J. Wargo (machinist, So. Norwalk, CT) and Jessie Meloon (New Castle)
Barbara Jean, b. 10/19/1926 in New Castle; tenth; Stephen J. Wargo (machinist, So. Norwalk, CT) and Jessie A.M. Meloon (New Castle)
Billie Patricia, b. 3/10/1930 in Portsmouth; twelfth; Stephen J. Wargo (machinist, So. Norwalk, CT) and Jessie A.M. Meloon (New Castle)
Charles Elliott, b. 7/28/1923 in New Castle; ninth; Stephen Wargo (machinist, So. Norwalk, CT) and Jessie A.M. Meloon (New Castle)
Frank Irving, b. 7/13/1928 in New Castle; eleventh; Stephen J. Wargo (machinist, So. Norwalk, CT) and Jessie A. Meloon (New Castle)
James, b. 10/31/1915 in New Castle; fourth; Stephen J. Wargo (machinist, So. Newark, CT) and Jessie A.M. Meloon (New Castle)
Mary, b. 2/18/1909 in New Castle; first; Steve J. Wargo (soldier, So. Norwalk, CT) and Jessie Meloon (New Castle)
Sarah Isabel, b. 12/27/1921 in New Castle; eighth; Stephen Wargo (machinist, So. Norwalk, CT) and Jessie A.M. Meloon (New Castle)

Stephen James, Jr., b. 4/7/1911 in New Castle; second; Stephen James
Wargo (machinist, USN, 22, So. Norwalk, CT) and Jessie
Meloon (24, New Castle)

William J., b. 4/4/1917 in New Castle; fifth; Steve J. Wargo
(machinist, So. Norwalk, CT) and Jessie Meloon (New Castle)

WATSON,
Kimberly Ann, b. 10/9/1969 in Portsmouth; Alan J. Watson (NH) and
Judy L. Clark (MA)

WATT,
Timothy Harold, b. 7/25/1962 in Portsmouth; second; Harold B. Watt
(NH) and Anita L. Sanford (NH)

WEBB,
Andrea M., b. 11/18/1953 in Portsmouth; fourth; Thomas H. Webb
(clerk, Navy Yard, ME) and Mary A. LaBrie (NH)

Susan E., b. 2/10/1952 in Portsmouth; third; Thomas H. Webb (clerk,
N. Base, ME) and Mary A. LaBrie (NH)

Thomas Henry, Jr., b. 4/10/1944 in Kittery, ME; first; Thomas H.
Webb (USNR, Kittery, ME) and Marie A. LaBrie (Portsmouth)

Virginia Alma, b. 11/24/1946 in Exeter; second; Thomas H. Webb
(clerk, navy yard, Kittery, ME) and Mary A. LaBrie (Portsmouth)

WEBBER,
Earl F., b. 10/27/1952 in Portsmouth; second; Fred St.C. Webber
(laborer, ME) and Olive M. Walsh (MA)

WELCH,
Francis Edward, b. 11/22/1946 in Portsmouth; first; Francis W.
Welch, Jr. (US Army, Reading, MA) and Charlotte Campbell
(New Castle)

WELLS,
Karen Patricia, b. 7/28/1969 in Portsmouth; James T. Wells (TX) and
Patricia E. Lane (NH)

Kim Marie, b. 9/14/1968 in Portsmouth; James T. Wells (TX) and Patricia E. Lane (NH)

WESTON,
Christine Ann, b. 3/18/1980; Robert Charles Weston, Jr. and Sheryl Ann Buckley

WHEELER,
Emma Katherine, b. 5/24/1996 in Portsmouth; Robert T. Wheeler and Katherine G. Wheeler

WHITAKER,
Irene, b. 8/31/1943 in Portsmouth; first; Nicholas Whitaker (bus driver, Avawam, KY) and Candous Deaton (Altro, KY)
Virginia Lee, b. 7/13/1943 in Portsmouth; first; Cadie Whitaker (Serg., USA, Avawam, KY) and Catherine R. Beyley (Hardbury, KY)

WHITCOMB,
Todd Ellis, b. 1/24/1972 in Portsmouth; Paul K. Whitcomb (NH) and Mary L. Ellis (NH)

WHITE,
Adam Jarrod, b. 2/24/1984 in Portsmouth; Richard H. White and Jan Rathgeber
Andrew B., b. 4/12/1940 in Portsmouth; second; Frederick S. White (rigger, New Castle) and Mary M. Odiorne (Rye)
Anna Belle, b. 9/16/1905 in New Castle; first; Andrew Bell White (machinist, 29, New Castle) and Octavia Becker (25, New Castle)
Frederick Seymore, b. 12/4/1909 in New Castle; second; Andrew B. White (machinist, New Castle) and Octavia Becker (New Castle)
Gail Ann, b. 5/6/1943 in Portsmouth; third; Charles D.A. White (major, USA, Newport News, VA) and Mary L. Stevens (Washington, DC)

Geraldine C., b. 11/5/1903 in New Castle; first; William G. White (engineer, 22, New Castle) and Clara M. Sheehan (26, Barnaby River, NB)

Rachel, b. 3/21/1973 in Portsmouth; Stephen White (MA) and Miriam Beth Novack (MA)

Richard Gordon, b. 3/4/1923 in New Castle; sixth; Arnold Bernard White (lighthouse keeper, New Castle) and Louise Ella Jordan (Cape Elizabeth, ME)

Richard H., b. 4/1/1953 in Portsmouth; first; Warren M. White (tug master, NH) and Jeanette I. White (ME)

Savanna Rebecca, b. 6/15/1996 in Dover; Zadoc L. White and Wendolyn L. Hammer

Sharon Lee, b. 9/25/1947 in Portsmouth; first; George L. White (mechanic, Rye Beach) and Loraine W. French (Laconia)

Sherri Linda, b. 1/16/1967 in Kittery, ME; second; Francis M. White (MA) and Ellen M. Randlov (MA)

Stephen Odiorne, b. 11/6/1947 in Portsmouth; third; Frederick S. White (master rigger, New Castle) and Mary M. Odiorne (Rye)

WHITEHOUSE,

Dustin Foss, b. 10/23/1991 in Portsmouth; Glenn F. Whitehouse and Jane Marie Whitehouse

Glenn Foss, b. 10/20/1964 in Portsmouth; second; Reginald E. Whitehouse (NH) and Marcia L. Foss (NH)

Marcie Lynn, b. 3/6/1971 in Portsmouth; Richard E. Whitehouse (NH) and Priscilla G. Harris (NH)

Mark Edward, b. 1/3/1964 in Portsmouth; first; Richard E. Whitehouse (NH) and Priscilla G. Harris (NH)

Melissa Ann, b. 6/21/1967 in Portsmouth; second; Richard E. Whitehouse (NH) and Priscilla G. Harris (NH)

Michele Ellen, b. 9/3/1965 in Portsmouth; first; John S. Whitehouse (NH) and Barbara A. Boucher (NH)

Scott Edward, b. 1/12/1963 in Portsmouth; first; Reginald E. Whitehouse (NH) and Marcia L. Foss (NH)

WHITLOCK,

Bertha Marguerite Moberg, b. 4/30/1911 in New Castle; fourth; Paul
LeRoy Whitlock (soldier, 30, Harrisburg, PA) and Ethel Manson
(26, Merrimac, MA)

Virginia Bell, b. 10/16/1909 in New Castle; third; Paul LeRoy
Whitlock (soldier, Harrisburg, PA) and Ethel Manson (Merrimac,
MA)

Walter Leroy, b. 1/31/1907 in New Castle; second; Paul LeRoy
Whitlock (soldier, 25, Harrisburg, PA) and Ethel Manson (22,
Merrimac, MA)

WILDRICKS,

Carolyn Newcomb, b. 4/1/1909 in New Castle; first; George A.
Wildricks (army officer, NY) and Marrion ----- (Omaha, NE);
residence - Fort Constitution

WILKINSON,

Henry Joseph, b. 2/1/1916 in New Castle; first; Henry J. Wilkinson
(soldier, Suncook) and Rose Black (Baltimore, MD); residence -
Ft. Constitution

Rosalie, b. 9/19/1917 in New Castle; second; Henry J. Wilkinson
(sergeant, USA, Suncook) and Rosalie Black (Baltimore, MD)

WILL,

Gerard Roy, b. 1/15/1941 in Portsmouth; eighth; George Burl Will
(1st sgt, USA, IL) and Daise Ellen Bradfield (Shawnee, OK);
residence - Fort Constitution

WILLIAMS,

Celia Florence, b. 6/10/1907 in New Castle; second; Chester Williams
(mason, 31, Lancaster So., PA) and Mabel Pridham (19, New
Castle)

Chester Elmer, b. 2/5/1906 in New Castle; first; Chester Williams
(stonemason, 30, Lancaster Co., PA) and Mabel Pridham (18,
New Castle)

Earl, b. 8/19/1923 in New Castle; sixth; Chester Williams (Sergt., USA, Christiania, PA) and Mabel Pridham (New Castle)

Richard Eugene, b. 9/23/1927 in New Castle; seventh; Chester Williams (sergeant, USA, Christiana, PA) and Mabel M. Pridham (New Castle)

WILLIAMSON,

Anna Dorothy, b. 10/20/1912 in New Castle; third; William H. Williamson (sergeant, USA, Minneapolis, MN) and Minnie C. Young (Alleghany, PA)

Kanoise Lee, b. 9/8/1975 at Pease AFB; Lee E. Williamson (NJ) and Constance A. Schlick (RI)

Reed Keener, b. 3/12/1997 in Portsmouth; J. T. Williamson and J. A. Williamson

WINSLOW,

Peter Adrian, b. 2/12/1995 in Portsmouth; Andrew R. Winslow and Christina VanKalen

WISE,

John Nathan, b. 11/6/1965 in Portsmouth; fourth; Roger L. Wise (OH) and Gayl Worden (NH)

WISEMAN,

John W., b. 8/16/1954 in Portsmouth; fourth; Edgar H. Wiseman (clerk, NH) and Shirley Glendenning (Canada)

P. E., 2d, b. 11/3/1951 in Portsmouth; third; Edgar H. Wiseman (truck driv., NH) and Shirley E. Glendenning (Canada)

WISWELL,

Kathleen Margaret, b. 10/29/1981; John M. Wiswell and Kathleen E. Shea

WOLFORD,

Ronald Glenn, b. 6/19/1959 in Portsmouth; first; Ronald G. Wolford, Sr. (OH) and Bette Linnette Mori (NH)

WOODMAN,
Ann H., b. 8/4/1954 in Portsmouth; third; Alfred K. Woodman
(Painter Navy Yard, ME) and Mary E. Horning (NH)

WOODS,
daughter, b. 12/7/1945 in Portsmouth; third; William A.H. Woods
(deceased, Woburn, MA) and Madeline Strouach (NS)

WOOLEY,
Megan Ann, b. 3/8/1991 in Portsmouth; Mark R. Wooley and Becky
Lee Palmer

WOURCE,
Richard, b. 12/25/1939 in Portsmouth; second; Donald R. Wource
(machinist, Springfield, VT) and Violet T. Paskell (Plattsburg,
NY)

WOZCIAH,
James H., b. 12/13/1945 in Portsmouth; first; James S. Wozciah
(laborer, Passaic, NJ) and Barbara H. Johnson (Portsmouth)

WYMAN,
Joseph C., b. 12/29/1911 in New Castle; fourth; Harry N. Wyman
(coppersmith, Bath, ME) and ----- Imphy (England)

YABLONSKY,
Cassandra Holly, b. 4/12/1966 in Kittery, ME; first; Richard E.
Yablonsky (MD) and Charlene S. Magoon (NH)

YEATON,
Mildred E., b. 9/6/1901 in New Castle; second; Henry S. Yeaton
(coppersmith, 32, New Castle) and Helen White (31, New Castle)

YOBLONSKY,
Richard Edward, Jr., b. 7/31/1970 in Kittery, ME; Richard E.
Yoblonsky (MD) and Charlene S. Magoon (NH)

YORK,

Michael James, b. 6/27/1960 in Kittery, ME; second; Charles T. York (VA) and Suzanne D. Harris (NH)

Michelle T., b. 6/25/1958; first; Charles Thomas York (VA) and Suzanne D. Harris (Portsmouth)

YOUART,

Richard, b. 3/27/1924 in New Castle; fifth; William T. Youart (US Army, Lancaster, PA) and Cecilia Walcott (Manchester, England)

ZANELLI,

Michael Joseph, b. 4/5/1962 in Portsmouth; second; Alfred W. Zanelli (MA) and Dorothy E. Lovelace (MA)

MARRIAGES

ADAMS,

Donald L. of Carmel, NY m. Barbara **Marshall** of Kittery, ME
9/24/1955 in New Castle; H - 22, USAF, b. NY, s/o Robert
Adams (NY) and Luella Tompkins (NY); W - 22, clerk-typist, b.
NH, d/o Charles Marshall (MA) and Elizabeth Bennett (NY)

George W. of Newtown, CT m. Christy **Cunningham** of Boston, MA
2/4/1989 in New Castle; H - s/o Alexander B. Adams and Lucy
D. Smith; W - d/o John M. Herlihy and Patricia M. Cunningham

Kevin Kenneth of Crofton, MD m. Josephine Ann **Grady** of Crofton,
MD 9/3/1978 in New Castle; H - s/o A. Kenneth Adams and Jane
F. Dougherty; W - d/o James B. Grady and Elizabeth Plum

ALBEE,

John of New Castle m. Nellie **Rickey** of Minneapolis, MN 2/15/1894
in Minneapolis, MN; H - 60, b. Bellingham, MA, s/o John Albee
and Esther Thayer; W - 30, b. Dayton, OH, d/o James Rickey and
Roealpha Jones

ALDRICH,

Jack William m. Ruth Susanne **Weeks** 9/13/1958 in Portsmouth; H -
33, 2d, b. MI, s/o Annette Spillers; W - 26, b. NH, d/o Edward A.
Weeks and Hilda Gillespie

ALLEY,

Warren A. of New Castle m. Florence **Crawford** of York, ME
11/3/1951 in Rockland, ME; H - 55, retired, 2d, b. Jonesport,
ME, s/o Arthur R. Alley (ME) and Alberta Faulkingham (ME);
W - 44, housewife, 2d, b. York, ME, d/o Joseph A. Briley (ME)
and Julia Moulton (ME)

ALLSBROOK,

R. B. of Roanoke Rapids, NC m. Barbara A. **Ruggles** of New Castle
6/16/1956 in New Castle; H - 27, US Navy, b. NC, s/o Julian R.
Allsbrook (NC) and Frances V. Brown (NC); W - 24, at home, b.
MA, d/o Carter K. Ruggles (MA) and Doris G. Saunders (MA)

ALMGREN,

George B., Jr. m. Margaret Jean **Nay** 10/30/1965 in Portsmouth; H - 27, b. MA, s/o George B. Almgren and Ingeborg Malmgren; W - 22, b. MA, d/o Phillip H. Nay and Dorothy A. Hurd

George B., Jr. of New Castle m. Nancy W. **Lloyd** of Portsmouth 7/17/1977 in Portsmouth; H - s/o George B. Almgren and Ingeborg Malmgren; W - d/o Theodore F. Weaver and Virginia Hughes

ALNAS,

Peter Andreas of New Castle m. Anna Louisa A. **Peterson** of New Castle 4/16/1927 in New Castle; H - 58, C.B.M., USN ret., 2d, b. Aalrund, Norway, s/o Ingbridt Alnas (mariner, Aalrund, Norway) and Karen Peterson (housewife, Brudal, Norway); W - 60, housekeeper, 3d, b. Molde, Norway, d/o Ammund Aaro (carpenter, Bulso, Norway) and Ingborg Aarones (housewife, Bulso, Norway)

AMAZEEN,

James M. of New Castle m. Nancy Dyer Anthony **Holden** of Portsmouth 5/29/1932 in Bartlett; H - 38, machinist helper, b. New Castle, s/o Granville Amazeen (New Castle) and Harriet K. Baker (housewife, New Castle); W - 37, housewife, 2d, b. Bristol, RI, d/o Hezekiah Anthony Cook (retired, Fall River, MA) and Hattie Estelle Pierce (housewife, Atlantic, GA)

Orville C. of New Castle m. Freda E. **Stenzel** of New Castle 1/1/1932 in New Castle; H - 47, packer, navy yard, b. New Castle, s/o Charles B. Amazeen (melter, navy yard, New Castle) and Jessie F. Bateno (New Castle); W - 38, housekeeper, b. Manchester, d/o Herman Stenzel (weaver, Germany) and Pauline Adams (Manchester)

Paul Gerard m. Caroline Jane **Ells** 8/26/1961 in Hampstead; H - 22, b. NH, s/o Gerard B. Amazeen and Elsie L. Jones; W - 18, b. MA, d/o Warren H. Ells and Alice M. Tillson

William G. of New Castle m. Ruth **Hoitt** of Portsmouth 11/8/1926 in Dover; H - 34, sheet metal worker, b. New Castle, s/o Granville

Amazeen (laborer, New Castle) and Harriet K. Baker (housewife, New Castle); W - 21, at home, 2d, b. Kittery, ME, d/o John S. Tilton (clerk, Portsmouth) and Edith Kendrick (housewife, Brockton, MA)

ANDREWS,

David B. of Cambridge, MA m. Joan **Wilson** of Boston, MA 1/18/1986 in New Castle; H - s/o Robert Angell Andrews and Joan Richards; W - d/o Lawrence Milo Wilson and Shirley M. Chrysler

James F. m. Terri L. **Butterfield** 8/16/1975 in Concord; H - s/o Robert F. Andrews and Annette Fowler; W - d/o Mason S. Butterfield and Geraldine F. Johnson

ARMITAGE,

Michael Lord m. Joanne Sylvia **Brunelle** 10/26/1963 in Berlin; H - 25, b. ME, s/o Perley E. Armitage and Elizabeth Lord; W - 21, b. NH, d/o Arthur J. Brunelle and Mary Bartoli

ARSENAULT,

Edmund J., III of New Castle m. Cathleen A. **Russo** of Portsmouth 12/24/1978 in Portsmouth; H - s/o Edmund J. Arsenault and Joanne Lamb; W - d/o John C. Russo and Eleanor Wade

Ernest L. of New Castle m. Karen A. **Liberty** of New Castle 1/12/1985 in Portsmouth; H - s/o Edmund Arsenault and Joanne Lamb; W - d/o Roger Liberty and Dorothy Coughig

ASPEN,

Erik S. of New Castle m. B. M. **McKensie** of New Castle 5/27/1949 in New Castle; H - 24, chauffeur, 2d, b. Brooklyn, NY, s/o Eroix A. Aspen (deceased, Norway) and Borgheld I. Wold (housewife, Norway); W - 21, waitress, b. Swainsboro, GA, d/o L. M. McKensie (GA) and Gertrude Watkins (GA)

Erik S. m. Louise M. **Boisvert** 11/28/1969 in New Castle; H - s/o Erolf Aspen and Borghild I. Wold; W - d/o Leon Girouard and Mary E. MacDaniels

ATWATER,

Donald V. of Ft. Fairfield, ME m. Dorothy T. **Cuskley** of New Castle 11/23/1920 in Portsmouth; H - 27, business man, b. Ft. Fairfield, ME, s/o Judson A. Atwater (farmer, Ft. Fairfield, ME) and Emma B. Rideout (housewife, Ft. Fairfield, ME); W - 24, civil service clerk, b. Cape Elizabeth, ME, d/o Henry M. Cuskley (lt. h. keep., Portland, ME) and Mary E. White (housewife, Portsmouth)

AUTAS,

Walter J. of Camp Langdon m. Anna D. **Waraksa** of Shamokin, PA 7/11/1942 in New Castle; H - 24, US Army, b. Newark, NJ, s/o Michael Autas (coal miner, Poland) and Mary Lobada (Poland); W - 22, shirt worker, b. Shamokin, PA, d/o Anthony Waraksa (grocer, Poland) and Anna Statasqenski (housewife, Poland)

AYKROYD,

Douglas S. m. Elizabeth A. **Rhoades** 7/12/1975 in New Castle; H - s/o Albert W. Aykroyd and Patricia Semler; W - d/o Leonard N. Rhoades and Jean Stone

BACHELDER,

Robert of Medford, MA m. Shirley **Lord** of Medford, MA 8/18/1940 in New Castle; H - 24, mechanic, b. Medford, MA, s/o Charles Bachelder (salesman, Bridgeport, CT) and Madeline Leavitt (at home, Medford, MA); W - 19, at home, b. W. Medford, MA, d/o James R. Lord (mariner, ret., Brookfield, ME) and Bessie Grimlaw (at home, Haverhill, MA)

BAILEY,

Roy O. of New Castle m. Doris E. **Shaw** of Portsmouth 5/30/1943 in New Castle; H - 26, coast artillery, b. Osseo, MI, s/o Oliver A. Bailey (machinist, Stanley, MI) and Jessie M. Rador (housewife, Portland, MI); W - 24, mach. op., b. S. Portland, ME, d/o Fred L. Shaw (pipe fitter, Portsmouth) and Delvina Perault (housewife, Rochester)

BAILY,

Theodore M., III of Decatur, GA m. Ellen C. K. **Murer** of New Castle 9/12/1987 in New Castle; H - s/o Theodore M. Baily, Jr. and Jean Sally Wilson; W - d/o Erik Murer and Inger Gierloff

BAKER,

Edward B. of New Castle m. Evelyn L. **Tarlton** of New Castle 11/6/1907 in New Castle; H - 41, laborer, b. No. Andover, MA, s/o George A. Baker (seaman, New Castle) and Abbie Woodbury (housewife, Haverhill, MA); W - 25, housewife, b. New Castle, d/o Elias Tarlton, Jr. (surfman, New Castle) and Carrie E. Poole (housewife, Isles of Shoals)

James H. of New Castle m. Ellen A. **Call** of Portsmouth 4/5/1893 in Portsmouth; H - 47, b. New Castle; W - 37, b. Kittery Point, ME

BAKETEL,

Sherman T. of Methuen, MA m. Helen C. **Epler** of Boston, MA 12/29/1929 in New Castle; H - 24, medical student, b. Methuen, MA, s/o Roy B. Baketel (physician, Pittsburgh, PA) and Helen Tenney (housewife, Methuen, MA); W - 24, nurse, b. Worcester, MA, d/o Percy H. Epler (ret. clergyman, Springfield, IL) and Helen York (housewife, New Haven, CT)

Sherman T. m. Marie B. **Hartshorn** 1/18/1968 in Manchester; H - b. MA, s/o Roy V. Baketel and Helen Tenney; W - b. NJ, d/o Thomas G. Barber and Frances M. Patterson

BALL,

Daniel R. of Greenland m. Susan C. **Mimnagh** of Greenland 9/20/1997 in New Castle

Frank M. m. Dorothy J. **Todd** 10/4/1969 in New Castle; H - s/o George B. Ball and Mary Brewster; W - d/o William H. Miller and Mary L. Jennings

Hayden M. of New Castle m. Nora J. **Hallice** of Milford 12/22/1995 in New Castle

Mark Thomas, Jr. of New Castle m. Linda Crowell **Rauchhaus** of New Castle 8/25/1994 in Portsmouth

BARBER,

Thomas H. of New Castle m. Clara A. **Hall** of New Castle 6/5/1898 in
New Castle; H - 44, surfman, USLSS, 2d, b. Boston, MA, s/o
William A. Barber (seaman, Liverpool, England) and Hannah
Murphy (Newport, RI) of Newport, RI; W - 40, b. New Castle,
d/o William Hall (seaman, New Castle) and Margaret Smith
(New Castle) of New Castle

Thomas H. of New Castle m. Ella Eudora **Morrell** of Cambridge, MA
6/5/1905 in North Cambridge, MA; H - 52, surfman, [3d], b.
Boston, MA, s/o William A. Barber (fisherman, Liverpool,
England) and Hannah Barber (Newport, RI); W - 39, companion,
b. Westport, NS, d/o John Morrell (sailor, Westport, NS) and
Annie Morrell (Westport, NS)

BARKER,

Floyd V. of New Castle m. Muriel G. **Hoyt** of Dover 11/28/1943 in
Newington; H - 28, soldier, b. Burlington, ME, s/o Fay T. Barker
(laborer, Burlington, ME) and Blanche L. Porter (housewife,
Lewiston, ME); W - 20, stud. nurse, b. Somerville, MA, d/o
Jackson W. Hoyt (laborer, Newington) and Cora J. Castella
(housewife, Cambridge, MA)

BARLOW,

Mark P. of New Castle m. Hannah R. **Zabarsky** of New Castle
10/20/1984 in Portsmouth; H - s/o Robert F. Barlow and Priscilla
Potter; W - d/o Melvin J. Zabarsky and Joyce Reopel

BARNARD,

Ralph of New Castle m. Vesta B. **Barber** of New Castle 5/1/1954 in
Portsmouth; H - 59, optometrist, 4th, b. NH, s/o James Barnard
(NH) and Ida M. Sargent (MA); W - 37, housewife, 2d, b. MA,
d/o Herbert Farrow (MA) and Zella B. Davis (VT)

BARRON,

John Edward of Portsmouth m. Mary C. **Sweetser** of New Castle
8/10/1957 in Portsmouth; H - 24, US Navy, b. NH, s/o John R.

Barron (MA) and Evelyn M. Hicks (NH); W - 20, legal secretary, b. NH, d/o John C. Sweetser (NH) and Harriette Stewart (NH)

BATCHELDER,

Cyrus P. of Boston, MA m. Lois A. **Rand** of New Castle 10/23/1895 in New Castle; H - 33, steward, b. Nottingham, s/o Charles H. Batchelder (Northwood) and Harriet Davis (Nottingham); W - 35, teacher, b. New Castle, d/o Thomas Rand (Rye) and Adaline Twombly (New Castle)

BATSON,

Wallace E. of New Castle m. Eleanor F. **Dixon** of Lynn, MA 2/19/1921 in Lynn, MA; H - 25, electrician, b. East Candia, s/o Samuel E. Batson (pipefitter, New Castle) and Florence G. Healey (housewife, Boston, MA); W - 20, clerk, b. Gloucester, MA, d/o Edward Dixon (New Castle, England) and Hattie G. Clark (housewife, Gloucester, MA)

BAYLESS,

Timothy H. of Cambridge, MA m. Nancy E. **Judkins** of Cambridge, MA 6/11/1983 in New Castle; H - s/o Terry S. Bayless and ----- Hatler; W - d/o Bradley C. Judkins and ----- Seaberry

BEAN,

Harold L. of New Castle m. Carmen R. **Gauvin** of Portsmouth 4/5/1943 in New Castle; H - 25, soldier, b. W. Farmington, ME, s/o Van A. Bean (laborer, Jay, ME) and Ruth Verral (Winthrop, ME); W - 19, shoe worker, b. Lewiston, ME, d/o Leon Gauvin (woodsman, Canada) and Medora Matthews (shoe stitcher, Augusta, ME)

BECKER,

Charles John m. Betty Ann **LaRose** 12/16/1967 in New Castle; H - 20, b. PA, s/o John J. Becker and Betty G. Kirtz; W - 19, b. NH, d/o Harold J. LaRose and Stella Karakostas

Chester A. of New Castle m. Martha B. **Amazeen** of New Castle
5/16/1901 in New Castle; H - 23, laborer, b. New Castle, s/o
Henry Becker (seaman, No. Berwick, ME) and Ellen Amazeen
(housewife, New Castle); W - 18, housewife, b. New Castle, d/o
Charles R. Amazeen (shoecutter, New Castle) and Jessie Batson
(housewife, New Castle)

Forrest Lyndon of New Castle m. Annie Laurel **Miller** of Portsmouth
8/17/1914 in Vassalboro, ME; H - 26, steamfitter, b. New Castle,
s/o Charles Henry Becker (fisherman, Kittery, ME) and Leona
Johnson Ricker (housewife, New Castle); W - 21, stenographer,
b. Riverside, ME, d/o Elijah Miller (farmer, No. Walpole, ME)
and Addie May Saggett (housewife, Ludlow, ME)

Henry of New Castle m. Dorothy M. **Shaffner** of Newburyport, MA
5/26/1933 in New Castle; H - 26, quartermaster, b. New Castle,
s/o Chester A. Becker (pipe fitter, New Castle) and Martha B.
Amazeen (at home, New Castle); W - 30, cost accountant, b.
Newburyport, MA, d/o George W. Shaffner (retired, NS) and
Elizabeth L. Libbey (at home, Newburyport, MA)

Joel of Hicksville, NY m. Carol Ann **Ledgard** of Hicksville, NY
8/18/1979 in New Castle; H - s/o Abraham Becker and Beatrice
Hirsch; W - d/o Edward Ledgard and Antoinette Mariano

Joseph of New Castle m. Elizabeth I. **Philbrick** of Rye 6/15/1904 in
Lynn, MA; H - 41, shoemaker, b. New Castle, s/o Charles E.
Becker (seaman, No. Berwick, ME) and Matilda Brown
(housewife, Kittery, ME); W - 33, housewife, b. Rye, d/o Joseph
N. Philbrick (farmer, Rye) and Annie Gwinn (housewife, East
Boston, MA)

Walter of New Castle m. Pauline T. **Blaisdell** of Portsmouth
7/25/1900 in Portsmouth; H - 26, surfman, b. New Castle, s/o
Charles Becker (seaman, Berwick, ME) and Esther M. Becker
(Kittery, ME); W - 27, b. York, ME, d/o Thomas Blaisdell
(carpenter, York, ME) and Nelena A. Blaisdell (Waterville, ME)

Walter M. of Portsmouth m. Dorothy M. **Lawrence** of New Castle
6/20/1936 in New Castle; H - 20, clerk, b. New Castle, s/o
Forrest L. Becker (pipe fitter, New Castle) and Ann L. Miller (at
home, Riverside, ME); W - 19, at home, b. St. Johnsbury, VT,

d/o Hardey Lawrence (carpenter, Waterford, VT) and Agnes L. Palmer (at home, Concord, VT)

BECKERT,
Walter Edward m. Evelyn Viola **Dame** 2/8/1966 in New Castle; H - 37, b. ME, s/o Harry W. Beckert and Mabel Kimball; W - 53, 2d, b. ME, d/o Harold R. Place and Estelle A. Hanscom

BEEVERS,
Harry A. of New Castle m. Phyllis M. **Gilliam** of New Castle 11/23/1932 in New Castle; H - 21, laborer, b. Lawrence, MA, s/o Arthur H. Beevers (salesman, Lawrence, MA) and Lillian Richardson (at home, Montreal, Canada); W - 19, at home, b. New Castle, d/o Claude C. Gilliam (electrician, Yale, VA) and Florence M. Batson (at home, Haverhill, MA)

BELL,
William H. of New Castle m. Jeanette E. **Toohill** of Rochester 4/15/1944 in New Castle; H - 26, US Army, b. Wollaston, MA, s/o Charles R. Bell (clerk, Canada) and Edith M. Cain (housewife, S. Weymouth, MA); W - 22, at home, b. Gorham, ME, d/o John J. Toohill (loom fixer, Saxonville, MA) and Velma H. Sawyer (housewife, Gray, ME)

BELMONT,
Michael John, III m. Christine Catherine **DeBlois** 9/6/1992 in Portsmouth

BENNETT,
Philip H. of New Castle m. Brenda L. **Doubleday** of New Castle 4/29/1995 in New Castle

BERGH,
Peter D. of New Castle m. Janet E. **Prince** of New Castle 5/27/1989 in New Castle; H - s/o Charles R. Bergh and Barbara Silverman; W - d/o Robert C. Prince and Thelma LeBlanc

BERRIMAN,
Thomas H. of New Castle m. Agnes G. **Bickford** of Damariscotta,
ME 7/17/1942 in New Castle; H - 28, US Army, b. England, s/o
William Berriman (Cong. minister, England) and Bessie Collette
(at home, England); W - 26, school teacher, b. Portland, ME, d/o
Irvin E. Bickford (salesman, Portland, ME) and Mary Murphy (at
home, Portland, ME)

BIANCHINO,
Daniel C. of New Castle m. Kathleen M. **Rogers** of New Castle
6/14/1981 in New Castle; H - s/o Americo Bianchino and
Eleanor Bolland; W - d/o Francis J. Rogers and Mildred R.
Collins

BLAISDELL,
Clyde Vincent of Portsmouth m. Mildred F. **Gilliam** of New Castle
3/2/1921 in Portsmouth; H - 30, machine operator, 2d, b.
Laconia, s/o Hosea F. Blaisdell (blacksmith, Gilford) and Annie
Roe (housewife, Belmont); W - 30, housewife, 2d, b. Haverhill,
MA, d/o S. E. Batson (pipefitter, New Castle) and Florence Healy
(housewife, Boston, MA)

BLISCO,
Robert H. of New Castle m. S. M. **Ducharme** of Portsmouth 7/7/1956
in Portsmouth; H - 27, doorman, Wentworth, b. PA, s/o Andrew
Blisco (PA) and Justine Dulpoc (Austria); W - 21, waitress, b.
NH, d/o Harry E. Ducharme (VT) and Margaret L. Houx (VT)

BOAZMAN,
Hurley O., III of Boise, ID m. Kari H. **Rasmussen** of Boise, ID
10/14/1990 in New Castle; H - s/o Hurley Boazman and
Jacqueline Dudack; W - d/o Carl Rasmussen and Margaret Hunt

BORDEN,
Andres E. of New Castle m. Sissel **Monsen** of Kittery, ME 1/31/1996
in New Castle

David A. m. Nancy Horner **Schwab** 7/27/1974 in New Castle; H - s/o Barry Borden and Juliana Holden; W - d/o Robert S. Horner and Virginia Hart

BOSWORTH,
Gregory M. m. Cassandra Kay **Hatch** 10/12/1991 in New Castle

BOUGHTON,
George W. of New Castle m. Roberta M. **Zengerle** of New Castle 6/5/1981 in New Castle; H - s/o Rufus E. Boughton and Helen R. Ferguson; W - d/o John R. Zengerle and Mae E. Williams

BRIGHAM,
John Clare m. Sheila Agnes **Mahoney** 3/30/1967 in Exeter; H - 23, b. OH, s/o Keston D. Brigham and Stella B. Weber; W - 24, b. NH, d/o William J. Mahoney and Elizabeth J. Brennan

BRISKAY,
Albert A. of Eliot, ME m. Laurel M. **Becker** of New Castle 10/18/1971 in Portsmouth; H - b. ME, s/o Martin Briskay and Mary Radcalls; W - b. ME, d/o Elijah Miller and Addie Mae Daggett

BROOKS,
Holman of Fort Constitution m. Eleanor **Cater** of Dover 1/8/1942 in Dover; H - 23, coast artillery, b. Stewartstown, s/o Harold E. Brooks (farmer, Stewartstown) and Marion McCornwell (housewife, Stewartstown); W - 21, salesgirl, b. Dover, d/o Fred A. Cater (clerk, Dover) and Ocee Sevigny (laundress, Somersworth)

BROUWER,
Johan M. S. of Portland, ME m. Jacqueline **Kelley** of New Castle 8/10/1990 in New Castle; H - s/o Johan Brouwer and Helen Heavenor; W - d/o John Kelley and Audrey Von Hasselyn

BROWN,

Alexander P. of Boston, MA m. Ella **Dinsmore** of Boston, MA
8/2/1902 in New Castle; H - 49, lawyer, b. Washington, DC, s/o
Austin Brown (lawyer, Washington, DC) and Katherine E.
Maxam (Boston, MA); W - 49, 2d, b. Charlestown, d/o Ebenezer
Dinsmore (Charlestown) and Fanny Willard (Charlestown)

Bryant M. of Monson, ME m. Stella V. **Vilandre** of Southbridge, MA
9/4/1951 in Portsmouth; H - 30, student, 2d, b. Parkman, ME,
s/o Oscar C. Brown (ME) and Katherine H. Crooker (ME); W -
36, dancer, 2d, b. Westville, MA, d/o Stephen Vilandre (MA) and
Rosa Frenier (MA)

Frank A. of New Castle m. Lucy M. **Hubley** of Portsmouth 9/27/1898
in Portsmouth; H - 27, shoecutter, b. Somerville, MA, s/o Charles
H. Brown (deceased, Lisbon) and Sarah D. Card (deceased); W -
19, b. Pleasantville, NS, d/o John Hubley (storekeeper, 56,
Pleasantville, NS) and Maria Crouse (49, Pleasantville, NS) of
Pleasantville, NS

Roger V. of New Castle m. Jacqueline M. **Lefavour** of New Castle
4/3/1982 in Strafford; H - s/o Paul V. Brown, Jr. and Glenvia
Arendt; W - d/o Ormand L. Pinneo and Georgette C. May

Walter D. of Westerly, RI m. Mary R. **Driscoll** of Portsmouth
5/29/1942 in New Castle; H - 24, coast artillery, b. Westerly, RI,
s/o Theodore J. Brown (Fall River, MA) and Phoebe J. Barras
(housewife, Westerly, RI); W - 16, shoe factory, b. Portsmouth,
d/o J. J. Driscoll, Jr. (truckman, Portsmouth) and Alice
Chamberlain (shoe factory, Portsmouth)

BUCKLEY,

David W. of New Castle m. Nancy J. **Hunter** of New Castle 2/4/1989
in Portsmouth; H - s/o William H. Buckley and Julianne Keenan;
W - d/o John B. Hunter, Jr. and Betty L. O'Grady

James William m. Dorothy Adeline **Minie** 7/9/1960 in New Castle; H
- 21, b. CT, s/o James W. Buckley and Anna M. Taylor; W - 38,
b. CT, d/o Leonard G. Minie and Marion C. Patterson

BUCKLIN,
Alan E. of New Castle m. Katherine M. **Ferland** of Portsmouth
6/9/1978 in New Castle; H - s/o Elwood Bucklin and Jane Rowe;
W - d/o Leo Ferland and Barbara Barton

BUDONSKI,
John R. of New Castle m. Marie **Aubert** of Somersworth 7/17/1942 in
Rollinsford; H - 22, US Army, b. Westport, CT, s/o Michael
Budonski (caretaker, Warsaw, Poland) and Julis Harco (Warsaw,
Poland); W - 19, Marks Bros., b. Somersworth, d/o John Aubert
(bleachery, Somersworth) and Rose Riberty (housewife,
Somersworth)

BURBECK,
Robert G. of New Castle m. Annie E. **Roberts** of Portsmouth
3/25/1943 in New Castle; H - 21, soldier, b. Lynn, MA, s/o Irvin
G. Burbeck (electrician, Newton, MA) and Marietta E. Berry
(housewife, Merrimack, MA); W - 21, cook, b. Levant, ME, d/o
Millard Roberts (farmer, Easton, ME) and Addie Teague
(housewife, Fort Fairfield, ME)

BURCH,
John B. E. of Los Angeles, CA m. Elizabeth F. **Jaffe** of Los Angeles,
CA 6/26/1977 in New Castle; H - s/o G.N. Blair Burch and
Althea Ward; W - d/o Rubin I. Jaffe and Barbara Weiss

BURKE,
John J. of New Castle m. Rosanna M. **Varden** of North Attleboro,
MA 6/18/1988 in Dover; H - s/o William M. Burke and Mary C.
Hayner; W - d/o John W.E. Varden and Rose M. Trigg
Philip A. of Billings, MT m. Anne H. **Harrington** of Billings, MT
8/21/1982 in New Castle; H - s/o Thomas C. Burke and Beatrice
Swift; W - d/o William F. Harrington and Margaret Hemingway

BUTCHER,

George of Midlothian, TX m. Frances L. **Back** of New Castle
8/16/1894 in Portsmouth; H - 28, b. Lancaster, TX, s/o George
Butcher and Mahala Barrow; W - 22, b. London, England, d/o
Francis Back and Emma L. Taylor

CALKINS,

Robert Allan m. Kathleen Ellen **Maynor** 8/10/1963 in New Castle; H
- 21, b. NY, s/o George F. Calkins and Gladys B. Knowlton; W -
20, b. NH, d/o Russell Maynor and Irene Herman

CALLAHAN,

Kevin J. of New Castle m. Deborah A. **Carrier** of Manchester
4/26/1985 in Portsmouth; H - s/o John Callahan and Virginia
Hurley; W - d/o Andre Carrier and Helen Fasekis

CALVERLEY,

Ernest A. m. Ellen L. **Lamond** 7/17/1976 in New Castle; H - s/o
Ernest Calverley and ----- Grout; W - d/o Allan A. Lamond and
Nancy Skillings

CAMPBELL,

C. W. of New Castle m. Virginia Ann **Sims** of Merchantville, NJ
8/27/1957 in Norwich, CT; H - 22, US Navy, b. NH, s/o W.
Campbell and K. Strachan; W - 18, waitress, b. NJ, d/o Benjamin
Sims and Virginia Rankin

Douglas of New Castle m. Stephanie A. **Miles** of Portsmouth
9/1/1984 in New Castle; H - s/o Donald Campbell and Patricia
Letts; W - d/o Nelson Miles and Doris Purchase

James Henry m. Cheryl Lee **Brissette** 10/15/1960 in Portsmouth; H -
19, b. NH, s/o Wentworth Campbell and Katherine A. Strahan;
W - 16, b. NY, d/o Benjamin A. Brissette and Cora K. Parlin

Kevin John m. Jerrilyn Phyllis **Sparks** 11/5/1966 in Portsmouth; H -
20, b. NH, s/o Wentworth Campbell and Katherine E. Strachan;
W - 18, b. MA, d/o Ralph H. Sparks and Phyllis C. Lefort

Richard J. of New Castle m. Carol Ann **Bennett** of New Castle 4/3/1996 in New Castle

CARBONETTI,

Louis J. of Roosevelt Island, NY m. Patricia J. **White** of Roosevelt Island, NY 8/25/1984 in New Castle; H - s/o Louis Carbonetti and Vivian Pellegrino; W - d/o Kenneth B. White and Joan Heard

CARPENTER,

Robert L., Jr. of New Castle m. Linda S. **Frampton** of New Castle 12/6/1980 in New Castle; H - s/o Robert L. Carpenter and Doris Wyman; W - d/o Harold V. Frampton and Katherine Hutchinson

CARTER,

William G. m. Susan T. **Parrish** 8/2/1975 in New Castle; H - s/o Joseph S. Carter and Betty Broadbent; W - d/o Hugh Parrish and Terese Sellers

CASSIDY,

Francis Edward m. Joyce Ellen **Rowe** 6/20/1992 in Rye

William J. of Charlestown, MA m. Joan F. **Buckley** of Charlestown, MA 9/23/1950 in New Castle; H - 21, assmb. man, b. MA, s/o William L. Cassidy (ME) and Catherine Houlihan (Ireland); W - 18, punch p. op., b. MA, d/o Robert F. Buckley (MA) and Alice C. Gatenby (England)

CASSO,

Anthony D. of New Castle m. Patricia A. **Smith** of Portsmouth 4/28/1984 in Portsmouth; H - s/o John R. Casso and Anna E. Murphy; W - d/o D'Thurlow Smith and Frances E. Noble

CERNY,

James W. m. Donna E. **Priestly** 6/21/1969 in L.B. Head; H - s/o Alvin J. Cerny and Julia C. Twomey; W - d/o William Priestly and Isadore E. Pridham

CHASE,

Charles S. of New Castle m. Ruth E. **Sloan** of New Castle 8/4/1937 in New Castle; H - 24, philatelist, b. Haverhill, MA, s/o Charles C. Chase (real estate, Haverhill, MA) and Susan Killiam (Topsfield, MA); W - 28, teacher, b. Manchester, d/o Alexander Sloan (ret. clergy, New York, NY) and Marie L. Halfman (at home, Philadelphia, PA)

Samuel H. m. Lea Anne **Golter** 7/20/1991 in Portsmouth

CHASTAIN,

William of New Castle m. Edith G.B. **Hannaford** of Woonsocket, RI 11/2/1942 in Woonsocket, RI; H - 31, seaman, 2d, b. LA, s/o James T. Chastain (retired, LA) and Maude Smith; W - 31, reg. nurse, 2d, b. Woonsocket, RI, d/o Verne Bassett (mechanic, Uxbridge, MA) and Carrie Holbrook (Woonsocket, RI)

CHEVRETTE,

Arthur J. of Fort Constitution m. Effie M. **Bullett** of Pittsfield, MA 11/13/1907 in New Castle; H - 22, soldier, b. Canada, s/o Charles Chevrette (laborer, Canada) and Lucie Brunell (Canada); W - 21, housewife, d/o John Bullett (laborer, Pittsfield, MA) and Mathilda Donneville (housewife, Canada)

CHILDS,

George W. m. Ethel F. **Kibler** 6/29/1968 in New Castle; H - b. Quebec, s/o Harba W. Childs and Annie A. Damon; W - b. MA, d/o Andrew T. Frost and Lydia Forbes

CLAPP,

Andrew D. of Eliot, ME m. Teresa A. **Borden** of Eliot, ME 9/18/1988 in New Castle; H - s/o Walter D. Clapp and Marion C. Hunt; W - d/o David Borden and Viviana Mendoza

CLARK,

Charles W., Jr. m. Sheila M. T. **Cameron** 5/11/1965 in New Castle; H - 28, b. NH, s/o Charles W. Clark and Albina Alessi; W - 20, b. Scotland, d/o Malcolm A. Cameron and Marion T. Herd

Charles W., Jr. m. Laurie **Page** 11/29/1975 in New Castle; H - s/o Charles W. Clark and Albina Alessi; W - d/o William L. Page and Lois T. Green

Henry W. m. Rose D. **Watson** 7/31/1966 in Boston, MA; H - 66, 2d, b. MA, s/o Charles M. Clark and Ella M. Sturgis; W - 50, 2d, b. NS, d/o Charles S. Davis and Elizabeth B. Powers

Joseph of New Castle m. Crescence E. **Smith** of New Castle 10/3/1930 in Ludlow, VT; H - 51, real estate, 2d, b. Cambridge, MA, s/o Elisha Clark (Bath, ME) and Eleanor Pettigrew (Portsmouth); W - 42, 2d, b. Jamaica Plain, MA, d/o Joseph Hertig (Boston, MA) and Crescence Wein (Boston, MA)

R. E., Capt. of New Castle m. Mary **Perkins** of Portsmouth 4/7/1943 in New Castle; H - 23, capt., USA, b. New London, CT, s/o Bert F. Clark (naval officer, Carbon, WY) and Francis L. Everts (Washington, DC); W - 21, secretary, b. Castine, ME, d/o Fred C. Perkins (carpenter, Castine, ME) and Hattie Sawyer (housewife, Castine, ME)

Ralph E. of Kittery, ME m. Addie M. **Meloon** of New Castle 2/14/1905 in New Castle; H - 29, druggist, b. Frankfort, ME, s/o John C. Clark (mason, Prospect, ME) and Sarah Rogers (housewife, Bristol, ME); W - 28, housewife, b. New Castle, d/o James M. Meloon (laborer, New Castle) and Charlotte Campbell (housewife, New Castle)

CLARKE, (see Clark)

Joseph of New Castle m. Crescence E. **Smith** 5/13/1927 in New Castle; H - 47, RE broker, ins., 2d, b. Cambridge, MA, s/o Elisha Clarke, Jr. (provision dealer, Bath, ME) and Eleanor A. Pettigrew (housewife, Portsmouth); W - 39, home, 2d, b. Jamaica Plains, MA, d/o Joseph Edward Hertig (fur. and steam't'r, Jamaica Plains, MA) and Crescence Theresa Wein (Jamaica Plains, MA)

CLAUSS,

Robert G. of Wakefield, MA m. Susan R. **Toomey** of Acton, MA 1/28/1984 in New Castle; H - s/o Robert Clauss and Dorothy Holycross; W - d/o Richard A. Toomey and Elizabeth Rylander

CLEMENS,

William G. of Rye Beach m. Pauline L. **Heinrich** of New Castle 3/25/1988 in Rye; H - s/o Harold V. Clemens and Eva M. Linchey; W - d/o Wesley Varney and Alta G. Parnham

CLENDENIN,

Gary K. m. Susan K. **Tabbutt** 10/11/1969 in New Castle; H - s/o Keith M. Clendenin and Bonnie J. Cloward; W - d/o Clifford C. Tabbutt and Arline R. Ricker

COFFIN,

Edward W. of Owls Head, ME m. Sallie G. **Smith** of Tenants Harbor, ME 9/6/1980 in New Castle; H - s/o Edward B. Coffin and Margaret Wejman; W - d/o Albert Dorman and Sallie Owings

COLE,

Arthur P. of Portsmouth m. Carol **Seybolt** of New Castle 6/7/1953 in New Castle; H - 25, ser. sta. att., b. NH, s/o Parker K. Cole (NH) and Olive T. Gardner (NH); W - 23, at home, b. NH, d/o John E. Seybolt (NY) and Carolyn W. Badger (NH)

COLLINS,

Edward C., III of Concord, MA m. Elizabeth M. **Lufkin** of Marblehead, MA 8/27/1983 in New Castle; H - s/o Edward C. Collins, II and Susan Prichard; W - d/o Chauncey F. Lufkin and Elizabeth Heard

CONKLIN,

Harry W. of Lakewood, NJ m. Iva F. **Reed** of New Castle 9/19/1950 in New Castle; H - 71, master plumber, 2d, b. NJ, s/o David L.

Conklin (NY) and Harriet Quackenbush (NY); W - 61, at home, 3d, b. NH, d/o Freeman Huntley (NH) and Ella Rogers (NH)

CONNELL,
Fintan J. H. m. Linda R. **Griebsch** 12/11/1976 in New Castle; H - s/o Vivian Connell and ----- Herrick; W - d/o Erich Voehringer and Eva Binder

CONSTANT,
Nazair George of Portsmouth m. Lucicone Dana **Gelinas** of Manchester 2/11/1918 in Manchester; H - 32, shoemaker, b. Epping, s/o Theophile Constant (shoeworker, Canada) and Mary Currier (Canada); W - 21, clerk, b. Manchester, d/o Joseph O. Gelinas (tailor, Canada) and Angerline Dieziel (Canada)

CORKUM,
Esrom of New Castle m. Julia H. **Nyberg** of Manchester 6/3/1896 in Manchester

CORRIVEAU,
Thomas A. of Rochester m. Martha **Prior** of New Castle 4/28/1990 in New Castle; H - s/o Henry Corriveau and Beatrice Gauthier; W - d/o Carl Prior and Margaret Badger

CORZATT,
Richard D. of New Castle m. Nancy F. **Euchner** of New Castle 7/22/1995 in New Castle

COYLE,
Frederick Michael m. Sue Elizabeth **Desmond** 10/18/1966 in Portsmouth; H - 19, b. NH, s/o Charles F. Coyle and Virginia L. White; W - 20, b. RI, d/o John E. Desmond and Virginia D. DaCosta

CRAIG,

William A. of New Castle m. Anna Grace **Elliott** of Wilkinsburg, PA
5/2/1941 in New Castle; H - 28, army officer, b. Ulrichville, OH,
s/o Harry Ross Craig (dentist, Armstrong Co., PA) and Helen
Marie Smith (housewife, Pittsburgh, PA); W - 23, stenographer,
b. Bridgeville, PA, d/o David J. Elliott (lumber estr.,
Wilkinsburg, PA) and Caroline C. Loch (housewife, McKeasport,
PA)

CREIGHTON,

David W. of Perth, NY m. Nettie M. **White** of New Castle 1/17/1899
in New Castle; H - 45, farmer, b. Perth, NY, s/o Duncan
Creighton (deceased, Perth, NY) and Ursula K. Creighton
(housewife, Perth, NY); W - 32, music teacher, b. New Castle,
d/o John V. White (carpenter, New Castle) and Miriam T. White
(deceased, New Castle)

CROCKET,

Douglas Robert m. Sandra Jayne **Jenkins** 7/5/1967 in New Castle; H -
50, 2d, b. MA, s/o Robert B. Crocket and Hilda Burhouse; W -
28, 2d, b. ME, d/o Joseph R. Smith and Elsie C. Hanlon

CROSBY,

Howard S. of Washington, DC m. Phyllis B. **McCarthy** of New
Castle 8/1/1953 in Portsmouth; H - 27, USN, b. CA, s/o Howard
H. Crosby (MA) and Georgie M. Armstrong (India); W - 24, at
home, b. MA, d/o Louis B. McCarthy (MA) and Gertrude Banks
(MA)

CROTHERS,

Edgar R. of New Castle m. Anne M. **Signorello** of New Castle
10/15/1988 in New Castle; H - s/o Edgar Crothers and Margaret
P. Beebe; W - d/o Joseph Signorello and Evelyn E. Gillis

CULLEN,
Paul Edward m. Pamela Elizabeth **Pitts** 6/12/1965 in Portsmouth; H - 21, b. NH, s/o Charles T. Cullen and Mary A. Monahan; W - 18, b. ME, d/o George S. Pitts and Virginia McCausland

CUMMINS,
Irving P. of New Castle m. Mary **Dundash** of New Castle 7/25/1925 in Portsmouth; H - 43, fireman, 2d, b. Lafayette, NJ, s/o William Cummins (retired, Ireland) and Alice Chircoyne (at home, NJ); W - 40, housekeeper, b. Ireland, d/o Richard Dundash (retired, Ireland) and Margaret Dundash (deceased, Ireland)

CUSHMAN,
William Edward m. Mary Margaret **Dawson** 4/14/1973 in Durham; H - s/o Rufus Cushman and Adele E. Schroeder; W - d/o Charles O. Dawson and Doris D. Smith

D'ANTONIO,
Michael B. of New Castle m. Toni E. **Raiten** of York, ME 6/3/1978 in Portsmouth; H - s/o Albert M. D'Antonio and Patricia Barr; W - d/o Allen Raiten and Marjorie Herfort

DAIN,
Robert W. m. Kim M. **Pridham** 4/23/1976 in New Castle; H - s/o John Dain and Joan Menken; W - d/o Frederick Pridham and Mary Moran

DALEY,
Peter, Jr. of Fort Constitution m. Mary E. **Desmanches** of Nashua 7/1/1920 in New Castle; H - 29, soldier, USA, b. Providence, RI, s/o Peter Daley (laborer, Ireland) and Jane McGaine (housewife, Ireland); W - 19, waitress, b. Nashua, d/o Henry Desmanches (laborer, Week Land., Canada) and Liza Perrault (housewife, PQ, Canada)

DAMON,

Kent Telfer of Boston, MA m. Lori Ann **Nollet** of Cambridge, MA 9/11/1993 in New Castle

DASKOSKI,

Raymond S. m. Karen L. **Newton** 7/17/1976 in New Castle; H - s/o Robert Daskoski and Shirley Barnaby; W - d/o Ray B. Newton and Ethel Herd

DAVIDSON,

David W. F. of Somersworth m. Michele L. **Arsenault** of New Castle 10/1/1983 in Portsmouth; H - s/o John E. Davidson, Jr. and Teresa Stowell; W - d/o Edmund J. Arsenault and Joanne Lamb

George of New Castle m. Josephine **Orde** of New Castle 11/23/1892 in Portsmouth; H - 30, b. New Castle; W - 28, b. Digby, NS

James D. of New Castle m. Gertrude **Mace** of Rye 11/6/1891 in Rye; H - 20, b. New Castle; W - 21, b. Rye

Merton O. of New Castle m. Frances M. **Bailey** of Portsmouth 10/9/1916 in Portsmouth; H - 23, draftsman, b. New Castle, s/o George H. Davidson (carpenter, New Castle) and Josephine Orde (Digby, NS); W - 21, school teacher, b. Portsmouth, d/o Charles E. Bailey (engineer, Portsmouth) and Ida Paine (Kittery, ME)

Reginald O. of New Castle m. Hazel E. **Ricker** of New Castle 12/31/1920 in New Castle; H - 20, shipfitter, b. New Castle, s/o George Davidson (carpenter, New Castle) and Josephine Orde (Digby, NS); W - 19, at home, b. New Castle, d/o George B. Ricker (boatswain, CG, New Castle) and Seddie White (housewife, New Castle)

Thomas of New Castle m. Lillian May **McPhee** of Kittery Point, ME 7/27/1931 in Little Harbor, Rye; H - 71, boat builder, 3d, b. New Castle, s/o Ralph Davidson (boat builder, New Castle) and Lucretia Harris (New London, CT); W - 42, at home, 2d, b. Portsmouth, d/o Charles S. Drown (sailmaker, Milton) and Sarah Jane Alton (Portsmouth)

DAY,

Gordon A. of Essex, MA m. Doris A. **Davis** of New Castle
6/30/1928 in Portsmouth; H - 21, coast guard, b. Essex, MA, s/o
Walter H. Day (truckman, Essex, MA) and Mary E. Haywood
(Essex, MA); W - 16, at home, b. Jonesport, ME, d/o Walter W.
Davis (Jonesport, ME) and Mary E. Alley

DECOFF,

Raymond W. of New Castle m. Blanche **Whitcomb** of Lunenburg,
MA 9/4/1918 in Cambridge, MA; H - 20, carpenter, b.
Fitchburg, MA, s/o John B. DeCoff (car inspector, East Boston,
MA) and Elner Oborne (Canada, PQ); W - 22, b. Lunenburg,
MA, d/o George Whitcomb (farmer, Pepperell, MA) and Jennie
Howard (Lunenburg, MA)

DEMAS,

Damon G. of Weston, MA m. Elaine M. **Rivard** of Weston, MA
9/23/1990 in New Castle; H - s/o George Demas and Victoria
Chiungos; W - d/o James Rivard and Margaret O'Sullivan

DENNIS,

Bradford C. of Newburyport, MA m. W. K. **Wilson** of New Castle
6/23/1956 in New Castle; H - 25, airplane mechanic, b. MA, s/o
Bradford C. Dennis (MA) and Mary Y. Curtis (MA); W - 22, at
home, 2d, b. NH, d/o Oscar C. Monro (NS) and Essie F. Ricker
(NH)

DEVANEY,

Thomas of Portsmouth m. Leslie Y. **Maxam** of New Castle 4/28/1984
in Portsmouth; H - s/o Thomas E. DeVaney and Rosetta
Drinkwater; W - d/o Simon Young and Audrey Orne

DEVENDORF,

David E. of New Haven, CT m. Aldona M. **Hamel** of New Haven, CT
8/12/1978 in New Castle; H - s/o Maurice Devendorf and -----
Franklin; W - d/o Frederick Hamel and ----- Pieslak

DEWHIRST,

Gary L. of New Castle m. Rebecca R. **Bergeron** of New Castle
11/29/1982 in Portsmouth; H - s/o A. N. Dewhirst, Jr. and Jean
Breckenridge; W - d/o John Randall and Pearl Payne

Gary Leigh m. Kathleen Ellen **Shea** 11/25/1967 in Portsmouth; H -
26, b. CA, s/o Arleigh N. Dewhirst and Margaret Breckenridge;
W - 21, b. NH, d/o Leo F. Shea and Ellen L. Robbins

DIAMENT,

Joseph m. Patti S. **Streiff** 8/7/1976 in New Castle; H - s/o Eli Diament
and Anne Koch; W - d/o Warren Streiff and Virginia Sidles

DIXON,

Richard F. m. Iris M. **Twidle** 6/20/1968 in Stratham; H - b. NH, s/o
Alden F. Dixon and Marjorie F. White; W - b. ME, d/o Fritz
Gnuirk and Gladys V. Wing

DOANE,

Valentine of Harwich, MA m. Louise C. **White** of New Castle
11/20/1901 in Boston, MA; H - 65, merchant, s/o Valentine
Doane (Harwich, MA) and Lydia Nickerson; W - 52, housewife,
d/o Albert White (New Castle) and Elizabeth Batson (New
Castle)

DORE,

John K., Jr. of Portsmouth m. Priscilla M. **Chase** of Hampton
10/8/1955 in New Castle; H - 35, NH state trooper, div., b. NH,
s/o John K. Dore (PA) and Luella M. Young (NH); W - 22,
hostess, b. MA, d/o Roy B. Chase (MA) and Elizabeth Whitley
(MA)

DOUBLEDAY,

Keenan David of Watertown, MA m. Elizabeth Mary **Dickey** of
Watertown, MA 6/4/1994 in New Castle

DOWNING,

Benjamin F. of Eliot, ME m. Arlene **Ricker** of New Castle
11/19/1926 in New Castle; H - 25, mechanic, b. Portsmouth, s/o
Henry Downing and Maude Downing; W - 18, b. New Castle, d/o
George B. Ricker (coast guard keeper, New Castle) and Sarah
White (New Castle)

DREW,

William Garvin, II m. Linda Ann **Florian** 8/5/1961 in Boston, MA; H
- 24, b. CA, s/o Garvin A. Drew and Lillian B. Jones; W - 22, b.
MA, d/o Kenneth A. Florian and Rosemary L. Moor

DUSO,

Carmi J. m. Phyllis C. **Dudley** 6/28/1969 in New Castle; H - s/o
Henry F. Duso and Linnie Benoit; W - d/o Homer D. Ovitt and
Maude L. Barnes

EARL,

Nellis C. of New Castle m. Phyllis A. **Payton** of Kittery, ME 8/7/1943
in New Castle; H - 23, coast artillery, b. New Milford, CT, s/o
Ivan H. Earl (contractor, Lansing, MI) and Grace E. Sharach
(housewife, New Milford, CT); W - 18, jr. clerk, b. Quincy, MA,
d/o Sydney Payton (Wollaston, MA) and Janet ----- (housewife,
Wollaston, MA)

EDWARDS,

Casey D. of New Castle m. Kimberly A. **Aremburg** of Greenland
8/12/1989 in Greenland; H - s/o Charles D. Edwards, Sr. and
Lois M. Frith; W - d/o Daniel R. Aremburg and Ellen K. Erwin

ELLIOTT,

Stewart S. m. Leah H. **Caswell** 6/7/1970 in Portsmouth; H - s/o
Edward P. Elliott and Eleanor Roosevelt; W - d/o Kenneth Y.
Caswell and Winifred M. Claus

ELLIS,

Arthur G. of Worcester, MA m. Sandra A. **Thomas** of Worcester, MA
10/9/1988 in New Castle; H - s/o Norman R. Ellis and Beverly J.
Oakes; W - d/o Walter G. Thomas and Patricia A. Mullin

ELLISON,

Arthur E. of Richmond, VA m. W. P. **Martin** of Marblehead, MA
6/23/1956 in New Castle; H - 30, surgeon, 2d, b. NY, s/o Arthur
E. Ellison (MA) and A. L. Tettemer (NY); W - 30, at home, 2d,
b. CT, d/o Joseph A. Pentland (CT) and Winifred M. Ryan (CT)

ELLKEWICZ,

Leonard B. of New Castle m. Rita M. **Boisvert** of Portsmouth
10/16/1943 in New Castle; H - 24, coast artillery, b. Manticoke,
PA, s/o Benjamin Ellkewicz (coal miner, Russia) and Mary Maga
(housewife, PA); W - 21, typist, b. Greenland, d/o John B.
Boisvert (blacksmith, Canada) and Mary J. Gulingo (housewife,
Canada)

EMERY,

Jotham of New Castle m. Rebecca B. **Janvrin** of Portsmouth
4/8/1897 in Portsmouth; H - 55, 2d, b. Biddeford, ME, s/o
Jotham Emery and Sarah Fernald; W - 67, 2d, b. Eliot, ME, d/o
Charles C. Tetherly and Rebecca P. Tetherly

Rufus J. of New Castle m. Josephine L. **Standish** of New Castle
10/29/1919 in Portsmouth; H - 41, general helper, b. New Castle,
s/o Jonathan Emery (laborer, Biddeford, ME) and Louise S.
Baker (at home, New Castle); W - 45, at home, 3d, b. Starks,
ME, d/o Moses P. Piper (farmer, Solon, ME) and Maria L.
Mashire (at home, Fryeburg, ME)

ERICKSON,

Allan R. m. Sue Anne **Sturtevant** 4/6/1974 in Portsmouth; H - s/o
Marvin K. Erickson and Etta Mae Towle; W - d/o Richard
Sturtevant and Mary Daly

FAGADORE,
John M. m. Elizabeth **Kennedy** 6/19/1976 in New Castle; H - s/o
John T. Fagadore and Rita Paskert; W - d/o Robert G. Kennedy
and Carol Brooks

FAIR,
Steven L. of Marblehead, MA m. Marta L. **Thornton** of Marblehead,
MA 1/10/1987 in New Castle; H - s/o Donald Fair and Royleen
Geiser; W - d/o Jack H. Thornton and Emma M. Boyce

FALLS,
Henry J. of New Castle m. Elizabeth **Durvali** of Scranton, PA
5/5/1945 in Portsmouth; H - 27, USC Artillery, b. Dun'more,
PA, s/o Henry Falls (machine op., Scranton, PA) and Helen
McBride (housewife, Hazleton, PA); W - 27, housewife, b.
Scranton, PA, d/o Romolo Durvali (defense wkr., Italy) and Rosa
Carta (housewife, Scranton, PA)

FAMOLARE,
John A. of New Castle Harbor m. Patricia C. **Hough** of Stratham
8/20/1993 in Gosport

FARDELMANN,
George of Salem, OR m. Janice **Pinhero** of Salem, OR 12/29/1995 in
New Castle

FARRINGTON,
William I. of Kittery, ME m. Elsie S. **Sylvester** of New Castle
9/12/1931 in Kittery, ME; H - 25, machine operator, b. Kittery,
ME, s/o Herbert O. Farrington (draughtsman, Portland, ME) and
Mary E. Hutchins (housewife, Canton, ME); W - 22, school
teacher, b. New Castle, d/o James E. Sylvester (shipfitter,
Quincy, MA) and Elsie Mary Fernald (housewife, Kittery, ME)

FERNALD,

Michael Edward m. Christina Jeanne **Pridham** 5/12/1973 in New Castle; H - s/o Charles E. Fernald and Mary Kalenian; W - d/o Stanley M. Pridham and Gloria Sawyer

FESSENDEN,

Chester James m. Nancy Marie **Andrews** 1/28/1961 in Portsmouth; H - 23, b. MA, s/o Chester J. Fessenden and Isabelle Sloan; W - 21, b. NH, d/o True J. Andrews and Mary E. Day

FIDES,

Peter J., II m. Brenda L. **Goldberg** 8/1/1976 in New Castle; H - s/o Forrest D. Fides and Frances Hatch; W - d/o David Goldberg and Beverly Walker

FINN,

Michael Paul of New Castle m. Carol Elizabeth **Croall** of Exeter 8/13/1994 in Hampton

FIORE,

Michael N. of New Castle m. Dorothy A. **Estes** of Somerville, MA 5/23/1943 in New Castle; H - 24, officer, USA, b. Revere, MA, s/o Vincuiso Fiore (barber, Italy) and Camilla Maffio (housewife, Italy); W - 29, sales prom., b. Pittsfield, MA, d/o Harold Estes (int. dec., N. Adams, MA) and Celia Kennedy (housewife, Pittsfield, MA)

FISHER,

Gary T. of Londonderry m. Diane A. **Miller** of New Castle 9/18/1982 in New Castle; H - s/o Lawrence Fisher and Jeanne Dohren; W - d/o John C. Miller and Nancy Mueller

FISK,

Eugene C. m. Holly L. **Young** 5/3/1975 in New Castle; H - s/o Charles Fisk and Marie Parrish; W - d/o Maynard Young and Hermelene Hubbard

Eugene C. m. Betty Ann **Quelch** 3/9/1991 in New Castle

FLEISHER,
John C. of New Castle m. Anne S. **Hess** of Durham 9/6/1980 in
Durham; H - s/o John C. Fleisher and Nettie V. Johnson; W - d/o
John F. Campbell and Mary Spillane

FLETCHER,
Norman A. of New Castle m. Mary **Fenton** of Dover 2/20/1943 in
New Castle; H - 21, coast artillery, b. Amherst, MA, s/o
Abraham Fletcher (pressman, England); W - 19, shoe shop, b.
Dover, d/o Daniel Fenton (belt factory, Dover) and Mari Rossiter
(housewife, Dover)
Royce Wayne m. Eleanor Newell **Marvin** 9/3/1960 in Portsmouth; H -
21, b. NM, s/o Cecil F. Fletcher and Viola L. Askins; W - 20, b.
MA, d/o Edward S. Marvin and Eleanor N. Jordan

FLYNN,
William L. of New Castle m. Lizzie **McDonald** of New Castle
7/7/1897 in New Castle; H - 46, 2d, b. New Castle, s/o James
Flynn and Martha Yeaton; W - 25, b. London, England, d/o
Angus McDonald and Lizzie McDonald

FOGG,
Rudolph J. of Dover m. Ruth J. **Groton** of New Castle 5/6/1950 in
Dover; H - 22, asst. mgr., b. NH, s/o John A. Fogg (NH) and
Alexandria M. Couture (NH); W - 20, clarostat, b. ME, d/o
Robert E. Groton (ME) and Ruth E. Gray (NH)

FOLLANSBEE,
Peter E. of New Castle m. Susan A. **Miller** of New Castle 9/19/1987
in New Castle; H - s/o Paul E. Follansbee and Barbara E.
Krieger; W - d/o John C. Miller and Nancy G. Muller

FORD,

George W. of New Castle m. Glenne E. **Tilley** of Portsmouth 9/20/1957 in Concord; H - 27, athletic director, b. NH, s/o Roland H. Ford (NH) and Margaret Lovejoy (NH); W - 18, secretary, b. NH, d/o John E. Tilley (NH) and Elizabeth Pearson (NH)

FOSS,

Gerald D. of Portsmouth m. Gertrude L. **Gilliam** of New Castle 6/3/1933 in Sanbornville; H - 22, clerk, b. So. Eliot, ME, s/o Herbert H. Foss (electrician, So. Berwick, ME) and Berenice D. Dixon (at home, So. Eliot, ME); W - 21, clerk, b. New Castle, d/o Claude C. Gilliam (electrician, Yale, VA) and Florence Mildred Batson (at home, Haverhill, MA)

Reginald Arthur of Malden, MA m. Evelyn Gertrude **Cousins** of New Castle 8/29/1931 in New Castle; H - 30, dispatcher, b. Rye, s/o Arthur M. Foss (painter, Rye) and Blanche Berry (at home, Rye); W - 22, registered nurse, b. Portsmouth, d/o Frank J. Cousins (machinist, Portsmouth) and Gertrude Jenness (at home, Rye)

FOSTER,

Dale G. of New Castle m. Vicki L. **House** of Greenland 10/29/1977 in Greenland; H - s/o Royce R. Foster and Carol L. Zink; W - d/o Raymond F. House and Mary F. Packard

FOWLER,

David Ernest of Arlington, MA m. Lillian L. **Butterworth** of Arlington, MA 9/29/1934 in New Castle; H - 46, electrician, 2d, b. Waltham, MA, s/o Josiah Fowler (blacksmith, St. Johns, NB) and Emma L. Bourne (housewife, Charlestown, MA); W - 42, clerk, r. of deeds, 2d, b. Ft. Payne, AL, d/o Frederick B. Doe (salesman, Thomaston, ME) and Lillian M. Urch (housewife, New Castle)

FOYE,

Donald Scott m. Susan Sherman **Amrol** 10/17/1992 in New Castle

FRAMPTON,

Damon H. m. Joann Louise **Petlick** 8/20/1965 in Portsmouth; H - 18, b. MD, s/o Harold V. Frampton and Katherine Hutchinson; W - 17, b. MI, d/o Casimis J. Petlick and Marion E. White

Damon H., II of New Castle m. Theresa M. **Christman** of Nottingham 6/11/1988 in Durham; H - s/o Damon H. Frampton and Joann L. Petlick; W - d/o Samuel J. Christman and Joan C. Dillenback

Marc Vernon of New Castle m. Bonnie Lee **Bryant** of Portsmouth 2/18/1978 in New Castle; H - s/o Harold V. Frampton and Katherine Hutchinson; W - d/o Ernest S. Bryant and Lorraine F. Dore

FREDRICKSON,

Gary R. m. Carol Ann **Gaudette** 12/7/1974; H - s/o George Fredrickson and Elaine Southwell; W - d/o Arthur Gaudette and Madeline Hebert

FREE,

Verne of New Castle m. Cora M. **Collins** of New Castle 1/5/1915 in New Castle; H - 24, soldier, b. PA, s/o H. A. Free (Ireland) and Anna Younger (Ireland); W - 21, housework, b. New Castle, d/o Luther P. Collins (fisherman, Kittery Point, ME) and Addie A. Simpson (housewife, New Castle)

FREEL,

Mark W. of New Castle m. Barbara **Stevens** of New Castle 8/28/1982 in Hanover; H - s/o C. Walker Freel and Thora Hansen; W - d/o Joseph C. Stevens and Jane Wurtz

FRENCH,

Jack of Portsmouth m. Sonja A. **Sullivan** of New Castle 8/27/1945 in New Castle; H - 24, USCG, b. Lincoln, NE, s/o Claude R. French (clerk, Lincoln, NE) and Claudia Chapman (housewife, Lincoln, NE); W - 18, welder, b. Brooklyn, NY, d/o Evolge Aspen (painter, Norway) and Borghild I. Wold (housewife, Norway)

Jack m. Katherine C. **Shapleigh** 6/9/1967 in Portsmouth; H - 45, 3d, b. NE, s/o Claude R. French and Claudea Chapman; W - 27, 3d, b. NH, d/o George A. Kent and Gladis R. Hopkinson

FRIES,

Robert George m. Vernice Ilene **Bennett** 1/18/1960 in New Castle; H - 24, b. NY, s/o Leo George Fries and Ines M. McNeil; W - 20, 2d, b. UT, d/o Ferron A. Christensen and Violet M. Cook

FROESE,

Ronald Keith m. Sherley Ann **Queen** 8/19/1962 in New Castle; H - 27, b. KA, s/o Gus V. Froese and Jesse J. Carey; W - 27, 2d, b. CA, d/o Cletus R. Proett and Mae R. Karr

FULLAM,

John B., Jr. m. Jill Elizabeth **Desmond** 6/10/1967 in Portsmouth; H - 22, b. NH, s/o John B. Fullam and Helen R. McLaughlin; W - 23, b. RI, d/o John E. Desmond and Virginia D. DaCosta

GABARDI,

Carlo Henry of New Castle m. Irene B. **Hebert** of Lowell, MA 9/6/1942 in Portsmouth; H - 33, coast artillery, b. Italy, s/o Peter Gabardi (bricklayer, Italy) and Rose Amprosali (Italy); W - 33, hairdresser, b. Canada, d/o Joseph Hebert (Canada) and Katherine Cross (housewife, Canada)

GAGE,

Thomas G. of New Castle m. Julia B. **Goodwin** of York, ME 1/31/1905 in Portsmouth; H - 23, carpenter, b. Dover, s/o Thomas F. Gage (carpenter, Dover) and Ida F. Brownell (housewife, Dover); W - 20, housewife, b. York, ME, d/o John Goodwin (mason, York, ME) and Hannah O. Donald (housewife, York, ME)

GAGNE,
Michael J. of New Castle m. Tobi L. **Evangelisti** of New Castle 7/12/1997 in New Castle

GAGNON,
Paul R. of Somersworth m. Ann L. **Lunt** of New Castle 8/20/1971 in Portsmouth; H - b. NH, s/o Leopold Gagnon and Dorothy P. Gelineau; W - b. NH, d/o Daniel E. Lunt and June F. Averill

GAILEY,
James R. of New Castle m. Wendy L. **Gilday** of Portsmouth 6/9/1984 in Rye; H - s/o John Gailey and Elizabeth Bolton; W - d/o Paul Gilday and Harriet Schofield

GALLANT,
Alfred Joseph m. Jane **Joaquin** 9/23/1961 in Portsmouth; H - 59, 2d, b. Canada, s/o Samuel Gallant and Mary Goodey; W - 51, b. PA, d/o George Joaquin and Maria Malent
Charles A., Jr. of Boston, MA m. Elizabeth **McDonough** of Boston, MA 10/16/1943 in New Castle; H - 26, longshoreman, b. Boston, MA, s/o Charles A. Gallant (coast guard, Boston, MA) and Genevieve Ford (Boston, MA); W - 21, at home, b. Boston, MA, d/o Richard McDonough (Ireland) and Esther McLaughlin (housewife, Boston, MA)

GARMARI,
David J. of Essex, MA m. Carla L. **Smith** of Essex, MA 4/30/1982 in New Castle; H - s/o Francis J. Garmari and Claire E. Bianco; W - d/o Bruce N. Smith and Norma L. Lagerstrom

GAZZA,
Mellio m. Linda L. **Chipman** 5/19/1968 in New Castle; H - b. PA, s/o Frank R. McClelland and Helen Percic; W - b. OK, d/o Samuel R. Hall and Lillian Burgess

GEARY,

Daniel E. of New Castle m. Christine A. **Dunnell** of Eliot, ME
12/22/1984 in New Castle; H - s/o Raymond F. Geary and Ann
C. Griffin; W - d/o Kenneth H. Johnson, Sr. and Aneta C. Shaub

GEBOW,

William G. of New Castle m. Debra P. **Meyer** of New Castle
12/17/1985 in Portsmouth; H - s/o William P. Gebow and Jean
E. Simpson; W - d/o Louis Meyer and Evelyn Judd

GEIB,

Robert Mark m. Joanna Fairbanks **Gough** 6/21/1958 in Hampton
Falls; H - 30, b. NY, s/o Jacob A. Geib and Edna Rall; W - 24, b.
RI, d/o Edward B. Gough and Gertrude O. Fairbanks

GEIGLEY,

John Davidson, Jr. of Kittery, ME m. Carol Anne **Pridham** of New
Castle 2/13/1979 in New Castle; H - s/o John D. Geigley and
Eleanor Smith; W - d/o Stanley M. Pridham and Gloria Sawyer

GELINAS,

Gerald George m. Nancy Ann **Evans** 2/8/1963 in Portsmouth; H - 18,
b. MA, s/o George A. Gelinas and Lea C. Brodeur; W - 16, b.
Newfoundland, d/o Wilbur L. Evans and Nannette Russell

GIANOTTI,

Michael Brian m. Janet Mae **Rowe** 10/23/1965 in New Castle; H - 19,
b. PA, s/o Charles F. Gianotti and Margaret S. Philbrick; W - 18,
b. ME, d/o Frederick Rowe and Marion I. Dickson

GIFT,

James J. of Salt Lake City, UT m. May P. **Gvozdenovic** of New
Castle 9/6/1980 in Portsmouth; H - s/o Byron Carl Gift and Jean
C. Hughes; W - d/o Frank M. Gvozdenovic and Mira Skaroupka

GILLIAM,
Claude C. of Yale, VA m. Florence M. **Batson** of New Castle
10/21/1909 in New Castle; H - 21, electrician, b. Yale, VA, s/o --
--- Gilliam (lumberman) and ----- Johnson (housewife, Yale,
VA); W - 19, b. Haverhill, MA, d/o ----- Batson (plumber, New
Castle) and ----- Healy (housewife, Boston, MA)

GILLIBRAND,
Gary m. Barbara A. **Coyle** 3/18/1972 in Portsmouth; H - s/o George
Gillibrand and Gretchen Sayward; W - d/o Charles Coyle and
Virginia White

GILLMORE,
John Henry of Portsmouth m. Mary Frances **Lacey** of New Castle
11/5/1942 in New Castle; H - 22, mariner, b. Ennis, TX, s/o
Harvey Gilmore (Little Rock, AR) and Minnie Jackson (Quanah,
TX); W - 17, at home, b. So. Portland, ME, d/o James F. Lacy
(sic) (Lowell, MA) and Isabel A. Sloan (housewife, Quebec,
Canada)

GLEASON,
Joel P. of Marblehead, MA m. Elise J. **Michaud** of Marblehead, MA
5/13/1978 in New Castle; H - s/o Arthur B. Gleason and
Josephine H. Rhones; W - d/o Gerard N. Michaud and Jacqueline
Deschamps

GOAN,
Edwin F. of Portland, ME m. Evelyn M. **Dotson** of Portland, ME
9/11/1952 in New Castle; H - 28, welder, b. ME, s/o Matthew A.
Goan and Ebba E. Lejonhud; W - 30, waitress, div., b. ME, d/o
Alvah S. Tibbetts and Eunice E. Alley

GODDARD,
Michael R. m. Lorna Jeanne **Healey** 4/19/1991 in New Castle

GOERSHEL,
Peter William of New Castle m. Elizabeth Ann **Gerdes** of New Castle 7/14/1984 in New Castle; H - s/o Paul W. Goershel, Jr. and Shirley E. Thorburn; W - d/o David F. Gerdes and Catherine McDermott

GOLDEN,
Eerin Kyle m. Karen Elizabeth **Passon** 2/18/1993 in Portsmouth

GOLDTHWAITE,
Willard C. of Gloucester, MA m. Christine **Richardson** of Gloucester, MA 3/16/1940 in New Castle; H - 28, chauffeur, b. Gloucester, MA, s/o George Goldthwaite (Gloucester, MA) and Mabel C. Wonson (saleslady, Gloucester, MA); W - 26, teacher, b. W. Somerville, MA, d/o Herman Richardson (salesman, Lowell, MA) and Lorena Sullivan (Gloucester, MA)

GORDON,
James J. of New Castle m. Elsie B. **Sargent** of New Castle 10/4/1984 in Portsmouth; H - s/o James A. Gordon and Catherine MacDonald; W - d/o Carroll L. Ford and Bertha N. Halliday

GRAAGE,
Eric C. of Washington, DC m. Susan R. **Lewis** of Washington, DC 6/16/1990 in New Castle; H - s/o Rolf Graage and Ursula Kowallik; W - d/o Kent Lewis and Beth Hobbs

GRAF,
Austin Paul of Revere, MA m. Evelyn L. **Holland** of Winthrop, MA 2/4/1940 in New Castle; H - 23, clerk, 2d, b. Revere, MA, s/o William C. Graf (printer, Malden, MA) and Florence Keeping (housewife, Boston, MA); W - 19, clerk, b. W. Roxbury, MA, d/o William Holland (electrician, Boston, MA) and Evelyn Rittinger (housewife, New York, NY)

GRAHAM,

Claude R. of New Castle m. Dora C. **O'Bannon** of New Castle
8/3/1943 in New Castle; H - 33, Lt., USA, b. Fredericton, MO,
s/o William P. Graham (miller, ret., MO) and Nellie B. Moore
(housewife, Fredericton, MO); W - 33, teacher, b. Rector, AR,
d/o Joseph W. O'Bannon (Fredericton, MO) and Mary R.
Thompson (housewife, Fredericton, MO)

GREENE,

William H. of Fall River, MA m. Joanne C. **Konarski** of Fall River,
MA 12/24/1941 in New Castle; H - 24, army cook, b. Fall River,
MA, s/o Cornelius Greene (US Eng. Dept., Springfield, MA) and
Ruby M. Gee (housewife, Fall River, MA); W - 21, floor lady, b.
Fall River, MA, d/o Victor Konarski (retired, Poland) and
Katherine Siergenza (Poland)

GREY,

Walter S. m. Kathleen B. **McDonough** 10/6/1973 in Portsmouth; H -
s/o Edwin W. Gray (sic) and Pearl Seavey; W - d/o John A. Berry
and Frances A. Meylert

GRICE,

Joseph E. of New Castle m. Mary A.T. **Royer** of Dover 2/13/1943 in
New Castle; H - 21, quartermaster, b. Jackson, MS, s/o Elmo B.
Grice (farmer, Jackson, MS) and Sarah Miller (housewife, MS);
W - 17, shoe shop, b. Dover, d/o Arthur Royer (navy yard,
Somersworth) and Leonie Doyen (Quebec)

GRIEVE,

Thomas J. of Bangor, ME m. Sadie B. **Ring** of New Castle
11/18/1912 in New Castle; H - 22, soldier, b. Brooklyn, NY, s/o
James Grieve (blacksmith, Scotland) and Margaret Dick
(housewife, Scotland); W - 22, 2d, b. Newington, d/o George
Ring (weaver, NS) and Carrie S. Hall (housewife, Portland, ME)

GRIFFIN,

Kenneth Leavy m. Joanne Ruth **Skidmore** 7/4/1960 in Portsmouth; H
- 22, b. FL, s/o Mitchell L. Griffin and Lillie G. Powell; W - 20,
b. NH, d/o Harry T. Skidmore and Mary A. Dwyer

Richard A. m. Joyce A. **Mikolyski** 2/17/1968 in Exeter; H - b. NH,
s/o Arnold H. Griffin and Dorothea G. Drew; W - b. NH, d/o
Edward J. Mikolyski and Mary P. Couillard

Robert F., Jr. of Kittery, ME m. Denise M. **Pridham** of New Castle
8/24/1979 in New Castle; H - s/o Robert F. Griffin and -----
Carpenter; W - d/o Frederick Pridham and Mary Moran

GUPTILL,

George M. of New Castle m. Eva M. **Manson** of New Castle 4/8/1917
in Dover; H - 22, electrician, b. Lubec, ME, s/o William B.
Guptill (USLSS, Lubec, ME) and Mary Davis (housewife, Lubec,
ME); W - 22, stenographer, b. New Castle, d/o George H.
Manson (shoemaker, New Castle) and Lillian Furbish
(housewife, Beverly, MA)

William B., Jr. of New Castle m. Ellen Crawford **Hoitt** of Durham
11/28/1925 in Durham; H - 35, clothing clerk, b. Charlestown,
MA, s/o William B. Guptill, Sr. (surfman, South Lubec, ME) and
Mary A. Davis (housewife, West Lubec, ME); W - 27, school
teacher, b. Durham, d/o George G. Hoitt (farmer, Lee) and Laura
M. Sleeper (housewife, Bristol)

GWOREK,

Jonathan D. of Boston, MA m. Amy Lee **Palmer** of Boston, MA
7/22/1995 in New Castle

HADKY,

Azzedine of Paris, France m. Lisa S. **Palais** of Paris, France
8/27/1983 in New Castle; H - s/o M'Hamed Hadky and Mina
Bent Essaleh; W - d/o Donald G. Palais and Judith A. Snyder

HAFF,

John C. of Brooklyn, NY m. Virginia A. **Cuskley** of New Castle
9/26/1936 in Portsmouth; H - 29, geologist, b. Brooklyn, NY, s/o
Buel C. Haff (lawyer, Brooklyn, NY) and Kate W. Coles
(Brooklyn, NY); W - 30, geologist, b. Cape Elizabeth, ME, d/o
Henry M. Cuskley (light keeper, Portland, ME) and Mary E.
White (at home, Portsmouth)

HAGAN,

James E., Jr. of Southern Pines, NC m. Charlotte F. **Belanger** of
Lawrence, MA 12/15/1990 in New Castle; H - s/o James Hagan
and Opie Sulcer; W - d/o Edward Belanger and Charlotte Barton

HALE,

Henry M. of New Castle m. Gladys **Lovering** of Moultonboro
2/21/1918 in Portsmouth; H - 25, soldier, USA, b. Conway, s/o
Frank W. Hale (station agent, Conway) and Henrietta Metcalf
(Conway); W - 22, b. Moultonboro, d/o Frank Lovering (doctor,
Moultonboro) and Josephine E. Hoyt (Moultonboro)

Lowell Wayne m. Nancy Louise **Amazeen** 9/3/1959 in Portsmouth; H
- 20, b. AR, s/o Clay A. Hale and Glyn O. Tallant; W - 19, b.
NH, d/o Gerard B. Amazeen and Elsie L. Jones

Shawn E. of Eliot, ME m. Lucero P. **Pena** of New Castle 8/28/1987 in
Portsmouth; H - s/o Lowell W. Hale and Nancy Amazeen; W -
d/o Carlos A. Pena and Ana Mercedes Rodriguez

HALL,

George K. of New Castle m. Elinor M. **Hackney** of Eliot, ME
9/24/1948 in Eliot, ME; H - 26, mechanic, b. Portsmouth, s/o
Winfred Hall and Eva Keen (housewife, Kittery, ME); W - 22,
sales clerk, b. York, ME, d/o Sidney Hackney (retired,
Manchester) and Effie Chase (housewife, York, ME)

HALLEY,

William I. of No. Randolph, MA m. Norma I. **Dunham** of Boston,
MA 11/10/1951 in New Castle; H - 26, draftsman, b. MA, s/o

James Halley, Sr. (Scotland) and Catherine Monro (Scotland); W
- 25, nurse, b. MA, d/o Louis J. Dunham (MA) and Charlotte E.
King (MA)

HALPIN,

Eugene M., Jr. m. Bonnie A. **MacDonald** 6/14/1975 in New Castle; H
- s/o Eugene M. Halpin and Audrey M. Rush; W - d/o Douglas
MacDonald and Margaret Snyder

HAMILLA,

John, Jr. of New Castle m. Lillian **Shaw** of Rochester 6/20/1943 in
New Castle; H - 30, coast artillery, b. Bridgeport, CT, s/o John
Hamilla (loom fixer, Czechoslovakia) and Anna Galyda
(Czechoslovakia); W - 19, waitress, b. Mexico, ME, d/o Wilfred
W. Shaw (paper mill, NB) and Ola Weeks (housewife, Mexico,
ME)

HAMILTON,

Clement of New Castle m. Phyllis **Stockwell** of Concord 8/5/1946 in
Concord; H - 21, store clerk, b. Belmont, s/o Eugene Hamilton
(storekeeper, Laconia) and Evelyn Clairmont (housewife,
Belmont); W - 21, nurse, b. Rochester, d/o John Stockwell
(farmer, Charleston, ME) and Jenny Mitchell (housewife, St.
John's, NB)

HANCOCK,

David A. of Houston, TX m. Janis K. **Sawtelle** of New Castle
3/13/1982 in New Castle; H - s/o David C. Hancock and Barbara
Rundlet; W - d/o Joseph G. Sawtelle and Jean E. Brown

HANEISEN,

Frank T. of New Castle m. Doris L. **Beane** of Portsmouth 6/12/1943
in New Castle; H - 22, coast artillery, b. Brooklyn, NY, s/o
Charles Haneisen (mgr. radio co., Brooklyn, NY) and Carolyn
Leifherto (housewife, Newburgh, NY); W - 22, clerk, b. Epping,

d/o Arthur L. Bean (sic) (foreman, Brentwood) and Elsie B.
Drowne (housewife, Sandown)

HANSCOM,
Albert W. of New Castle m. Mary B. **Neal** of New Castle 4/30/1896
in Portsmouth
Albert W. of New Castle m. Delia H. **Austin** of Hamilton, MA
1/20/1915 in New Castle; H - 72, carpenter, 4th, wid., b. Eliot,
ME, s/o Stephen Hanscom (carpenter, Eliot, ME) and Olive
Hanscom (housewife, Eliot, ME); W - 67, housewife, 2d, wid., b.
Salem, MA, d/o Israel Norwood (carpenter, Gloucester, MA) and
Lucretia Yeaton (housewife, New Castle)

HARRINGTON,
John Leo m. Gail D. M. **Griffin** 8/24/1963 in Portsmouth; H - 21, b.
MA, s/o Edward J. Harrington and Helen A. Satkowski; W - 19,
b. NH, d/o Arnold Griffin and Dorothea G. Drew

HARRIS,
Bevual J. of New Castle m. Pauline D. **Stenzel** of Manchester
10/1/1938 in New Castle; H - 20, seaman, b. New Castle, s/o
Joseph Harris (machinist, Springfield, OH) and Katherine Nugent
(housewife, Newfoundland); W - 23, housework, b. Manchester,
d/o Otto Stenzel (chef, Germany) and Sadie Ring (Fall River,
MA)
Bevuell J. of New Castle m. Pauline D. **Harris** of Portsmouth
10/21/1949 in New Castle; H - 31, laborer, 2d, b. New Castle,
s/o Joseph Harris (MO) and Katherine Nugent (Canada); W - 34,
home, 2d, b. Manchester, d/o Otto F. Stenzel (Germany) and
Sadie Riley (MA)
Bevuell J. of New Castle m. Pauline D. **Harris** of New Castle
1/30/1954 in Portsmouth; H - 35, engineer, 4th, b. NH, s/o
Joseph T. Harris (MO) and Katherine Nugent (Newfoundland);
W - 38, housewife, 3rd, b. NH, d/o Otto Stenzel (Germany) and
Sadie Riley

HARRISON,

Carl. E., Jr. of Hanover m. Elizabeth V. **Margeson** of New Castle 12/27/1953 in New Castle; H - 22, student, b. IN, s/o Carl. E. Harrison, Sr. (IN) and Helen R. Woodall (IN); W - 20, student, b. AL, d/o Ralph C. Margeson (NH) and Hildegarde B. Szepinski (VA)

Edward G. of New Castle m. Thelma L. **Foss** of Dover 2/14/1942 in New Castle; H - 23, coast artillery, b. Freeport, ME, s/o William Harrison (shipyard wkr., Bath, ME) and Mary Clement (housewife, Brunswick, ME); W - 21, secretary, b. Dover, d/o Harold M. Foss (inspector, Dover) and Bertha Meserve (housewife, Dover)

HARTSHORN,

B. M. of New Castle m. Marie B. **White** of Ridgewood, NJ 9/5/1957 in Portsmouth; H - 65, retired, 2d, b. MA, s/o M. B. Hartshorn (VT) and Mary E. Murray (MA); W - 62, housewife, b. NJ, d/o Thomas G. Barber (NJ) and F. M. Patterson (NY)

HAY,

Thomas H. of New Castle m. Lizzie S. **Meloon** of New Castle 3/16/1904 in Portsmouth; H - 26, soldier, b. Morristown, NJ, s/o George Hay (merchant) and Rebecca Hay (housewife, Ireland); W - 19, housewife, b. New Castle, d/o Amory J. Meloon (carpenter, New Castle) and Sarah E. Yeaton (housewife, New Castle)

HAYNES,

Lawrence G. of New Castle m. Muriel C. **Burgess** of Bath, ME 9/16/1938 in Bath, ME; H - 40, fireman, b. Northeast Harbor, ME, s/o George E. Haynes (mason, ME) and Ethel Gott (housewife, Boothbay, ME); W - 28, housework, b. Bath, ME, d/o Alexander Burgess (boiler maker, Bath, ME) and Catherine Belanger (housewife, Bath, ME)

HAYWOOD,

LeRoy W. of New Castle m. Ellen I. **Winn** of Portsmouth 1/27/1912 in New Castle; H - 21, electrician's helper, b. New Castle, s/o Thomas Haywood (real estate, Portsmouth) and Dolly F. Amazeen (housewife, New Castle); W - 20, b. Brentwood, d/o Wilbur F. Winn (carpenter, Tuftonboro) and Estella Henderson (housewife, Staten Island, NY)

LeRoy W. m. Florina **Kitchen** 9/14/1968 in Portsmouth; H - b. NH, s/o Thomas Haywood and Dolly F. Amazeen; W - b. ME, d/o Joseph Murray and Virginia Duby

Nathaniel H. m. Mildred Bevans **Gaudet** 10/21/1961 in Portsmouth; H - 50, 2d, b. CT, s/o Archibald A. Haywood and Laura I. Hebbard; W - 51, 3d, b. CT, d/o Levi Bevans and Eleanor Birney

HEYWOOD,

Ruel Everett of Franklin, MA m. Hazel Mary **Buchanan** of Franklin, MA 8/10/1932 in New Castle; H - 51, supt. woolen mill, 2d, b. Central Falls, RI, s/o Frederick Heywood (Stalybridge, England) and Martha Louise Green (Ashton, RI); W - 44, at home, 2d, b. Woonsocket, RI, d/o William A. Booth (retired, England) and Harriet A. Smith (at home, Springfield, MA)

HICKS,

Terry A. of Stamford, CT m. Nancy Ann **Brown** of Stamford, CT 7/15/1995 in New Castle

HIXON,

Lucius C. of Grand Island, NE m. M. Theresa R. **Rand** of Boston, MA 5/4/1899 in Grand Island, NE; H - 43, contractor, b. Oil City, PA, s/o Henry B. Hixon (VA) and Eliza Hixon (PA); W - 34, nurse, b. New Castle, d/o Thomas Rand (Rye) and Adeline Twombly (New Castle)

HODGDON,

John F. of New Castle m. Greta B. **Beal** of New Castle 6/13/1938 in Hampton; H - 20, mach. op., b. Augusta, MA, s/o Myrtle

Hodgdon (at home, Clinton, ME); W - 21, at home, b. Jonesport, ME, d/o Ernest R. Beal (surfman CG, Jonesport, ME) and Edith Woodward (at home, Jonesport, ME)

John F., Jr. m. Jeanne B. **Muir** 9/16/1975 in Portsmouth; H - s/o John F. Hodgdon and Greta Beal; W - d/o Robert M. Muir and Margaret A. Motter

HODGKINS,

James W. m. Anne Louise **Hourihan** 7/17/1965 in Dover; H - 23, b. MA, s/o William Hodgkins and Marie L. Lyons; W - 21, b. NH, d/o Raymond Hourihan and Beatrice D. Mayrand

HOES,

John S. of NY m. Mercie **Walford** of New Castle 10/2/1954 in Portsmouth; H - 37, physician, 2d, b. NY, s/o Ernest P. Hoes (NY) and Louise Nesbit (MO); W - 35, artist, 2d, b. MA, d/o H. S. McKee Clay (PA) and Mercie Tarbell (MA)

HOLLAND,

William W. of Wellesley, MA m. Jonatha **Allen** of Newtonville, MA 6/14/1986 in New Castle; H - s/o Henry Holland and Elizabeth Adams; W - d/o Paul Adams and Judith Simmons

HOLMES,

Warren E. of New Castle m. Sylvia E. **Pio** of Portsmouth 8/7/1922 in Portsmouth; H - 21, beltmaker, b. Brighton, MA, s/o Harry Holmes (carpenter, Cambridge, MA) and Ella M. Erb (at home, Wolfeboro); W - 17, at home, b. ME, d/o Charles E. Pio (carpenter) and Ida M. Garland (at home, ME)

HOOD,

Jonathan L. of Westwood, MA m. Patricia A. **O'Connor** of New Castle 11/17/1990 in Portsmouth; H - s/o Leo Hood and Mary DiAnni; W - d/o William O'Connor and Margaret Chandler

HOPWOOD,

Paul m. Mary **Pickett** 9/21/1959 in New Castle; H - 25, b. NH, s/o
Walter Hopwood and Isabelle J. Gysen; W - 24, b. NH, d/o
Charlie W. Pickett and Gertrude E. Maertins

Walter of New Castle m. Marion E. **Petlick** of New Castle 12/19/1953
in Keene; H - 53, super. Navy Yard, 2d, b. ME, s/o John
Hopwood (England) and Sarah Batho (England); W - 33, clerk,
2d, b. NH, d/o Arnold B. White (NH) and Louise E. Jordan (ME)

HORNER,

Henry C. of New Castle m. Mary Ann **Knight** of Worcester, MA
8/9/1986 in New Castle; H - s/o Robert S. Horner and Virginia
V. Hart; W - d/o Chester P. Gifford and Mary Hunter Wilcox

Henry Chandler of New Castle m. Nancy Scribner **Pyle** of Farmington
4/7/1978 in New Castle; H - s/o Robert S. Horner and Virginia
V. Hart; W - d/o Richard B. Pyle and ----- Broughton

Robert S. of Brewer, ME m. Virginia V. **Hart** of New Castle 9/7/1927
in New Castle; H - 25, mgr. tannery, b. Melrose, MA, s/o
Thomas J. Horner (minister, Green Co., PA) and Flora B. Horner
(home, Boston, MA); W - 25, home, b. Manchester, d/o J. Ben
Hart (cert. public acct., Portsmouth) and Alice C. Chandler
(home, Manchester)

HORTON,

Daniel P. m. Marcia B. **Hersey** 11/17/1973 in New Castle; H - s/o
John A. Horton and Dorothy I. Olsen; W - d/o Walter F. Hersey
and Helen Clark

HOUGHTON,

Robert W. of New Castle m. Esther E. **Holton** of Dover 1/10/1942 in
New Castle; H - 24, soldier, b. Bangor, ME, s/o Lloyd Houghton
(superintendent, Bangor, ME) and Villa C. Brooker (housewife,
Bangor, ME); W - 31, restaurant, b. Wells, ME, d/o Willie H.
Hilton (sic) (retired, Wells, ME) and Mabel Hatch (housewife,
Wells, ME)

HOUSE,

Wilford E. of New Castle m. Bertha M. **Staples** of Oakland, ME 11/28/1943 in New Castle; H - 33, coast artillery, b. Derby, VT, s/o John House (stone mason, VT) and Hattie Kennedy (VT); W - 27, clerk, b. Oakland, ME, d/o Frank Brooks (spinner, Oakland, ME) and Emma Kennedy (housewife, Oakland, ME)

HOWE,

Dennis Allen m. Deborah Terhune **Marvin** 11/6/1959 in Stratham; H - 20, b. NH, s/o Edmond S. Howe and Hazel G. Reed; W - 18, b. MA, d/o Edward S. Marvin and Eleanor N. Jordan

HOWELL,

Richard L. of Kittery, ME m. Trudi E. **Bernardi** of Kittery, ME 12/31/1981 in New Castle; H - s/o Charles E. Howell and Virginia L. Golden; W - d/o Bruno Bernardi and Marilyn Olsen

HUBBARD,

Thomas T. of Harwich, MA m. Julie A. **Warn** of New Castle 10/28/1979 in New Castle; H - s/o Edward Hubbard and Virginia Davis; W - d/o Julius G. Schreibner and ----- Chapin

HUBBELL,

Roger Kingsley of Newtonville, MA m. Ethel Mabelle **Pierce** of Newtonville, MA 11/24/1928 in New Castle; H - 30, salesman, b. Lancaster, MA, s/o Chauncey G. Hubbell (statistician, Lexington, MA) and Alice D. Slade (at home, Lexington, MA); W - 29, teacher, b. Portland, ME, d/o Frank A. Pierce (expressman, Portland, ME) and Ida Fuller (at home, Portland, ME)

HUBLEY,

Lorin E. of New Castle m. Sophia C. **Hanson** of Portsmouth 12/25/1893 in Portsmouth; H - 33, b. New Castle; W - 30, b. Guttenberg, Sweden

HUMPHREYS,

Cecil Charles m. Lois Alba **Davis** 9/23/1961 in New Castle; H - 57, 2d, b. NH, s/o Charles W. Humphreys and Lydia A. Shannon; W - 45, 3d, b. ME, d/o Clarence C. Hall and Ella M. Moody

HUNING,

Harold W., II m. Sharin Lee **Ward** 9/2/1963 in New Castle; H - 26, b. MO, s/o Harold W. Huning and Ida M. Champlain; W - 19, b. WA, s/o Harold J. Ward and Dorothy M. Grant

HUSSEY,

Edward C. of Boston, MA m. Nora **Summers** of Boston, MA 1/23/1944 in New Castle; H - 36, coast artillery, b. Newfoundland, s/o Benjamin Hussey (carpenter, Newfoundland) and Maude Kane (Newfoundland); W - 36, at home, b. Ireland, d/o Martin Summers (Ireland) and Judith Cahill (Ireland)

HUTCHINS,

Henry E. of New Castle m. Estella T. **Kinnear** of New Castle 10/5/1904 in New Castle; H - 24, merchant, b. Wells, ME, s/o Henry W. Hutchins (laborer, Wells, ME) and Nellie L. Hatch (housewife, Wells, ME); W - 19, housewife, b. Somerville, MA, d/o Lewis E. Kinnear (carpenter, New Castle) and Susan E. Gildart (housewife, St. John, NB)

HUTCHINSON,

Albert W. m. Sharon A. **Colpritt** 2/15/1963 in Portsmouth; H - 20, b. NH, s/o Arthur W. Hutchinson and Ruth E. Mori; W - 18, b. ME, d/o Linwood R. Colpritt and Gwendolyn Hartley

HUTTON,

Mark G. of New Castle m. Thalia **Ravlin** of New Castle 7/26/1986 in New Castle; H - s/o John G. Hutton and Barbara Coon; W - d/o Winston C. Ravlin and Catherine Rich

IRELAND,

John M. m. Joann L. **Frampton** 12/20/1975 in New Castle; H - s/o Frank N. Ireland and Elenor Chapman; W - d/o Casimer J. Petlick and Marion E. White

IRWIN,

James R., Jr. of Laconia m. Elaine **Ruggles** of New Castle 4/27/1957 in Hampton; H - 32, boat dealer, b. NH, s/o James R. Irwin (MA) and Ella J. Henry (MA); W - 23, at home, b. MA, d/o Carter K. Ruggles (MA) and Doris G. Sanders (MA)

JACKSON,

Thomas G. of New Castle m. Eva B. **Amazeen** of New Castle 9/11/1901 in New Castle; H - 25, soldier, b. Hazelville, DE, s/o James W. Jackson (mail carrier, Canton, DE) and Emma J. Guessford (housewife, Canton, DE); W - 21, b. New Castle, d/o Granville Amazeen (laborer, New Castle) and Hattie Baker (housewife, New Castle)

JACOBSON,

Robert A. m. Margaret E. **Call** 9/25/1976 in North Hampton; H - s/o Birger E. Jacobson and Alice E. Orr; W - d/o Wallace R. Jacques and Marion Wiggin

JAMESON,

Charles of Wakefield, MA m. Marion J. **Flynn** of Haverhill, MA 8/30/1934 in New Castle; H - 40, manufacturer, 2d, b. Gloucester, MA, s/o William A. Jameson (retired, Boston, MA) and Hattie Hoskins (at home, Gloucester, MA); W - 28, private secretary, b. New Bedford, MA, d/o John Flynn (Wareham, MA) and Mary Higgins (at home, Providence, RI)

JAMIESON,

Charles D. m. Terry A. **Brigham** 6/5/1976 in Portsmouth; H - s/o Neil D. Jamieson and Dora M. Munster; W - d/o Roy C. Brigham and Germaine L. Quirk

JEFFERSON,

Steven B. of Rye m. Elizabeth A. **Phelps** of Rye 8/27/1977 in New
Castle; H - s/o Charles E. Jefferson and Barbara A. Isherwood;
W - d/o Philip D. Phelps and Elizabeth F. Fitzgerald

JENKINS,

James W. of Morristown, NJ m. Ann E. **Baker** of Morristown, NJ
3/4/1979 in New Castle; H - s/o William C. Jenkins and Susan D.
Berry; W - d/o O. Gordon Baker and Fannie A. Davis

JENNESS,

Willard M. of New Castle m. Emily **Wharton** of Worcester, MA
10/30/1901 in Worcester, MA; H - 30, carpenter, b. Rye, s/o
Albert D. Jenness (gardener, Rye) and Clara J. Jenness
(housewife, Rye); W - 24, housewife, b Worcester, MA, d/o
William Warton (gardener, Tralee, OH) and Ann B. Hassett
(housewife, Tralee, OH)

JENNINGS,

William L. of New Castle m. Blanche J. **Gage** of New Castle
12/2/1902 in New Castle; H - 22, soldier, b. Gilbraltar, s/o
Thomas J. Jennings (timekeeper, Plymouth, England) and Ida C.
Basden (housewife, Plymouth, England); W - 27, housewife, b.
Dover, d/o Thomas Gage (carpenter, Dover) and Ida F. Brownell
(housewife, Dover)

JOHNSON,

Andrew William of New Castle m. Pauline **Bergeron** of Keene
11/26/1942 in New Castle; H - 23, coast artillery, b. Nashua, s/o
John W. Johnson (shoe shop, Providence, RI) and Jessie M.
Lessard (housewife, Nashua); W - 27, sup. weaver, b. Keene, d/o
Peter A. Bergeron (clerk, Keene) and Flora Putnam
Donald K. m. Karen **Aspen** 9/7/1974 in New Castle; H - s/o Dan E.
Johnson and ----- Anderson; W - d/o Erick S. Aspen and Bessie
McKenzie

JONES,

Foster Tarlton m. Nancy Priscilla **Beane** 9/6/1963 in Rye; H - 21, b. NH, s/o Robert S. Jones and Beverly J. Tarlton; W - 21, b. NH, d/o Urban A. Beane and Virginia J. Lamson

Jesse C. of New Castle m. Olympia **Melitus** of Dover 10/31/1943 in Seabrook; H - 26, coast artillery, b. NC, s/o James Jones (NC) and Edna Maradic (NC); W - 19, spinner, b. Dover, d/o Arthur Melitus (weaver, Greece) and Stella Demopoulos (housewife, Greece)

JORDAN,

Lewis Ledger of Tampa, FL m. Anna Mary **Harricon** of Houston, TX 6/30/1929 in New Castle; H - 25, seaman, Sub. USN, b. Chipley, FL, s/o Thomas W. Jordan (realtor, Chipley, FL) and Mamie Morgan (Augusta, GA); W - 30, housewife, 3d, b. Rye, d/o George A. Locke (Rt. CG surfman, Rye) and Marguerite Gilles (housewife, Rye)

KAROLKIEWICZ,

Raymond m. Bette G. **Vennard** 11/28/1970 in Portsmouth; H - s/o Edward Karolkiewicz and Jennie Swierz; W - d/o Eliton Vennard and Helen Harris

KAROSIS,

Robert J. of New Castle m. Lauren A. **Erlandson** of New Castle 2/6/1988 in Rye; H - s/o John G. Karosis and Josephine P. Corraccio; W - d/o Paul K. Erlandson and Elizabeth Cummings

KAU,

Jan Richard of Eugene, OR m. Anne Greenough **Udaloy** of Missoula, MT 6/21/1986 in New Castle; H - s/o Louis Kau and Wilma Dace; W - d/o John Udaloy and Judith Greenough

KAYLOR,

Rant B. of Fort Constitution m. Armina **Getty** of Pittsfield, MA 5/25/1909 in New Castle; H - 26, soldier, b. Bristol, VA, s/o -----

Kaylor (lumberman) and ----- Harlow (housewife); W - 27, 2d, b. VT, d/o ----- Donnevilla (housewife, Montreal, Canada)

KELLENBECK,
W., Jr. of New Castle m. G. H. **Harris** of Perham, ME 10/8/1948 in Perham, ME; H - 18, US Army, b. Portsmouth, s/o W. R. Kellenbeck (electrician, Portsmouth) and L. Ruth Morrill (hostess, Portsmouth); W - 18, student, b. Perham, ME, d/o W. I. Harris (mechanic, Perham, ME) and Lena M. Huston (housewife, Perham, ME)

KELLEY,
Gerald John, Jr. of Portsmouth m. Vale Maria **Farrar** of New Castle 6/25/1994 in New Castle

KENYON,
David Carl m. Pamela Sue **Snyder** 11/25/1967 in New Castle; H - 20, b. RI, s/o John B. Kenyon and Mary E. Houde; W - 20, b. NY, d/o William L. Snyder and Jean P. Wojcak

KIMBALL,
Ivory G. of Hooksett m. Margaret E. **Anderson** of New Castle 8/12/1950 in New Castle; H - 35, cert'g officer, b. NH, s/o Guy C. Kimball (NH) and Laura M. Cole (MA); W - 30, school teacher, b. ME, d/o Olaf Anderson (Sweden) and K. H. Blind'svig (Norway)
Kenneth B. of So. Poland, ME m. Mildred M. **Timmons** of Windham, ME 6/11/1933 in New Castle; H - 29, dept. of agri., ME, b. Hanover, ME, s/o John Kimball (farmer, Rumford, ME) and Minna Saunders (at home, Hanover, ME); W - 25, maid, b. Farmington, ME, d/o Robert Timmons (farmer, Cape Breton, Canada) and Grace Johnson (at home, New Castle, NB)

KING,
Emery C. of New Castle m. Elinor F. **Paul** of Eliot, ME 2/3/1950 in Cape Porpoise, ME; H - 20, USCG, b. Portsmouth, s/o Paul J.

King (Melrose, MA) and Clara N. Currier (New Castle); W - 18, assy. worker, b. Eliot, ME, d/o Moses M. Paul (Eliot, ME) and Gertrude R. Shapleigh (Eliot, ME)

Frank Oakes m. Sherry Anne **DeMars** 8/10/1963 in New Castle; H - 21, b. NH, s/o Linn A. King and Mary A. Little; W - 19, b. MI, d/o Arthur J. DeMars and Mae H. Potter

Linn A. of New Castle m. Mary A. **Little** of Kittery, ME 6/18/1938 in Portsmouth; H -24, draftsman, b. Methuen, MA, s/o Frank A. King (carpenter, Raynham, MA) and Irene Brackett (housewife, Providence, RI); W - 19, at home, b. Kittery, ME, d/o Herbert O. Little (electrician, Augusta, ME) and Viola Stacey (housewife, Eliot, ME)

KINGSLEY,

Herbert L. of Wentworth Hotel m. Lillie A. **Crabtree** of Wentworth Hotel 5/27/1922 in Portsmouth; H - 36, gardener, b. Fitzwilliam, s/o George Kingsley (farmer, NY) and Fanny Chase (NY); W - 34, chambermaid, b. Carthage, NC, d/o Henry Crabtree (farmer, Carthage, NC) and Susana Bretton (Carthage, NC)

KLEIN,

William Arthur of Belchertown, MA m. Jennifer Marie **Bliss** of Belchertown, MA 7/2/1994 in New Castle

KLICK,

Rollin G. m. Hattie Lynn **Blumer** 8/12/1991 in New Castle

KYLE,

D. Scott of Hyde Park, MA m. Karen E. D. **Passon** of New Castle 5/21/1982 in New Castle; H - s/o Donald W. Kyle and Beverly Gardener; W - d/o Jack Passon and Jean Doe

LABOSSIERE,

Michael J. of Cape Neddick, ME m. Melanie S. **Dunbar** of Cape Neddick, ME 9/11/1993 in New Castle

LACOSTE,

Edward William of Worcester, MA m. Sarah Lydia **Mallett** of Rochester 12/18/1942 in New Castle; H - 21, cook, b. Leicester, MA, s/o Joseph A. LaCoste (truck driver, Quebec, Canada) and Emma E. Lessard (Norfolk, ND); W - 19, shoe shop, b. Rochester, d/o Harry A. Mallett (laborer, PEI) and Jane Quelch (housewife, England)

LANE,

Dean S. of Kittery, ME m. Tracy L. **Miles** of New Castle 10/27/1990 in New Castle; H - s/o Jacqueline Lane; W - d/o Arthur Miles and Shirley Owaley

LANHAM,

William E. of Kittery, ME m. Ruth E. **Hutchinson** of New Castle 11/12/1977 in New Castle; H - s/o Elwood E. Lanham and Eleanor E. Boger; W - d/o Albert E. Mori and Hilda Ricker

LANNI,

Paul A. of New Castle m. Roberta **Winkler** of Manchester 8/21/1943 in New Castle; H - 27, army officer, b. Lawrence, MA, s/o Albert Lanni (yard hand, Italy) and Annie Ruggiero (housewife, Italy); W - 20, jr. clerk, b. Manchester, d/o Gustave Winkler (foreman, Austria) and Lillian Barnes (housewife, Clinton, MA)

LANSING,

Michael A. of New Castle m. Debraane **Severns** of Portsmouth 5/28/1983 in New Castle; H - s/o Gerald R. Lansing and Gail Webb; W - d/o Chesley Severns and Jo-Anne Withee

LAPORE,

Carmen J. m. Virginia A. **Parker** 11/27/1967 in New Castle; H - b. MA, s/o Antonio Lepore (sic) and Lydia Maffie; W - b. NH, d/o Thomas H. Webb and Mary A. LaBrie

LAVERDIERE,

L. T. of Lewiston, ME m. Virginia Lee **Childs** of Lewiston, ME 3/31/1956 in New Castle; H - 32, dental technician, 2d, b. ME, s/o John B. Laverdiere (ME) and Evelyn Janelle (ME); W - 31, photographer, b. ME, d/o Clinton W. Childs (ME) and L. M. Campbell (MA)

LAYMAN,

Craig L. of Portsmouth m. Mary Kathryn **Kennedy** of Portsmouth 7/10/1993 in New Castle

LEARY,

Arthur T. of New Castle m. Helen G. **MacKay** of Eliot, ME 8/29/1925 in Portland, ME; H - 20, machinist, b. Boston, MA, s/o Thomas A. Leary (mach. helper, Boston, MA) and Josephine McKenna (housewife, Ireland); W - 19, b. NS, d/o George MacKay (carpenter, NS) and Martha Hanscom (housewife, Eliot, ME)

LEAVITT,

Charles F. of Harpswell, ME m. Gladys F. **Carver** of West Bowdoin, ME 5/2/1907 in Portsmouth; H - 25, fisherman, 2d, b. Harpswell, ME, s/o Israel E. Leavitt (fisherman, Harpswell, ME) and Eliza McKenney (housewife, Biddeford, ME); W - 16, servant, b. Auburn, ME, d/o Wilbert S. Carver (farmer, Rockland, ME) and Isabel Carver (housewife, Portland, ME)

LESSLEY,

Frank R. of New Castle m. Emily **Detrick** of Newmarket 10/4/1920 in New Castle; H - 21, soldier, USA, b. Clascow, MD, s/o William T. Lessley (farmer, Glasgow, MO) and Laura Stanley (housewife, Glasgow, MO); W - 18, housekeeper, b. Springfield, MA, d/o Emil Detrick (farmer, Springfield, MA) and Agnes Huber (housewife, Newmarket)

LETENDRE,

Jon G. of Denver, CO m. Ellen M. **Custer** of Denver, CO 6/21/1997 in New Castle

LEWIS,

Michael A. of New Castle m. Lorinda A. **Bradley** of Portsmouth 8/13/1988 in Portsmouth; H - s/o Maurice A. Lewis and Marie Carles; W - d/o Charles Bradley and Patsy B. Woton

LINEHAM,

John D. of Middleton, MA m. Nancy J. **Shipley** of Middleton, MA 6/23/1990 in New Castle; H - s/o Paul Lineham and Ann Southword; W - d/o Eugene Shipley and Geraldine Laffin

LIPSON,

Steve m. Pamela Jane **Groton** 8/18/1973 in New Castle; H - s/o Samuel Lipson and ----- Stotland; W - d/o Richard Groton and Miriam Herrick

LITTLEFIELD,

Oliver M. of New Castle m. Eleanor O. **Moulton** of Kittery Point, ME 5/30/1911 in New Castle; H - 23, painter, b. New Castle, s/o Oliver C. Littlefield (seaman, Ogunquit, ME) and Susan F. Trussell (housewife, New Castle); W - 20, b. York, ME, d/o Henry L. Moulton (fireman, York, ME) and Sarah O. Goodwin (housewife, York, ME)

LIZAK,

Matthew C. m. Lilath M. **Estes** 10/27/1972 in Portsmouth; H - s/o Frank Lizak and Mary Seaman; W - d/o Walter Estes and Mary Merrill

LOCKE,

Wallace W. of Fort Constitution m. Winifred M. **Pollard** of Keene 9/11/1942 in Franklin; H - 21, coast artillery, b. Barnstead, s/o Elias W. Locke (teamster, Haverhill, MA) and Elsie M. Garrick

(Jamaica Plains, MA); W - 18, shop worker, b. Marlow, d/o
Lewis C. Pollard (engineer, Marlow) and Louise LaPage
(housewife, Gilsum)

LOMBARDO,

James A. m. Deborah **Alessi** 10/16/1976 in New Castle; H - s/o John
Lombardo and Ellen Johnson; W - d/o Carlo Alessi and Rowena
Furey

LONG,

Scott A. of New Castle m. Jacqueline A. **Nolan** of Orlando, FL
6/22/1989 in New Castle; H - s/o William F. Long and Tamara
Toupher; W - d/o Gerald Nolan and Margaret A. Roynan

LORD,

Lawrence Shaw m. Nell **Strasner** 10/9/1959 in New Castle; H - 46,
2d, b. ME, s/o Leonard M. Lord and Nellie E. Reed; W - 46, 2d,
b. AR, d/o Andrew C. Custer and Ada C. Bedwell

Norman E. of Fort Constitution m. Dorothy **Doyle** of New Castle
7/7/1942 in New Castle; H - 25, US Army, b. Tuftonboro, s/o
Harvey J. Lord (lumberman, Ossipee) and Clara Nichols
(Ossipee); W - 26, waitress, b. Boston, MA, d/o Henry Doyle
(fish cutter, Chelsea, MA) and Margaret Raymond (at home,
Chelsea, MA)

LOVEWELL,

Leroy Elwood m. Bette Lynette **Sanborn** 6/28/1992 in New Castle

LOWE,

John G. m. Leni C. **Langendoen** 6/5/1976 in New Castle; H - s/o Otis
R. Lowe and Helen Weber; W - d/o Johannes deJager and
Catharina Weening

Robert J. m. Janice E. **Hodgdon** 11/7/1968 in New Castle; H - b. WV,
s/o Robert H. Lowe and Nora L. Hamm; W - b. NH, d/o John F.
Hodgdon, Sr. and Greta B. Beal

LUDGATE,
William F. of Fort Constitution m. Helen M. **Carmack** of Robinson,
IL 8/4/1920 in New Castle; H - 24, sergt., USA, b. Chicago, IL,
s/o Joseph Ludgate (evangelist, London, England) and Nellie M.
Ryerson (housewife, Patterson, NJ); W - 21, b. Flat Rock, IL, d/o
Daniel E. Carmack (contractor, Muncie, IN) and Helen Marie
(housewife, Muncie, IN)

LUNDY,
Everett E. of New Castle m. Mearl V. **Peavey** of Laconia 4/5/1944 in
New Castle; H - 24, coast artillery, b. Westboro, ME, s/o Robert
C. Lundy (truck driver, Westport, ME) and Ruth A. Varney
(housewife, S. Windham, ME); W - 18, shoe shop, b. Laconia,
d/o Harry Peavey (janitor, Ashland) and Mary L. Dionne
(housewife, Salem, MA)

LYCZAK,
Alfred A. of New Castle m. Dorothy **Weeks** of Portsmouth 2/6/1944
in New Castle; H - 30, coast artillery, b. Burlington, NJ, s/o John
Lyczak (Poland) and Anna Potts (housewife, Poland); W - 25,
telephone op., b. Portsmouth, d/o Arthur Weeks (carpenter,
Wakefield) and Marion Wallace (housewife, Boston, MA)

MACDONALD,
Roderick M. m. Susan O. **Eldredge** 4/19/1975 in New Castle; H - s/o
Douglas MacDonald and Margaret Snyder; W - d/o Edgar
Eldredge and Arlene Creeden

MACDOUGALL,
James R. of New Castle m. Lisa M. **Nadeau** of New Castle 6/21/1986
in Allenstown; H - s/o John Andrew MacDougall and Janet
Pauline Leafe; W - d/o Arthur N. Nadeau and Claudette J. Cyr

MACE,

Michael T. of New Castle m. Paula K. **Brooks** of New Castle 8/4/1984 in New Castle; H - s/o William J. Mace and Mary A. Jackson; W - d/o Craig Brook and Joan LaBranche

MACINNIS,

John Dan m. Adele **MacInnis** 10/14/1992 in New Castle

MACKINTOSH,

Robin G. J. m. Wendy Ellen **Boutilier** 1/6/1974 in New Castle; H - s/o Arthur Mackintosh and Margaret Denne; W - d/o Robert J. Boutilier and Betty Heuer

MACLENNAN,

Douglas A. of Portsmouth m. Susan D. **Reid** of New Castle 1/2/1983 in Durham; H - s/o Lorne D. MacLellan and Florence Pratt; W - d/o Thomas Reid and Theresa Murphy

MADDOCK,

Scott J. of Portsmouth m. Heidi J. **Snyder** of New Castle 5/7/1977 in New Castle; H - s/o Richard Maddock and Phyliss Elwell; W - d/o William Snyder and Jean Wojciak

MAGOON,

Bert C. of New Castle m. Nellie G. **Poole** of New Castle 9/19/1908 in New Castle; H - 24, soldier, b. Danville, VT, s/o Joseph Magoon and Emma Magoon; W - 33, at home, b. New Castle, d/o John C. Poole (watchman, ME) and Angeline E. Caswell (housewife, Rye)

Dennis Proctor m. Joan Frances **Hale** 5/7/1960 in New Castle; H - 24, b. NH, s/o Hollis C. Magoon and Carrie Proctor; W - 21, b. NY, d/o George C. Hale and Hazel E. Bussmann

MAHER,
Raymond J., Jr. m. Lee F. **Shea** 10/11/1969 in Portsmouth; H - s/o
Raymond J. Maher and Agnes C. Perkins; W - d/o Leo F. Shea
and Ellen L. Robbins

MAHONEY,
Michael Parker of Kittery, ME m. Lisa Marie **Pace** of Kittery, ME
12/3/1993 in New Castle

MALLER,
Christopher S. of Hull's Cove, ME m. Isabelle **Birsdall** of New Castle
9/17/1977 in New Castle; H - s/o John F. Maller and Evadne
Burglund; W - d/o Gregg C. Birdsall and Natalie Audibert

MALONEY,
John J., 3d of Stamford, CT m. Mary E. **Glassmeyer** of New Canaan,
CT 8/28/1971 in New Castle; H - b. VA, s/o John J. Maloney
and Rachel M. Dutcher; W - b. NH, d/o Edward Glassmeyer and
Caroline E. Fellows

MANSON,
Andrew of New Castle m. Hannah **Manson** of New Castle 5/24/1896
in Greenland
George H. of New Castle m. Lillian F. **Furbush** of Beverly, MA
6/28/1891; H - 21, b. New Castle; W - 22, b. Beverly, MA
George H. of New Castle m. Marie E. **Marshall** of Lynn, MA
7/12/1913 in Portsmouth; H - 43, shoemaker, 3d, b. New Castle,
s/o Hiram Manson (laborer, Kittery, ME) and Hannah Bell
(housewife, New Castle); W - 33, shoemaker, b. Canada, d/o
Lazare Marshall (laborer, Canada) and Selina King (housewife,
Canada)

MARANHAS,
Charles P. m. Cynthia J. **D'Antonio** 8/23/1975 in Portsmouth; H - s/o
Francis Maranhas and Virginia Small; W - d/o Albert D'Antonio
and Patricia Barr

MARGESON,

Robert K. m. Robin H. **Hovenden** 4/2/1972 in Portsmouth; H - s/o Richman Margeson and Miriam King; W - d/o Thomas R. Hovenden and Lucy Kilmer

Robert King m. Joanne Marcia **Adams** 2/7/1959 in Portsmouth; H - 23, b. NH, s/o Richman S. Margeson and Sarah M. King; W - 18, b. ME, d/o Woodbury S. Adams and Anita T. Van Guns

MARPLE,

Terry Forman of Jackson, NJ m. Anna Adele **Hayward** of Jackson, NJ 10/4/1980 in New Castle; H - s/o John R. Marple and Irene Forman; W - d/o Max Grossman and Katherine Brand

MARSDEN,

Thomas, Jr. of Durham m. Edith H. **Witham** of New Castle 9/4/`937 in Portsmouth; H - 25, horticulturist, b. Saugus, MA, s/o Thomas Marsden (machinist, Billerica, MA) and Susan Jenkins (at home, PEI); W - 25, ceramist, b. Fitchburg, MA, d/o Gardner Witham (sheet metal worker, Conway) and Alice Gray (at home, Portsmouth)

MARSH,

Charles D. of Rutland, MA m. Eileen **Cowperthwaite** of Hartford, CT 8/15/1943 in New Castle; H - 22, coast artillery, b. Holden, MA, s/o Francis E. Marsh (chauffeur, Rutland, MA) and Selma M. Solin (housewife, Worcester, MA); W - 19, ins. clerk, b. Methuen, MA, d/o Sidney Cowperthwaite (Lawrence, MA) and Marie Wright (def. worker, Malden, MA)

MARTIN,

Jeffrey of New Castle m. Lisa D. **Patat** of Greenland 9/19/1985 in Farmington; H - s/o John Martin and Ann Parnham; W - d/o Carroll Patat and Dorothy Roy

MARVIN,

Oliver Wheeler of New Castle m. Gertrude **Limington** of Brooklyn, NY 2/10/1926 in New York, NY; H - 24, attorney at law, b. New Castle, s/o Oliver B. Marvin (salesman, Portsmouth) and Idella W. Marvin (housewife, Lynn, MA); W - 18, student, b. Brooklyn, NY, d/o Frank Limington (civil engineer, Brooklyn, NY) and Kittie Limington (housewife, Brooklyn, NY)

William E. m. Carla P. **Creighton** 6/1/1974 in New Castle; H - s/o Edward S. Marvin and Eleanor Jordan; W - d/o Carl E. Johnson and Ruth Lear

William E. m. Carolyn B. **Bouffard** of New Castle 12/31/1982 in New Castle; H - s/o Edward S. Marvin and Eleanor Jordan; W - d/o Maynard Bryant and Dorothy Davis

MASKIN,

Eric S. of Boston, MA m. Gayle E. **Sawtelle** of Boston, MA 2/27/1983 in New Castle; H - s/o Meyer Maskin and Bernice Rabkin; W - d/o Joseph G. Sawtelle and Jean E. Brown

MATHEWS,

Paul G. of Deerfield m. Molly **Grant** of New Castle 9/10/1993 in New Castle

MATTHEWS,

Donald C. of Bar Mills, ME m. Helen P. **Hill** of Bar Mills, ME 1/5/1955 in New Castle; H - 41, elec. appl. service man, div., b. MA, s/o Charles Matthews (PEI) and Bertha A. O'Connor (MA); W - 32, housewife, div., b. ME, d/o Raymond C. Dwyer (ME) and Hazel B. Oliver (ME)

MAXAM,

Welcom E. of Springfield, MA m. Ida M. **Poole** of New Castle 10/1/1902 in New Castle; H - 27, US Armory, b. Dickerson, NY, s/o Oscar A. Maxam (carpenter) and Mattie S. Hatch (Brushton, NY); W - 26, housewife, b. New Castle, d/o John Poole (watchman, Edgecomb, ME) and Angeline Caswell (housewife, Rye)

MAYER,
Robert T. of North Hampton m. Anne E. **Finn** of New Castle 5/13/1979 in New Castle; H - s/o Raymond C. Meyer and Doris M. Travers; W - d/o Philip P. Finn and Ann Jane Theiler

McBRIDE,
W. Henry of New Castle m. Mary Jean **Sargent** of New Castle 2/6/1912 in Bangor, ME; H - 59, clergyman, 2d, b. Lindsay, NB, s/o Thomas McBride (farmer, Lindsay, NB) and Letitia Bond (housewife, Lindsay, NB); W - 49, housewife, 2d, d/o James Folleys (mason, St. Stephens, NB) and Jean Robertson (housewife, Aberdeen, Scotland)

McCABE,
Frederic C., Jr. m. Merrilee E. **Roberts** 8/23/1969 in Portsmouth; H - s/o Frederic C. McCabe and Grace Boehner; W - d/o Wesley F. Roberts and Esther L. Livingstone

McCARRON,
Thomas D. of New Castle m. Terrie L. **Harmon** of New Castle 10/5/1989 in New Castle; H - s/o William E. McCarron and Frances E. Edwards; W - d/o Lyle Harmon and Phyllis Stuart

McCORMACK,
John N. of New Castle m. Kerin A. **Henderson** of New Castle 6/13/1987 in New Castle; H - s/o John F. McCormack and Catherine Noll; W - d/o Donald G. Henderson and Sheila Pumpa

McDANIELS,
Donald Melvin m. Tania Elsie **Amazeen** 9/24/1960 in Portsmouth; H - 21, b. NY, s/o Charles M. McDaniels and Doris E. Miles; W - 18, b. NH, d/o Gerard B. Amazeen and Elsie L. Jones

McDONALD,

Leo T. of Haverhill, MA m. Mary T. **Verombec** of Haverhill, MA
1/31/1955 in New Castle; H - 51, RR retired, div., b. MA, s/o
William McDonald (MA) and Matilda E. Phillips (MA); W - 45,
housewife, b. MA, d/o Victor Veromec (Poland) and Rose M.
Topa (Poland)

McGRAW,

Kenneth of St. Louis, MO m. Miriam C. **Jones** of New Castle
10/19/1946 in New Castle; H - 24, US Army, b. St. Louis, MO,
s/o Charles McGraw (St. Louis, MO) and Grace Gasperson
(housewife, Eureka, MO); W - 21, housewife, 2d, b. New Castle,
d/o Haven Johnson (gen. contractor, York, ME) and Annie
Goodwin (Boston, MA)

McKENNEY,

William R. m. Charlotte **Thompson** 4/4/1970 in New Castle; H - s/o
Ernest C. McKenney and Rita A. Regan; W - d/o Carlo Alessi
and Rowena S. Furey

McLAUGHLIN,

Edward Thomas of New Castle m. Anna Belle **McGeoghegan** of
Somerville, MA 10/22/1933 in Somerville, MA; H - 36,
gardener, b. Hingham, MA, s/o Patrick McLaughlin and Mary E.
Fee; W - 28, maid, b. Co. Donegal, Ireland, d/o James
McGeoghegan and Mary E. Harkins

McMULLEN,

Edwin M., Jr. of Madison, NJ m. Susan E. **Steele** of Madison, NJ
8/31/1986 in New Castle; H - s/o Edwin W. McMullen and
Virginia Rowe; W - d/o Wayne W. Steele and Marion C. Hughes

MELKONIAN,

Harry m. Claire Marie **Haggerty** 1/28/1959 in New Castle; H - 31, b.
MA, s/o Melkon K. Melkonian and Madeline Dourian; W - 29,
2d, b. MA, d/o John P. Dinan and Mildred A. Logan

MELOON,

Alfred of New Castle m. Claire C. **Schurman** of New Castle
12/15/1944 in New Castle; H - 40, caretaker, b. New Castle, s/o
George S. Meloon (teamster, New Castle) and Julia Healey
(Ireland); W - 46, at home, b. Greenland, d/o Joseph L. Schurman
(insurance, NS) and Annie Badger (housewife, Newington)

George B. of New Castle m. Julia **Healey** of Portsmouth 10/20/1903
in Portsmouth; H - 24, laborer, b. New Castle, s/o Alfred Meloon
(New Castle) and Susan Yeaton (New Castle); W - 22,
housewife, b. Ireland, d/o Jeremiah Healey (Ireland)

MERCIER,

Joseph H. of New Castle m. Ruth A. **Colman** of Portsmouth
2/12/1943 in New Castle; H - 25, coast artillery, b. Webster,
MA, s/o Joseph H. Mercier (steeplejack, Fitchburg, MA) and
Alexina ----- (housewife, Manton, MA); W - 18, at home, b.
Portsmouth, d/o Lincoln Coleman (sic) (ant. dealer, Portsmouth)
and Alma Underhill (Portsmouth)

MIKSCH,

Levin A. of New Castle m. Alice C. **Coleman** of Rochester 9/2/1943
in New Castle; H - 29, army officer, b. Bethlehem, PA, s/o
Franklin Miksch (tech. eng., Bethlehem, PA) and Blanche A.
Moyer (housewife, Bethlehem, PA); W - 24, gov. clerk, b.
Amesbury, MA, d/o Arthur E. Coleman (England) and Alice C.
Sargent (Merrimack, MA)

MILES,

Arthur Lamprey m. Shirley Louise **Owsley** 7/21/1964 in New Castle;
H - 20, b. NH, s/o Shirley E. Miles and Martha B. Trefethen; W -
23, b. NH, d/o Raymond J. Owsley and Mary E. Horning

MILLER,

Daniel F. of New Castle m. Arta **Manson** of New Castle 9/18/1902 in
New Castle; H - 23, soldier, b. So. Hampton, England, s/o Joseph
Miller (carpenter, So. Hampton, England) and Sarah Hubbard

(housewife, So. Hampton, England); W - 17, housewife, b. New
Castle, d/o Andrew Manson (molder, New Castle) and Hannah
Manson

MILNE,
William A. of Fort Constitution m. Constance **Morrison** of Fort
Constitution 4/6/1922 in New Castle; H - 27, soldier, b.
Somerville, MA, s/o Alexander Milne (farmer, Mt. Vernon) and
Flora V. Hadervolets; W - 18, clerk, b. Boston, MA, d/o George
Morrison (contractor) and Gertrude Bigley (teacher of domestics,
Boston, MA)

MORAITES,
James M. of Haverhill, MA m. Joan M. **Amato** of Haverhill, MA
6/24/1995 in New Castle

MORGAN,
Patrick W. of New Castle m. Rebecca L. **Coutermarsh** of New Castle
5/31/1997 in New Castle

MORI,
Charles A. of New Castle m. Ellen J. **Page** of Greenland 2/23/1954 in
Greenland; H - 22, laborer, b. NH, s/o Albert Mori (Italy) and
Hilda G. Ricker (NH); W - 20, clerk, b. NH, d/o Willard R. Page
and Helen Bartosh (MA)

MORRILL,
Eugene C. m. Mary G. **Sturtevant** 10/3/1970 in Portsmouth; H - s/o
Harris W. Morrill and Doris P. Maxam; W - d/o Bernard F. Daly
and Yvonne Carignan

MORRIS,
Thomas S. of New Castle m. Eva R. **General** of Dorchester, MA
6/22/1919 in New Castle; H - 30, hotel cook, b. Canada, s/o
Joseph Morris (stone cutter, Canada) and Birthena Morris
(Bethlehem); W - 23, store clerk, b. Providence, RI, d/o Jacob

General (store keeper, Providence, RI) and Ada General (Providence, RI)

MUIR,

William C. of Concord m. B. H. **Hayden** of New Castle 8/28/1948 in New Castle; H - 28, student, b. Clinton, MA, s/o Roy C. Muir (w'sale drug ex., Clinton, MA) and Caroline A. Bowen (housewife, Clinton, MA); W - 23, N.E. Tel. Co., b. Portsmouth, d/o W. C. Hayden (draftsman, Eliot, ME) and M. E. Yeaton (supervisor, New Castle)

MULLIS,

Douglas W. of Boston, MA m. Margaret J. **Watts** of Waban, MA 2/7/1981 in New Castle; H - s/o Wallace G. Mullis and Vivian W. Breitkreitz; W - d/o Boyd E. Watts and ----- Mason

MUNRO,

Benjamin R. m. Germaine M. **Mayo** 3/11/1959 in Dover; H - 20, b. NH, s/o Carl Munro and Essie F. Ricker; W - 31, 2d, b. NH, d/o Walter H. Jewell and Gladys C. Saville

MURDOCK,

Burton K., Jr. of Kennebunk, ME m. Frances E. **Caswell** of New Castle 7/16/1955 in Portsmouth; H - 31, engineer naval base, b. ME, s/o Burton K. Murdock (ME) and Florence M. Thayer (ME); W - 34, draftsman naval base, b. NH, d/o Alvah L. Caswell (NH) and J. H. Trecartin (ME)

MURR,

William Harvey m. Janet Neal **Champagne** 4/8/1961 in Portsmouth; H - 20, b. Canada, s/o Harvey Harold Murr and Rose Catherine Powell; W - 20, b. MA, d/o Earl E. Champagne and Marion O. Gilkey

MURRAY,
Wayne E. of New Castle m. Jaclyn M. **Adams** of New Castle
7/14/1997 in New Castle

NANCARROW,
James S. of Rochester m. Christina J. **Fernald** of New Castle
9/19/1979 in Hampton; H - s/o Stanley Nancarrow and Madeline
Moule; W - d/o Stanley M. Pridham and Gloria Sawyer

NEVIN,
Raymond G. m. Cheryl I. **French** 5/31/1969 in New Castle; H - s/o
Raymond C. Nevin and Elizabeth Kresge; W - d/o Jack French
and Sonja Aspen

NEWMAN,
John Paul of New Castle m. Margaret Mary **Walsh** of New Castle
12/31/1994 in Durham

NEWTON,
Byron G. of New Castle m. Judith E. **Poirier** of Portsmouth
7/30/1977 in New Castle; H - s/o Ray B. Newton and Ethel
Hurd; W - d/o Charles S. Paul and Patricia A. Martin

NICHOLS,
Charles C., Jr. m. Rhonda R. **Newton** 10/5/1974 in Hampton; H - s/o
Charles C. Nichols and Margaret Glodas; W - d/o Ray B. Newton
and Ethel Hurd

NILES,
George S., Jr. of Nashua m. Cheryl J. **Bucklin** of New Castle
6/26/1971 in New Castle; H - b. CT, s/o George S. Niles, Sr. and
Elizabeth A. Meader; W - b. MD, d/o Elwood A. Bucklin and
Jane L. Rowe

NOLD,

Roger B. of Portsmouth m. Jane B. **Abernathy** of New Castle
12/24/1980 in New Castle; H - s/o George W. Nold and Virginia
F. Byam; W - d/o E. W. Bigger and Willia M. Williamson

NOSEWORTHY,

Randall of Hull, MA m. Elsie K. **Littlefield** of New Castle 12/12/1932
in New Castle; H - 24, ord., USA, b. Newfoundland, s/o Levi
Noseworthy (religious work, Newfoundland) and Bridget Burns
(Newfoundland); W - 19, at home, b. Portsmouth, d/o Oliver M.
Littlefield (painter, New Castle) and Eleanor O. Moulton (at
home, York, ME)

NOYES,

David C. of New Castle m. Elizabeth **Fletcher** of New Castle
3/18/1945 in New Castle; H - 21, USNR, b. New Castle, s/o
Frederick R. Noyes (Windsor, ME) and Alice M. Robinson
(housewife, New Castle); W - 19, clerk, b. Madison, ME, d/o
Walter S. Fletcher (rigger, Navy Yard, Stark, ME) and Gladys
Blackwell (housewife, Madison, ME)

NUNMAKER,

D. John of New Castle m. Susan Pauline **Pulyak** of Portsmouth
5/21/1978 in Portsmouth; H - s/o David J. Nunmaker and R.
Louise Denny; W - d/o George Pulyak and Goldie Thomas

O'BRIEN,

John Edward of Portsmouth m. Paula T. **Pridham** of New Castle
10/19/1957 in Portsmouth; H - 25, construction worker, b. NH,
s/o William P. O'Brien (ME) and Grace H. Donovan (PEI); W -
22, telephone operator, b. NH, d/o G. S. Pridham, Jr. (NH) and
Ellen C. Crockett (NH)

O'LEARY,

Patrick J. of Mt. Pleasant, SC m. Mary C. **Holst** of Mt. Pleasant, SC 12/29/1990 in New Castle; H - s/o Joseph O'Leary and Catherine Herbert; W - d/o William Holst and Lottie McGrane

O'NEIL,

Edward Franklin of So. Berwick, ME m. Ethelle Mae **Remick** of Kittery, ME 2/9/1935 in Portsmouth; H - 36, mill, b. So. Berwick, ME, s/o Daniel O'Neil (mill, So. Berwick, ME) and Sarah Sullivan (housewife, So. Berwick, ME); W - 23, hairdresser, b. Eliot, ME, s/o Myron S. Remick (navy yard, Eliot, ME) and Florence Moulton (at home, York, ME)

OBREGON,

Charles of New Castle m. Camilla **Bova** of Lawrence, MA 2/8/1943 in New Castle; H - 23, coast artillery, b. Temple, AZ, s/o Peter Obregon (harvester, Temple, AZ) and Rita Arbizo (housewife, Temple, AZ); W - 19, at home b. Lawrence, MA, d/o Peter Bova (musician, Italy) and Marie ----- (Italy)

OGLES,

Lucian G. of Springfield, MO m. Gertrude M. **Robinson** of New Castle 6/14/1920 in New Castle; H - 25, electrician, b. Bowling Green, KY, s/o William M. Ogles (tel. elec., Bowling Green, KY) and Lula A. Whitlock (housewife, Bowling Green, KY); W - 20, bank clerk, b. New Castle, d/o Fabius W. Robinson (gen. helper, Kittery, ME) and Annie L. Card (housewife, New Castle)

Lucien G. of Springfield, MO m. Edith Marion **Rand** of Portsmouth 7/7/1923 in Exeter; H - 27, electrician, 2d, wid., b. Bowling Green, KY, s/o William M. Ogles (telephone elec., Bowling Green, KY) and Lula S. Whitlock (housewife, Bowling Green, KY); W - 26, nurse, b. Portsmouth, d/o Walter S. Rand (teamster, Portsmouth) and Mary S. Stoddard (at home, Portsmouth)

OLDMIXON,

John Clark m. Donna Mae **Howe** 4/10/1965 in New Castle; H - 21, b. ME, s/o Robert G. Oldmixon and Barbara T. Brooks; W - 18, b. ME, d/o Archer W. Bucklin and Lena M. Howe

OLIVER,

Horatio N. of New Castle m. Louise T. **Pitman** of Manchester 1/17/1916 in Manchester; H - 36, clerk, 2d, b. Philadelphia, PA, s/o Horatio N. Oliver (electrotyper, Philadelphia, PA) and Emma Forst (Philadelphia, PA); W - 28, 2d, b. Boston, MA, d/o William O'Donnell (Ireland) and Norah Foley (Ireland)

Robert of New Castle m. Nellie **Costo** of New Castle 12/25/1895 in Portsmouth; H - 52, laborer, 2d, b. New Castle, s/o Benjamin Oliver (New Castle) and Abigail ----- (New Castle); W - 30, b. Killarney, Ireland, d/o Thomas Costo (Killarney, Ireland) and Nellie ----- (Killarney, Ireland)

OSGOOD,

Warren T. of New Castle m. Emily H. **Jarvais** of Readsboro, VT 7/6/1918 in New Castle; H - 34, general helper, b. Allenstown, s/o Warren A. Osgood (farmer, Allenstown) and Eudora H. Truesdell (Monmouth, ME); W - 25, bookkeeper, b. Readsboro, VT, d/o Joseph Jarvais (farmer, Canada) and Harriet Douglass (Milton, VT)

OTT,

Alva Edison m. Margaret White **Dickson** 8/27/1959 in New Castle; H - 69, 2d, b. NJ, s/o Frederick P. Ott and Emma H. Miller; W - 64, 2d, b. TX, d/o Justin C. White and Jennie Dann

OUELLETTE,

David A. m. Sylvia M. **Labbe** 5/10/1975 in Colebrook; H - s/o Albert Ouellette and Barbara Stevens; W - d/o John Labbe and Marcelle Roy

PACE,

Brandt Paris m. Sandra Lee **Harris** 11/5/1966 in Portsmouth; H - 24, b. NH, s/o Erwin Brand Pace and Laurence M. Bilodeau; W - 20, b. NH, d/o Bevuell J. Harris and Pauline D. Stenzel

PAGE,

Frederick S. of New Castle m. Lucile **Dore** of Portsmouth 10/31/1942 in Portsmouth; H - 25, lineman, b. Portsmouth, s/o William F. Page (tel. installer, Portsmouth) and Bertha Seaward (housewife, Kittery, ME); W - 20, mach. opr., b. Portsmouth, d/o John L. Dore (USN ret., Albany, NY) and Lucile M. Young (housewife, Newport)

PAINE,

Joseph S. of New Castle m. Edith M. **Simpson** of New Castle 7/13/1903 in Portsmouth; H - 21, baker, b. Mt. Vernon, KY, s/o Moses Paine (Lexington, KY) and Sarah Cummings (Mt. Vernon, KY); W - 16, housewife, b. New Castle, d/o Alexis A. Yeaton (New Castle) and Addie Simpson (housewife, New Castle)

PALMER,

Franklin James m. Martha Ann **Emerson** 12/27/1967 in Newmarket; H - 21, b. NH, s/o Franklin J. Palmer and Mary L. Evans; W - 20, b. PA, d/o Mark F. Emerson and Winifred C. Moody

PANARESE,

Ralph R. m. Nancy C. **LaRose** 6/28/1968 in Portsmouth; H - b. NH, s/o Joseph Panarese and Vera Male; W - b. NH, d/o Harold LaRose and Stella Karakostas

PARKER,

Donald Edward m. Virginia Anne **Webb** 9/3/1965 in Portsmouth; H - 22, b. TN, s/o Edward M. Parker and Margaret E. Bush; W - 18, b. NH, d/o Thomas H. Webb and Mary A. LaBrie

Sheridan K. of New Castle m. Darla C. **Springer** of Tampa, FL
5/10/1980 in Londonderry; H - s/o Frank Parker and Esther
Craig; W - d/o Norman D. Springer and Myrtle S. Roberts

PARRELLA,
David P. of Waltham, MA m. Lorrie E. **Shea** of New Castle 6/3/1989
in Portsmouth; H - s/o Ernest J. Parrella and Angelina L.
Mobilia; W - d/o Leo F. Shea and Ellen L. Robbins

PARSONS,
Ronald R. of New Castle m. Joan Kelly **Jule** of Portsmouth 2/7/1987
in Portsmouth; H - s/o Raymond N. Parsons and Helen Mullan;
W - d/o James Kelly and Charlotte Kidney

PATTEN,
George A. m. Juliana **Fern** 4/1/1974 in New Castle; H - s/o George A.
Patten and Mildred Cook; W - d/o Jules J. Fern and Elizabeth
Koehler
George Alfred m. Mildred Cook **Patten** 7/30/1965 in Portsmouth; H -
42, 2d, b. NH, s/o Karl L. Patten and Margaret W. George; W -
43, 2d, b. RI, d/o James Cook and Gladys M. Truesdale

PAULMAN,
Oswald S. of New Castle m. Valerie M. **Hartman** of New Castle
1/31/1986 in Portsmouth; H - s/o Borge Paulman and Monseratte
Roman; W - d/o Lyle Hartman and Grace Jackson

PERKINS,
Earnest L. of Portsmouth m. Theresa **Procassio** of Portsmouth
2/19/1942 in New Castle; H - 23, US Marine, b. Niantic, CT, s/o
Joseph H. Perkins (gardener, Niantic, CT) and Ozelia M. Machee
(housewife, Willimantic, CT); W - 23, domestic, b. Portsmouth,
d/o Leonardo Procassio (garageman, Italy) and Pia Fracassi
(housewife, Italy)
Harold W. of Kennebunkport, ME m. Sarah A. **Horning** of New
Castle 12/28/1953 in Hampton; H - 64, painter, 2d, b. ME, s/o

158

Charles H. Perkins (ME) and Alice J. Hanson (ME); W - 46, housework, b. NH, d/o Andrew J. Horning (OH) and Ivalean Emery (NH)

PERRY,
Paul Francis m. Mary Elizabeth **Hughes** 2/8/1960 in Portsmouth; H - 31, b. NH, s/o Mary G. Perry; W - 32, 2d, d/o Harry S. MacLeod and Helen Nearhood

PETERS,
Leigh m. Andrea **Webb** 4/8/1973 in New Castle; H - s/o Reginald S. Peters and Naomi Skillings; W - d/o Thomas Webb and Mary Labrie

PETLICK,
Charles A. m. Michele P. **Roy** 5/24/1969 in Portsmouth; H - s/o Casimer J. Petlick and Marion E. White; W - d/o Thomas L. Roy and Patricia M. Tergesen
Charles A. m. Charlene M. **Neves** 5/25/1974 in New Castle; H - s/o Casimer Petlick and Marion White; W - d/o Charlie R. McKie and ----- Mobley

PETTICH,
Casimir J. of New Castle m. Marion E. **White** of New Castle 10/2/1943 in Portsmouth; H - 25, coast artillery, b. Benton Harbor, MI, s/o Charles J. Pettich (painter, dec., B. Harbor, MI) and Elsie Olkowski (housewife, B. Harbor, MI); W - 23, jr. typist, b. Portsmouth, d/o Arnold B. White (coast guard, New Castle) and Louise Jordan (housewife, Cape Elizabeth, ME)

PHANEUF,
Robert D. of Eliot, ME m. Patricia B. **Calderara** of South Berwick, ME 9/25/1993 in New Castle

159

PHILBRICK,

Paul Brian m. Peggy Beth **Patten** 1/15/1972 in Portsmouth; H - s/o
  Moulton E. Philbrick and Gene C. Baker; W - d/o George A.
  Patten and Mildred Cook

PHILBROOK,

John E. of New Castle m. Donna M. **Fairbrother** of New Castle
  2/18/1984 in New Castle; H - s/o John B. Philbrook and Martha
  Merrill; W - d/o Don R. Fairbrother and Mary Shields

PHILLIPS,

Norman Ray of Lisbon Falls, ME m. Elizabeth F. **Lally** of Lowell,
  MA 9/14/1942 in New Castle; H - 23, soldier, USA, b. Lowell,
  MA, s/o Ray M. Phillips (steamfitter, Lewiston, ME) and Harriet
  I. Reynolds (housewife, Lisbon Falls, ME); W - 29, seamstress,
  b. Lowell, MA, d/o Thomas H. Lally (retired, Lowell, MA) and
  Margaret Macguire (housewife, Lowell, MA)

PICHE,

Gordon Grant m. Ruth Jane **Grady** 4/24/1965 in Portsmouth; H - 22,
  b. NH, s/o Daniel E. Piche and Oravilla M. Grant; W - 21, b. PA,
  d/o James B. Grady and Josephine E. Plum

PICKETT,

Robert Jaffrey m. Annegret Ruth **Niehaus** 7/4/1961 in New Castle; H
  - 31, b. NH, s/o Charles W. Pickett and Gertrude E. Maertins; W
  - 30, b. Germany, d/o Alfred Niehaus and Elfriede W. Weiss

PINGREE,

Stanley C. of New Castle m. Wilda **Holt** of New Castle 1/20/1978 in
  Portsmouth; H - s/o Fred. W. Pingree and Arvilla Gordon; W -
  d/o Joseph Masse and Rose Cloutier

William L. of New Castle m. Judith C. **Kamakas** of Rye 8/30/1996 in
  Portsmouth

PIPER,

Raymond A. of New Castle m. Grace **Small** of Portsmouth 2/11/1922 in New Castle; H - 47, contractor, 2d, b. Starks, ME, s/o Moses P. Piper (lumberman, Starks, ME) and Maria L. Mosher (housewife, Starks, ME); W - 53, housewife, 2d, b. Groton, MA, d/o Nathan P. Culver (farmer, Bath) and Mary Farnsworth (housewife, Groton, MA)

PITTS,

Hal R. of New Castle m. Penny L. **Sharon** of Rumney 6/6/1981 in New Castle; H - s/o Frederick P. Pitts and Greselda N. Strasner; W - d/o Conrad Dow and Marietta McKee

PITTSLEY,

Walter R. of Middleboro, MA m. Mary T. **Gravelin** of Pembroke, MA 8/6/1949 in Farmington; H - 24, mechanic, b. Middleboro, MA, s/o Walter L. Pittsley (MA) and E. A. Rogers (MA); W - 18, home, b. Hyannis, MA, d/o Peter D. Gravelin (VT) and Thelma E. Ray (NH)

PLASKET,

Irving of New Castle m. Doris A. **Story** of Dover 9/26/1943 in New Castle; H - 29, US Army, b. Brooklyn, NY, s/o Herman Plasket (watchman, Germany) and Mary Stubing (New York, NY); W - 36, stenographer, b. Gloucester, MA, d/o Andrew T. Story (fisherman, Sweden) and Elsie O. Nelson (housewife, Sweden)

PLUMER,

Herbert E. of No. Hampton m. Elizabeth G. **Johantgen** of New Castle 12/16/1951 in Rye; H - 50, M.D., 2d, b. Union, ME, s/o Herbert H. Plumer (ME) and Alice L. Southworth (ME); W - 50, nurse, 2d, b. MA, d/o Franklin H. Grier (MD) and Gertrude L. Flint (MA)

Michael R. m. Devon E. **Draffen** 9/28/1974 in New Castle; H - s/o Robert H. Plumer and Virginia J. Smith; W - d/o Harold Draffen and Joan Goebel

PONGRACE,

Donald Ross of Rye m. Marcia Anne **Call** of New Castle 10/13/1979 in North Hampton; H - s/o Donald D. Pongrace and Mary L. Maury; W - d/o Thomas E. Call, Jr. and Margaret E. Jacques

POOLE,

Kendrick W. of New Castle m. Roberta E. **Groton** of So. Berwick, ME 4/13/1934 in Portsmouth; H - 21, salesman, b. New Castle, s/o Wayne D. Poole (plumber, New Castle) and Alice G. Winn (Boston, MA); W - 18, at home, b. Portsmouth, d/o Robert E. Groton (brakeman, Augusta, ME) and Ruth E. Gray (at home, Portsmouth)

Robert W. of New Castle m. Pamela S. **Aspen** of New Castle 10/30/1971 in New Castle; H - b. NH, s/o Kendrick W. Poole and Roberta Groton; W - b. NH, d/o Erik S. Aspen and Bessie May MacKenzie

Wayne D., Jr. of New Castle m. Mary **White** of Portsmouth 6/13/1938 in Hampton; H - 27, painter, b. New Castle, s/o Wayne D. Poole (plumber, New Castle) and Alice G. Winn (Boston, MA); W - 26, waitress, b. Jonesport, ME, d/o Bert White (laborer, Jonesport, ME) and Carrie Banks (at home, Machias, ME)

PRATT,

Charles E. of New Castle m. Dianne M. **Moore** of Dover 3/3/1979 in Dover; H - s/o Edwin F. Pratt and Phyliss Spaulding; W - d/o Robert A. Moore and Phyliss Downs

PRIDHAM,

D. W. of New Castle m. E. J. **Lydston** of Portsmouth 8/25/1957 in New Castle; H - 21, accountant, b. NH, s/o S. W. Pridham (NH) and Jeanne L. Cochrane (MA); W - 19, secretary, b. NH, d/o Floyd L. Lydston (ME) and E. A. Robbins (ME)

David C. m. Elaine I. **Keating** 7/14/1974 in New Castle; H - s/o Douglas C. Pridham and Arline Cousins; W - d/o Thomas J. Keating and Edna Smith

Donald F. m. Karen L. **Sorensen** 4/5/1975 in Portsmouth; H - s/o
Douglas Pridham and Arline Cousins; W - d/o George Sorensen
and Mary Ellis

Elmer S. of New Castle m. Ethel O. **Poole** of New Castle 9/16/1903 in
Portsmouth; H - 24, shoecutter, b. New Castle, s/o John Pridham
(New Castle) and Mary C. Ruee (Eliot, ME); W - 24, housewife,
b. New Castle, d/o John Poole and Angeline Caswell (housewife,
Rye)

Isaac C.H. of New Castle m. Lena **Lowe** of New Castle 11/21/1921 in
Portsmouth; H - 50, gardener, b. New Castle, s/o John Pridham
(fisherman, New Castle) and Mary Ruee (housekeeper, Kittery,
ME); W - 48, housekeeper, 2d, b. Isles of Shoals, d/o Edwin A.
Caswell (gardener, Rye) and Lucy Hart (housekeeper, Isles of
Shoals)

Stanley W. of New Castle m. Jeanne Logan **Cochrane** of New Castle
5/10/1931 in Portsmouth; H - 19, auto mechanic, b. New Castle,
s/o Elmer S. Pridham (shoe cutter, New Castle) and Ethel O.
Poole (at home, New Castle); W - 21, at home, b. Boston, MA,
d/o Archie Cochrane (soldier, USA, Portland, ME) and
Wilhelmina Willard (So. Portland, ME)

Worth Ruee of New Castle m. Mina Josephine **Bedell** of Kittery Point,
ME 2/4/1931 in Portsmouth; H - 22, chauffeur, b. Portsmouth,
s/o John W. Pridham (coast guard, New Castle) and Anna F.
Bates (at home, Cambridge, MA); W - 19, at home, b. Kittery
Point, ME, d/o Henry Allen Bedell (driller, navy yard, Kittery
Point, ME) and Angie Melissa Blake (at home, Kittery Point,
ME)

PRIESTLEY,

William of New Castle m. Elizabeth Isadore **Pridham** of New Castle
7/11/1935 in New Castle; H - 21, chauffeur, b. Barre, MA, s/o
Hector Priestley (caretaker, Nottingham, England) and Sarah Ann
Wise (at home, Nottingham, England); W - 19, at home, b. New
Castle, d/o Elmer S. Pridham (shoe cutter, New Castle) and Ethel
O. Poole (at home, New Castle)

William R. of New Castle m. Loretta Jean **Cruz** of Portsmouth 7/20/1957 in New Castle; H - 21, power plant operator, b. NH, s/o William Priestley (NH) and E. I. Pridham (NH); W - 21, secretary, b. CA, d/o Lorenzo D. Cruz (Phillipines) and Edna M. Gonnier (MA)

PROHASKA,
Roy J. of New Castle m. Maude E. **Metcalfe** of Peacham, VT 10/3/1916 in Peacham, VT; H - 27, grocer, b. Hull, MA, s/o Charles F. Prohaska (carpenter, Austria) and Sadie Card (New Castle); W - 24, b. Danville, VT, d/o Burgess J. Metcalfe (farmer, Lewis, NY) and Nellie M. Merritt (Danville, VT)

QUINLAN,
Jeremiah P. m. Marguerite F. **O'Neill** 11/15/1964 in New Castle; H - 54, 3d, b. NJ, s/o Jeremiah T. Quinlan and Helen O'Keefe; W - 45, 2d, b. NY, d/o Archibald T. Kienzle and Margaret M. Taylor

QUIRK,
Edmund F. m. Mary T. **Pridham** 2/14/1976 in New Castle; H - s/o James Quirk and Clara Wentworth; W - d/o John Moran and Laura Moran

RADEMACHER,
Michael W. of Boston, MA m. Anne C. **Schwab** of Boston, MA 9/6/1997 in New Castle

RAND,
Philip S. of New Castle m. Marguerite **Merrill** of New Castle 4/3/1920 in New Castle; H - 22, deputy col., b. Kittery, ME, s/o William G. Rand (marine eng., high seas) and Sophie M. Sylvester (housewife, Quincy, MA); W - 23, housework, b. Franklin, d/o Gilbert S. Merrill (papermaker, Cumberland Co., MD) and Margaret Carroll (housewife, Queenstown Is.)

RANDALL,

Harold B. of Cape Neddick, ME m. Ruth Ann **Smith** of Milwaukee, WI 3/20/1942 in New Castle; H - 22, signal corps, b. Prewaukee, WI, s/o William Randall (bar tender, Palymire, WI) and Leila Erherdt (housewife, Johnston City, IL); W - 18, stenographer, b. Milwaukee, WI, d/o Edward Smith (RR switchman, Fond du lac, WI) and Estelle Meagher (housewife, Oshkosh, WI)

RANSDORF,

James D. of New Castle m. Rita A. **Rich** of Portsmouth 10/19/1989 in Greenland; H - s/o James L. Ransdorf and Patsy C. Whykoff; W - d/o Harold E. Hutchins and Deloris A. Myers

REDDEN,

William H. of New Castle m. Juliet **Webster** of New Castle 12/19/1903 in New Castle; H - 49, carpenter, 2d, b. Falmouth, NC, s/o Dennis Redden (seaman, Falmouth, NC) and Mary Hazlett (housewife); W - 44, housewife, 3d, b. York, ME, d/o Rufus M. Emery (carpenter, Sanford, ME) and Julia A. Fernald (housewife, York, ME)

REDFIELD,

Leon James m. Leona Madeline **Smart** 12/27/1958 in Stratham; H - 44, b. NH, s/o Amiziah J. Redfield and Mary Ducey; W - 43, 3d, b. NH, d/o George B. Ricker and Sarah E. White

REMICK,

Stanton G. of Rye m. Elizabeth M. **Prohaska** of New Castle 10/1/1936 in New Castle; H - 20, mechanic, b. Rye, s/o Austin F. Remick (coast guard, Rye) and Julia Blute (housewife, Rye); W - 19, beautician, b. Portsmouth, d/o Roy J. Prohaska (grocer, Hull, MA) and Maude Metcalf (at home, Danville, VT)

REMONDI,

Joseph F., Jr. of Brighton, MA m. Maureen P. **O'Connor** of New Castle 6/25/1983 in Portsmouth; H - s/o Joseph F. Remondi, Sr. and ----- Peters; W - d/o William J. O'Connor and ----- Chandler

REYNOLDS,

Walter L. of New Castle m. Arlene N. **Vendasi** of Somersworth 7/23/1977 in Portsmouth; H - s/o Harold Reynolds and Jennie Rittenhouse; W - d/o Romeo Jacques and Angele Tanguay

RICH,

Lonnie C. of Alexandria, VA m. Marcia Anne **Call** of Alexandria, VA 11/18/1995 in New Castle

RICHARDSON,

Bruce Winter m. Marcia **Hartford** 6/23/1959 in Portsmouth; H - 21, b. NH, s/o Herman W. Richardson and Jessie R. Shurman; W - 22, b. VT, d/o Chester P. Hartford and Geraldine Conner

Hermon W. of Gloucester, MA m. Jennie Beane **Schurman** of New Castle 5/20/1934 in New Castle; H - 44, salesman, 2d, b. Lowell, MA, s/o Almon L. Richardson (Woburn, MA) and Louise S. Winter (Fredericton, NB); W - 32, bookkeeper, b. Greenland, d/o Joseph L. Schurman (insurance, Rawden, NS) and Annie Badger (at home, Newington)

RICKER,

George B. of New Castle m. Sadie E. **White** of New Castle 6/15/1898 in New Castle; H - 22, surfman, b. New Castle, s/o Samuel Ricker (laborer, 43, New Castle) and Esther Pridham (39, New Castle) of Portsmouth; W - 24, b. New Castle, d/o Charles H. White (deceased, New Castle) and Sarah F. Randall (64, New Castle) of New Castle

George B. m. Donna R. **Robinson** 5/22/1970 in New Castle; H - s/o Lyndon H. Ricker and Louise E. Gaudreault; W - d/o Roger I. Moore and Muriel E. Greenwood

George B. of New Castle m. Janis D. **Hopkins** of New Castle 10/8/1994 in Portsmouth

RINKER,
Travis F. of Greenlawn, NY m. Rene H. **Danko** of Greenlawn, NY 10/12/1996 in New Castle

ROBINSON,
E. Fremont of New Castle m. Carrie **Lyman** of Greenville 8/24/1916 in Greenville; H - 27, USN officer, b. New Castle, s/o Fabius Robinson (laborer, New Castle) and Annie L. Card (New Castle); W - 30, teacher, b. Mainstee, MI, d/o A. Hubert Lyman (druggist, Huntington, MA) and Julie E. Barnard (Richard, ME)

J. William of New Castle m. Estelle M. **Redington** of New Castle 11/17/1908 in New Castle; H - 51, painter, b. Isles of Shoals, s/o John H. Robinson (sea captain, Isles of Shoals) and Mary A. Becker (housewife, Fort Constitution); W - 49, trained nurse, b. Eastport, ME, d/o John Gore Redington (farmer, England) and Elmira G. Trott (housewife, Eastport, ME)

Jeffrey D. of Kittery Point, ME m. Elisabeth S. **Kinney** of New Castle 4/18/1987 in Portsmouth; H - s/o Darroll E. Robinson and Ardelle L. Briggs; W - d/o Douglas M. Kinney and Martha G. Snowdon

Kelly of Marblehead, MA m. Emily E. **Michaud** of Marblehead, MA 2/17/1979 in New Castle; H - s/o Wade Robinson and Jean Roberts; W - d/o Gerald Michaud and Jacqueline Deschamp

William Y. m. Juanita Ardis **Cook** 6/15/1973 in New Castle; H - s/o David B. Robinson and Thelma Mae Young; W - d/o William Cook and Zelma Cilley

ROGERS,
Harvey Lyndon m. Barbara Lee **Yeaton** 12/29/1962 in Portsmouth; H - 29, 2d, b. NH, s/o Harvey E. Rogers and Leona M. Ricker; W - 19, b. NH, d/o Earle M. Yeaton and Phyllis L. McIntosh

ROLLINS,
Daniel J. m. Tara Lyn **Chase** 4/13/1991 in New Castle

ROONEY,
Thomas P. of Washington, DC m. Dani M. **McLaughlin** of
Washington, DC 11/4/1995 in New Castle

ROTH,
George P. of Amesbury, MA m. Alice L. **Amazeen** of New Castle
11/11/1891 in New Castle; H - 23, b. West Newbury, MA; W -
22, b. New Castle

ROWELL,
Gorham N. m. Brenda W. **Heath** 12/10/1973 in Portsmouth; H - s/o
Gardner L. Rowell and Ethelwyn N. Nickerson; W - d/o F. Weld
Heath and Patricia Barry

ROWLEY,
Clark W., Jr. of New Castle m. Marjorie A. **Lamb** of Portsmouth
9/3/1956 in Portsmouth; H - 18, US Navy, b. WA, s/o Clark W.
Rowley (WA) and C. M. McKinney (WA); W - 18, at home, b.
NH, d/o Ernest E. Lamb (NH) and Louise C. Allen (ME)

RUBINO,
Thomas S. of New Castle m. Amelita **DiAngelo** of Pittsburgh, PA
4/26/1943 in New Castle; H - 23, soldier, b. Weltsville, OH, s/o
Joseph Rubino (wholesale prod., Italy) and Josephine LaScola
(housewife, Italy); W - 19, fac. worker, b. Pittsburgh, PA, d/o
Bon'ture D'Angelo (laborer, Italy) and Elvita Petrares
(housewife, Italy)

RUMORE,
Joseph, Jr. m. Diane M. **Thomits** 1/6/1969 in Portsmouth; H - s/o Joe
D. Rumore and Carmen Ruiz; W - d/o Albert R. Thomits and
Myrtle M. Harris

RUTH,

Leo J. m. Ariel E. **Findora** 9/20/1976 in Portsmouth; H - s/o Joseph B. Ruth and Mary Woblan; W - d/o Bernard Mulroy and Ariel Meeker

SAMUELS,

George F. of New Castle m. Joanne **Goodman** of New Castle 12/19/1981 in Portsmouth; H - s/o George F. Samuels and Gabriella Lavetsky; W - d/o Bernard A. Goodman and June Chase

SANDLER,

Stuart Arthur m. Marjorie L. **Fewings** 10/9/1969 in Manchester; H - s/o Barney Sandler and Jennie Shafran; W - d/o Reginald J. Coombs and Winifred Stephens

SARKISSIAN,

Steven A. of Newburyport, MA m. Barbara A. **Hall** of Newburyport, MA 9/30/1978 in New Castle; H - s/o Edward Sarkissian and Marion Avedisian; W - d/o Wilfred H. Hall and Emily Heizer

SAWYER,

Eric m. Julie Lynne **Levesque** 11/15/1991 in New Castle
Stephen Daniel m. Judith Annette **LaRose** 7/10/1965 in Portsmouth; H - 21, b. NH, s/o James F. Sawyer and Frances E. Goodrich; W - 18, b. NH, d/o Loring P. LaRose and Lucille E. Lacey

SCARPONI,

Calvin D. m. Patricia A. **O'Leary** 11/12/1976 in New Castle; H - s/o Edmund T. Scarponi and Barbara Callahan; W - d/o Bartholomew O. O'Leary and Ida Laprise

SCHARTNER,

Matthew Edward of New Castle m. Christine Renee **Louis** of New Castle 9/10/1994 in Sandwich

SCHEMBRI,

Lawrence L. of Cambridge, MA m. Elizabeth B. **Springer** of Cambridge, MA 6/16/1984 in New Castle; H - s/o Joseph Schembri and Edith Muller; W - d/o Clinton H. Springer and Francesca Judkins

SCHOFIELD,

Roger F. of Abington, MA m. Ann T. **Copley** of New Castle 4/7/1951 in Portsmouth; H - 21, Navy, b. MA, s/o Royal L. Schofield (NS) and Jean Campbell (NS); W - 19, clerk, b. NH, d/o James R. Copley (KY) and Theresa Joyce (Ireland)

SCHULTZ,

William E. of Knoxville, TN m. Elsie L. **Cliffe** of New Castle 5/24/1944 in New Castle; H - 23, US Army, b. Knoxville, TN, s/o Franklin L. Schultz (farmer, Serville, TN) and Duliah M. Butler (housewife, TN); W - 25, spar, b. England, d/o George C. Cliffe (marine eng., England) and Carrie Johnson (housewife, England)

SCHULTZE,

Timothy A. of Menands, NY m. Leslie Anne **Ringham** of Liverpool,. NY 4/22/1995 in New Castle

SCHUPP,

James B. m. Linda A. **Pillsbury** 12/13/1969 in Portsmouth; H - s/o Wayne E. Schupp and Cherie Matthews; W - d/o Frederic E. Pillsbury and Marguerite M. Clark

SCHWAB,

Peter Baldwin m. Nancy Hart **Horner** 6/11/1966 in New Castle; H - 21, b. PA, d/o Peter B. deV. Schwab and Augusta Achilles; W - 22, b. MA, d/o Robert S. Horner and Virginia V. Hart

SCOTT,

Lawrence J. of Easton, PA m. Leah Nell **Kimball** of New Castle 6/15/1957 in New Castle; H - 21, student, b. MI, s/o Lloyd L. Scott (MI) and Jean H. Hodgins (MI); W - 22, assistant engineer, b. NH, d/o G. H. Kimball (NH) and Madeline A. Dozois (NH)

Richard A. m. Carolyn F. **Kelly** 8/10/1968 in Portsmouth; H - b. OR, s/o Philip C. Scott and Alice P. Meadows; W - b. LA, d/o Emmitte J. Kelly and Joyce M. Poimboeuc

SEAGREN,

Leonard A. of Portsmouth m. Nancy J. **Hammond** of New Castle 5/3/1980 in New Castle; H - s/o C. A. Seagren and Marion Redding; W - d/o Norman Wheeler and ----- Radcliffe

SEAVEY,

Dana R. of York, ME m. Kimberly A. **Gagne** of York, ME 5/13/1989 in New Castle; H - s/o Fred Seavey and Barbara M. Hammond; W - d/o Roland W. Gagne and Marlene L. Heilman

SELLERS,

John M. m. Christine E. **Wilson** 8/10/1968 in Newington; H - b. IN, s/o John G. Sellers and Mildred R. Marshall; W - b. Japan, d/o Donald M. Wilson and Meta A. Flothmeier

SEWALL,

Peter of Eustis, ME m. Louise May **Snook** of Eustis, ME 4/20/1980 in New Castle; H - s/o Kenneth W. Sewall and Regina M. Corsi; W - d/o Paul E. Snook and Frances Rand

SHEEHY,

Frederick B., Jr. of New Castle m. Elizabeth A. **Harrison** of Rye 3/5/1983 in Portsmouth; H - s/o Frederick Sheehy, Sr. and Catherine J. Markey; W - d/o Edward A. Harrison and Cecile M. Wilson

SHEFFIELD,
Michael A. m. Mary Ellen **D'Antonio** 4/24/1976 in Portsmouth; H -
s/o Merle G. Sheffield and Joyce D. Roscoe; W - d/o Albert M.
D'Antonio and Patricia Barr

SHEPARD,
John R. of New Castle m. Margaret F. **Chandler** of Portsmouth
2/17/1943 in New Castle; H - 24, coast artillery, b. Gorham, IL,
s/o Michael Shepard (MO, farmer) and Rose E. Edwards
(housewife, Ava, IL); W - 19, tele. op., b. Portsmouth, d/o Harold
Chandler (insurance, Canada) and Theresa Wood (elec. wkr.,
Portsmouth)

SHORT,
Larry T. of Chapel Hill, NC m. Angela **DeBellis** of Highwood, IL
9/12/1987 in New Castle; H - s/o Thomas Russell Short and
Rubelle L. Harris; W - d/o Antonio DeBellis and Vincenza
Roppo

SHULDMAN,
Mitchell D. m. Diane Louise **Schaefer** 8/11/1991 in Portsmouth

SKIDMORE,
Harry T. m. Mary M. **Hanson** 6/11/1969 in Portsmouth; H - s/o
Woodford D. Skidmore; W - d/o Patrick Malloy and Delia J.
Coyne

SLOCUM,
Lee E. of Melrose, MA m. Cheryl A. **Caswell** of Cambridge, MA
5/17/1986 in New Castle; H - s/o George Slocum and Marjorie
Peabody; W - d/o Frank J. Caswell and Ann Fanfesti

SMERIGLIO,
John B. m. Kathleen L. **DeCourcy** 5/15/1976 in Portsmouth; H - s/o
James Smeriglio and Camille Caputi; W - d/o John DeCourcy and
Ruth Hassett

SMITH,

Arthur C. of New Castle m. Nellie M. **Grace** of New Castle
7/15/1916 in Portsmouth; H - 38, painter, 2d, b. Isles of Shoals,
s/o Charles A. Smith (fish market, Portsmouth) and Ada M.
Smith (dressmaker, Portsmouth); W - 30, domestic, b. Rochester,
d/o William D. Grace (janitor, Kittery Point, ME) and Adella M.
Clarke (Kittery Point, ME)

Bruce N., Jr. of New Castle m. Cheryl L. **Anderson** of Portsmouth
8/25/1984 in New Castle; H - s/o Bruce N. Smith and Norma
Lagerstrom; W - d/o Elton R. Anderson and Nancy Poole

Bruce W. of New Castle m. Karole A. **Pinney** of Greenland 5/7/1977
in Greenland; H - s/o Bruce N. Smith and Norma L. Lagestrom;
W - d/o Richard B. Pinney and Jane Arendt

Francis L. of New Castle m. Luella A. **Collins** of New Castle 2/6/1912
in New Castle; H - 25, corporal, USA, b. Friend, NE, s/o George
C. Smith (farmer) and Hattie A. Farrill (housewife); W - 19, b.
New Castle, d/o Luther P. Collins (fisherman, Kittery Point, ME)
and Addie A. Simpson (housewife, New Castle)

Fred of New Castle m. Bertha L.M. **Robertson** of Norton Sta., NB
9/8/1919 in New Castle; H - 23, soldier, USA, b. Portsmouth, s/o
Albert Smith (carpenter, Portsmouth) and Blanch E. Berry (at
home, Rye); W - 24, laundress, b. Norton Sta., NB, d/o Joseph D.
Robertson (farmer, Norton Sta., NB) and Mary L. Gildred (at
home, St. Johns, NB)

Harry W. of New Castle m. Frances M. **Perkins** of Portsmouth
10/28/1935 in New Castle; H - 19, button worker, b. New Castle,
s/o Francis Smith (US soldier, IA) and Luella Collins (New
Castle); W - 17, at home, b. Dorchester, MA, d/o Charles N.
Perkins (painter, MA) and Emeline L. Wakeham (MA)

James B., II m. Sandra Marie **Gleason** 10/12/1965 in Portsmouth; H -
21, b. TX, s/o James B. Smith and Margaret M. Tasher; W - 22,
b. MA, d/o Charles A. Gleason and Mary J. Rigali

Lester E. of Salem, MA m. Helen E. **Hanscom** of Salem, MA
6/27/1920 in New Castle; H - 26, clerk, b. Salem, MA, s/o Albert
C. Smith (sales stables, Chelsea, MA) and Nettie L. Buldsted
(housewife, Beverly, MA); H - 26, tele. operator, b. Salem, MA,

d/o Jttai P. Hanscom (cus. house jan., Salem, MA) and Florence
T. Martin (housewife, Salem, MA)

Maxwell Ayer of Tamworth m. Izola M. **Prohaska** of New Castle
8/17/1941 in New Castle; H - 27, pneu. tool wkr., b. Hardwick,
VT, s/o Lamont C. Smith (stationary eng., St. Johnsbury, VT)
and Gladys F. Ayer (housewife, Stannard, VT); W - 28, social
worker, b. New Castle, d/o C. Prohaska, Jr. (cont. builder,
Boston, MA) and Ida Murray (housewife, Carbonear, NF)

Russell F. of Gloucester, MA m. B. J. **Winchester** of Gloucester, MA
6/18/1955 in New Castle; H - 30, fish worker, b. MA, s/o Louis
F. Smith (NS) and Charlotte G. Call (MA); W - 19, at home, div.,
b. CA, d/o Lyle T. Rumsey (OK) and E. N. Cassingham (KS)

Wendell Tyng of New Castle m. Virginia Lee **Corliss** of Laconia
9/24/1942 in Laconia; H - 21, USNR, b. Portland, ME, s/o
Wendell T. Smith (sales mgr., Portland, ME) and Myrle
Townsend (at home, Alfred, ME); W - 20, stenographer, b.
Laconia, d/o Haven E. Corliss (st. high. dept., Weirs) and Esther
P. Jenkins (at home, Atlantic, MA)

SNOOK,
Paul E., Jr. of New Castle m. Carolyn A. **Cocklin** of New Castle
5/20/1990 in New Castle; H - s/o Paul E. Snook and Frances
Rand; W - d/o Thomas Cocklin and Barbara Sawyer

SNOW,
Christopher Dunlap m. Melissa Lee **Hussey** 7/11/1992 in New Castle

SNYDER,
Peter S. of New Castle m. Bonnie Jean **Wing** of Greenland 6/2/1984
in New Castle; H - s/o William L. Snyder and Jean P. Wojciak;
W - d/o Elmer F. Wing and Martha I. Brackett

William J. of New Castle m. Jean **Wojciaki** of New Castle 5/29/1947
in Berwick, ME; H - 23, laborer, b. New Castle, s/o Harold
Snyder (US Army, Centralia, IL) and Alice Mulvan; W - 21, at
home, b. Holyoke, MA, d/o Stanley Wojciaki (Poland) and -----
(Tupper Lake, NY)

SOUSA,

Manuel of Fall River, MA m. Louise **Clough** of Kittery, ME
12/30/1944 in New Castle; H - 25, mach., USA, b. Fall River,
MA, s/o Nicholas Sousa (machinist, Azores) and Maria Perreira
(housewife, Azores); W - 19, stenographer, b. Portsmouth, d/o
Chester L. Clough (letter car., Portsmouth) and Emma Perry
(machinist, Woodsville)

SPEAR,

Charles Graffam m. Kay Frances **Pecunies** 10/15/1966 in Portsmouth;
H - 39, 2d, b. ME, s/o Charles G. Spear and Alice Eva Anthony;
W - 33, b. NH, d/o John T. Pecunies and Emma C. Henderson

Franklin E. of Lisbon m. Maud Gibson **Wilmarth** of New Castle
6/27/1907 in Portsmouth; H - 35, physician, b. Charlotte, VT, s/o
Oscar E. Spear (farmer, Charlotte, VT) and Caroline E. Wilder
(housewife, Stratford, VT); W - 35, teacher, b. Guelph, Canada,
d/o John M. Gibson (teacher, Guelph, Canada) and Sophronia
Mason (housewife, Brookline, VT)

SPONSLER,

James E., Jr. of Kittery Point, ME m. Holly Lynn **Covel** of Kittery
Point, ME 4/26/1997 in New Castle

SPRAGGINS,

Cecil Wayne m. Elsie Mary **LaRose** 12/15/1959 in New Castle; H -
21, b. FL, s/o Cecil E. Spraggins and Wilma Smith; W - 17, b.
NH, d/o Harold J. LaRose and Stella Karakostas

STACK,

Dennis John of Chicago, IL m. Marie Genevieve **White** of San
Francisco, CA 11/7/1942 in New Castle; H - 26, lieut., USA, b.
Chicago, IL, s/o Maurice W. Stack (ret. city fire., Ireland) and
Catharine Stack (housewife, Columbus C., IN); W - 27, typist-
clerk, b. San Francisco, CA, d/o James N. White (longshoreman,
Sacramento, CA) and Mary L. White (housewife, San Francisco,
CA)

STACY,

Russell James of Belmont, MA m. Mildred Josephine **Leary** of New Castle 10/16/1932 in Portsmouth; H - 23, clerk, b. Cambridge, MA, s/o Clifford Stacy (garage manager, NS) and Edna Munday (at home, NS); W - 20, at home, b. Portsmouth, d/o Thomas A. Leary (laborer, Boston, MA) and Josephine McKenna (at home, Ireland)

STANDISH,

Myles of New Castle m. Mary **MacArthur** of Manchester 9/9/1925 in Portsmouth; H - 28, machine operator, b. Anson, ME, s/o Fred D. Standish (spinner, Flagstaff, ME) and Josephine Piper (housewife, Starks, ME); W - 33, office work, b. Manchester, d/o William MacArthur (dyer, Paisley, Scotland) and Mary Cunningham (at home, Glasgow, Scotland)

STEELE,

Dana A. of FL m. Elizabeth H. **Warren** of New Castle 12/8/1938 in New Castle; H - 47, none, b. Cincinnati, OH, s/o Frederick L. Steele (was retired, Strafford) and Alice H. Allen (at home, Cincinnati, OH); W - 31, at home, b. Manchester, d/o George H. Warren (lawyer) and Mary H. Palmer (at home, Groton, MA)

STEVENS,

Hamilton Brooks of New Castle m. Margaret **Pesce** of New Castle 1/17/1996 in New Castle

Lester F. of New Castle m. Frances L. **Brown** of Portsmouth 6/20/1943 in New Castle; H - 22, coast artillery, b. Baltimore, MD, s/o Edgar L. Stevens (male nurse, Southbridge, MA) and Hazel Summers (MD); W - 19, jr. clerk, b. Portsmouth, d/o Howard M. Brown (machinist, Portsmouth) and Ethel M. Smith (housewife, Portsmouth)

Robert G., Jr. of New Castle m. Pamela A. **Richard** of Dover 7/2/1988 in New Castle; H - s/o Robert G. Stevens and Susan L. Chase; W - d/o Edgar A. Richard and Norma F. Cass

STEWART,

Hugh R., Jr. of Portland, ME m. Jacqueline H. **Kitchen** of New Castle 12/15/1951 in Portsmouth; H - 21, UAAF, b. MS, s/o Hugh R. Stewart, Sr. (MS) and Mary L. McCarley (MS); W - 21, receptionist, b. NY, d/o John R. Kitchen (England) and Florina Murray (ME)

Maxwell D. m. Eileen F. **Coyle** 7/28/1969 in Portsmouth; H - s/o Maxwell Howard and Marguerite Gauvin; W - d/o Charles Coyle and Virginia White

Robert K. of New Castle m. Caroline E. **Flagg** of New Castle 12/17/1977 in New Castle; H - s/o Robert Stewart and Adeline Simmons; W - d/o Chester Williams and Mabel Pridham

STRANGE,

Fred, Jr. m. Bette J. **Harrison** 11/4/1972 in Portsmouth; H - s/o Fred Strange and Mary Holmes; W - d/o Robert Harrison and Bette Lowell

STRINGHAM,

Peter S. of New Castle m. Carol A. **Fitzgerald** of Stratham 8/27/1988 in New Castle; H - s/o Edward B. Stringham and Mary A. Dresser; W - d/o Francis A. Fitzgerald and Diana K. Hutchinson

STRYD,

Peter J. of Kalamazoo, MI m. Tena **Van Woodloos** of Kalamazoo, MI 5/18/1942 in Portsmouth; H - 28, coast artillery, b. Netherlands, s/o Jacob Stryd (celery farmer, Netherlands) and Mary de Regt (Netherlands); W - 28, factory wkr., b. Kalamazoo, MI, d/o Joseph Van Woodloos (Netherlands)

STURGIS,

George A. of New Castle m. Maureen **Kelley** of New Castle 8/25/1984 in New Castle; H - s/o William Sturgis and Georgette Fortin; W - d/o Hartley F. Kelley and Virginia Day

SULLIVAN,

David R. of Dorchester, MA m. Katherine **O'Connor** of New Castle
1/3/1981 in Portsmouth; H - s/o Timothy F. Sullivan and
Penelope Odessey; W - d/o William J. O'Connor and Margaret
Chandler

SUTTER,

William W. of Houston, TX m. Ruth L. **Czerwinski** of Boston, MA
12/2/1955 in New Castle; H - 21, US Navy, b. TX, s/o B. E.
Funderbunk (TX) and Mary E. Ringo (KY); W - 21, lab. tech., b.
MA, d/o Edward A. Czerwinski (MA) and Olgo Kimmert
(Germany)

SWEETSER,

John Clifford m. Jane Thwaites **Wood** 10/31/1959 in Portsmouth; H -
48, 2d, b. NH, s/o John G. Sweetser and Mabel Jones; W - 41, b.
Scotland, d/o Newton W. Wood and Jane Thwaites

SYKES,

C. Jeremy of Warren, MA m. Karyl M. **Scott** of Reading, MA
8/6/1983 in New Castle; H - s/o Charles M. Sykes and Barbara
Eaton; W - d/o William C. Scott and Lucille M. Rossignol

SYLVESTER,

James, Jr. of New Castle m. Bessie J. **Langley** of So. Eliot, ME
10/24/1925 in Portsmouth; H - 23, clerk, b. Cambridge, MA, s/o
James F. Sylvester (shipfitter, Quincy, MA) and Elsie M. Fernald
(at home, Kittery, ME); W - 18, at home, b. So. Eliot, ME, d/o
Walter Langley (carpenter, York, ME) and Anna Tobey (at home,
So. Eliot, ME)

TABBUTT,

Stephen R. of New Castle m. Tami S. **Sarters** of New Castle
6/27/1981 in New Castle; H - s/o Richard C. Tabbutt and Sylvia
Harrison; W - d/o Charles Stokes and Reva A. White

TACKETT,
Roy of New Castle m. Anna K. **Bozzocchi** of Portsmouth 12/19/1943 in New Castle; H - 25, coast artillery, b. WV, s/o Milton R. Tackett (farmer, WV) and Ellen Gilmerabro (housewife, WV); W - 22, navy yard, b. Portsmouth, d/o Enrico Bozzocchi (shoe shop, Italy) and Rosa Moroncelli (housewife, Italy)

TARANTINO,
Christopher E. of Washington, DC m. Emily Jean **Harville** of New Castle 7/17/1993 in Portsmouth

TARATUS,
Mark N. m. Kathleen Ann **Roy** 6/29/1991 in New Castle

TARBELL,
Thomas of Los Gatos, CA m. Annette S. **Young** of Los Gatos, CA 6/2/1990 in New Castle; H - s/o Edmund Tarbell and Barbara Penrose; W - d/o Gordon Young and Wendy Faber

TARLTON,
Charles C. of New Castle m. Mary L. **Emery** of New Castle 9/25/1894 in Portsmouth; H - 31, b. New Castle, s/o Nathan B.F. Tarlton and Eliza J. Frost; W - 22, b. New Castle, d/o Jonathan Emery and Louisa Baker

Thaddeus of New Castle m. Harriet L. **Franklin** of New Castle 2/23/1895 in Portsmouth; H - 62, postmaster, b. New Castle, s/o John Tarlton (New Castle) and Ann E. Vennard (New Castle); W - 48, b. New Castle, d/o William H. Franklin and Maria T. White

THACHER,
Jeffrey S. of So. Berwick, ME m. Amanda E. **Silva** of New Castle 5/13/1989 in New Castle; H - s/o Jack L. Thacher and Elisabeth Singleton; W - d/o J. Donald Silva and Lucy A. Niles

THEOBALD,

Roderick M. of Rollinsford m. Karoline L. **Kimball** of New Castle
8/9/1986 in New Castle; H - s/o William L. Theobald and
Patricia Martin; W - d/o Ivory G. Kimball and Margaret
Anderson

THEODOSSIOU,

Dimitrios T. of Dedham, MA m. Donna L. **Jennings** of New Castle
5/21/1983 in Portsmouth; H - s/o Herculis Theodossiou and
Manianthi Vardaxis; W - d/o Richard Jennings and Patricia D.
Campbell

THERIAULT,

William P. m. Kathleen E. **Gordon** 2/14/1976 in Portsmouth; H - s/o
Albert E. Theriault and Blanche E. Zalansky; W - d/o James J.
Gordon and Helen Berner

William Paul of Kittery, ME m. Virginia Anne **Lepore** of New Castle
1/18/1980 in New Castle; H - s/o Albert E. Theriault and
Blanche C. Zalansky; W - d/o Thomas H. Webb and Mary A.
LaBrie

THINNESS,

Henry A., Jr. of New Castle m. Marion Grace **Ripley** of Portsmouth
8/9/1942 in New Castle; H - 24, 2d Lt., USA, b. Camden, NJ, s/o
Henry A. Thinness (sorter, Richmond, VA) and Viola Sackarnd
(at home, Camden, NJ); W - 26, bookkeeper, b. Wilson Mills,
ME, d/o Roland H. Ripley (machinist, Magalloway, ME) and
Emma M. Marsh (at home, Cambridge, MA)

THOMAS,

Carlton A., Jr. m. Barbara Louise **Brown** 12/9/1967 in Portsmouth; H
- 25, 2d, b. NH, s/o Carlton Thomas, Sr. and Marjorie Parker; W
- 23, 2d, b. NH, d/o Myron H. Hapgood and Helen M. Day

Donald B. of Portsmouth m. Shirley L. **Kellenbeck** of Portsmouth
9/10/1950 in New Castle; H - 28, crane op., b. MA, s/o George

C. Thomas (MA) and Nina E. Bartlett (NH); W - 21, clerk, b.
NH, d/o William R. Kellenbeck (NH) and Livina R. Morrill (NH)
Elwood R. m. Cynthia A. **Nichols** 12/19/1970 in Portsmouth; H - s/o
Harold B. Thomas and Lucy J. Farnham; W - d/o Gordon
Pridham and Niola Noyes
Peter O. of New Castle m. Janice M. **Owen** of Portsmouth 7/14/1990
in New Castle; H - s/o Clayton Nichols and Cynthia Pridham; W
- d/o Jerry Owen and Lorraine Gorman

THOMITS,
Albert R., Jr. m. Ilya **Wuelper** 6/27/1970 in New Castle; H - s/o
Albert R. Thomits and Myrtle M. Harris; W - d/o Louis F.
Wuelper and Marion Klecka

THOMPSON,
Alden H. of New Castle m. Mary Belle **Goodwin** of Portsmouth
10/31/1942 in Portsmouth; H - 34, storekeeper, b. Rollinsford,
s/o Charles A. Thompson (lumber dealer, So. Berwick, ME) and
Elizabeth Johnson (housewife, York, ME); W - 38, stenographer,
b. Portsmouth, d/o Charles Goodwin (retired, NS) and
Wilhelmina McKinnon (housewife, NS)

THORP,
Richard m. Janice Loretta **Barnes** 6/17/1961 in Portsmouth; H - 22, b.
ME, s/o John C. Thorp and Priscilla Alden; W - 21, b. VT, d/o
Dwight F. Barnes and Aubrey Gilchrist

THORVALDSON,
Bill R. m. Roberta M. **Wharton** 5/26/1972 in Exeter; H - s/o Sverre
Thorvaldson and Olga Groskopf; W - d/o Robert M. Green and
Dora E. Edwards

THYNG,
Alan R. m. Bonnie S. **Hart** 12/28/1970 in Somersworth; H - s/o
Arthur L. Thyng and Verna Foss; W - d/o Dwinal L. Hart and
Anna E. Doherty

Arthur L., Jr. of New Castle m. Susan Evelyn **Cousens** of Milford
8/8/1984 in Milford; H - s/o Arthur L. Thyng, Sr. and Verna A.
Foss; W - d/o William Cousens and Marion B. Lorette
Larry C. m. Wanda J. **McGee** 3/3/1973 in Rye Beach; H - s/o Arthur
L. Thyng and Verna Foss; W - d/o Otis McGee and Rosalene
Bronzetti

TIBBETTS,
Fred W. of New Castle m. Fannie C. **White** of New Castle 6/5/1901 in
Portsmouth; H - 28, surfman, b. Boothbay Harbor, ME, s/o
Elephalet Tibbetts (boatbuilder, Linnekin, ME) and Ellen Adams
(housewife, East Boothbay, ME); W - 25, housewife, b. New
Castle, d/o Charles H. White (seaman, New Castle) and Sarah F.
Randall (housewife, New Castle)

TOMMOLA,
William C. of York, ME m. Marilyn H. **Prescott** of No. Hampton
6/20/1971 in New Castle; H - b. RI, s/o Walter Tommola and
Henni Pylvanainon; W - b. MA, d/o Charles S. Prescott and
Rosealice Hargraves

TOOMEY,
Richard A. of Ft. Foster, ME m. Elizabeth **Rylander** of New Castle
10/24/1943 in Portsmouth; H - 25, Lt., USA, b. Danvers, MA,
s/o John P. Toomey (shoemaker, Danvers, MA) and Margaret
Hayden (housewife, Peabody, MA); W - 22, med. secre., b.
Newton, MA, d/o Thor A. Rylander (marine corps, Milton, MA)
and Myra Neal (housewife, Boston, MA)

TRACEY,
Sean M. of New Castle m. Lina M. **Carrillo** of New Castle 2/18/1996
in New Castle

TRAFTON,
Bradley C. of Kittery, ME m. Kris A. **Russell** of Kittery, ME
12/4/1981 in New Castle; H - s/o Bradley G. Trafton and Helen
L. Lutts; W - d/o James C. Russell and Wilma Mittlesteadt

TRAUGUT,
Bryant of New London, CT m. Dorothy **Stickles** of Portsmouth
9/7/1929 in New Castle; H - 21, radio off., US Sub., b. Brooklyn,
NY, s/o Fred Traugut (technical eng., Astoria, LI) and Laura
Minard (housewife, Astoria, LI); W - 18, at home, b. Portsmouth,
d/o Abraham Stickles (shipfitter, navy yard, North Adams, MA)
and Ida Stanley (at home, Portsmouth)

TRUEMAN,
Glenn F. m. Rebecca Marie **Powers** 9/21/1991 in New Castle

TRUSLOW,
E. William of New Castle m. Danna N. **Butler** of New Castle
8/2/1980 in New Castle; H - s/o E. W. Truslow and Mary Powell;
W - d/o Thomas G. Butler and Margaret Hatch

TRYON,
Bruce Bower of Norwood, MA m. Marilyn Hubbard **Francis** of
Norwood, MA 10/22/1994 in New Castle

TURNER,
John J.S., Jr. of New Castle m. Ethel **Manson** of New Castle
8/25/1903 in Portsmouth; H - 22, engineer, b. ND, d/o John J.S.
Turner (ND) and Elizabeth Hooper (NY); W - 18, housewife, b.
New Castle, d/o Andrew Manson (Kittery, ME) and Hannah Bell
(New Castle)

TWIDEL,
Michael A. of New Castle m. Wendy M. **Garland** of New Castle
7/12/1997 in New Durham

TYSNES,

Ove Alf of Oslo, Norway m. Sissel **Nielson** of Marblehead, MA
7/3/1993 in New Castle

VADALA,

John Edward of Rye m. Bonnie Anne **Robbins** of New Castle
6/16/1993 in Portsmouth

VANDENBERG,

J. A. of Andover, MA m. Eva Louise **Cohen** of Andover, MA
9/29/1956 in New Castle; H - 48, consulting engineer, 2d, b.
Netherlands, s/o A. van den Bergh (Netherlands) and Betje Knurr
(Netherlands); W - 34, secretary, b. Netherlands, d/o Maurito J.
Cohen (Netherlands) and Louise Wynberg (Netherlands)

VOLKMAN,

William J. of New Castle m. Dorothy J. **Moore** of Milford 6/25/1938
in Milford; H - 28, teacher, b. Manchester, s/o Henry Volkman
(textile worker, Germany) and Minnie Luecht (domestic,
Germany); W - 20, at home, b. Nashua, d/o George W. Moore
(plumber, Warwick, MA) and L. June Hodgman (housewife,
Mason)

VOLPE,

Matthew J. of New Castle m. Jorja M. **Dozet** of Kittery, ME 9/4/1993
in New Castle

WALZ,

Elmer Henry of New Castle m. Thelma Marie **Winker** of Carroll, IA
4/4/1942 in New Castle; H - 27, coast artillery, b. Carroll, IA, s/o
John B. Walz (retired, Carroll, IA) and Henrietta Searke (Carroll,
IA); W - 23, teleph. opr., b. Carroll, IA, d/o Arthur E. Winker
(mechanic, Carroll, IA) and Henrietta Rust (housewife, Arcadia,
IA)

WARD,

Dane M. of West Palm Beach, FL m. Jennifer A. **Stringham** of New
Castle 8/8/1987 in New Castle; H - s/o Gerald G. Ward and
Carol S. Underhill; W - d/o Edward B. Stringham and Mary Anne
Dresser

Harold Francis, Jr. m. Judith Estelle **Tabbutt** 9/23/1961 in New
Castle; H - 22, b. MA, s/o Harold F. Ward and Theresa
McGlynn; W - 21, b. NH, d/o Clifford C. Tabbutt and Arline R.
Ricker

WARNER,

Robert E., Jr. of New Castle m. Merrie L. **Mangold** of New Castle
11/11/1978 in New Castle; H - s/o Robert E. Warner and Frances
E. Merrill; W - d/o John Mangold and Margaret Anderson

WASIHEWSKI,

Joseph J. of Fort Constitution m. Doris May **Hughes** of Portsmouth
7/4/1942 in Seabrook; H - 28, soldier, b. Norwichtown, CT, s/o
Stanley Wasihewski (foreman, Poland) and Josephine -----
(housewife, Poland); W - 22, postal clerk, b. Pike, d/o Frank
Hughes (Whitefield) and Marion Craig (housewife, Pike)

WATKINS,

James F., Jr. of Amesbury, MA m. Elizabeth A. **Groton** of New
Castle 11/13/1982 in Portsmouth; H - s/o James F. Watkins, Sr.
and Gertrude M. LaFontaine; W - d/o Richard W. Groton and
Miriam E. Herrick

WEBB,

George Lumus m. Elizabeth Louise **Smith** 6/23/1962 in Milton; H -
21, b. Boston, MA, s/o James Gordon and Helen Burner; W - 20,
b. Milton, d/o George Smith and Janet Williams

WELCH,

Francis E. of New Castle m. Marguerite T. **Kluesner** of Portsmouth
6/12/1982 in Portsmouth; H - s/o Francis W. Welch and

Charlotte Campbell; W - d/o Edwin F. Conner and Margaret Carroll

WENTWORTH,

Clifton Lawrence m. Alice Frances **McCormack** 7/14/1962 in Portsmouth; H - 22, b. MA, s/o Herman Wentworth and Ruth V. Whitehouse; W - 18, b. NY, d/o Edward McCormack and Mary A. Campbell

WETZEL,

Raymond E., Jr. of Eliot, ME m. Joellen P. **McKinney** of Kittery, ME 5/21/1983 in New Castle; H - s/o Raymond Wetzel, Sr. and Virginia Dame; W - d/o George A. Pilgrim and Joan E. Reynolds

WHEELER,

Howard W. of Rumney m. Esther **Thornton** of Manchester 10/30/1942 in New Castle; H - 31, lieut., USA, b. Nashua, s/o Charles Wheeler (carpenter, Stow, MA) and Nettie Wheeler (housewife, Hollis); W - 30, teacher, b. Manchester, d/o John Thornton (fireman, Manchester) and Ida Dekmelt (housewife, Manchester)

WHEELOCK,

Geoffrey M. of Boston, MA m. Mary B. **Wendell** of Boston, MA 9/8/1902 in New Castle; H - 22, clerk, b. Shanghai, China, s/o Thomas R. Wheelock (Annapolis, NS) and Edith H. Clark (Boston, MA); W - 19, b. Boston, MA, d/o Barrett Wendell (Boston, MA) and Edith Greenough (Swampscott, MA)

WHITAKER,

Cadie of New Castle m. Catherine R. **Begley** of New Castle 10/1/1942 in New Castle; H - 23, coast artillery, b. Hazard, KY, s/o Wess Whitaker (veterinary, Avawam, KY) and Eunice Shepherd (housewife, Avawam, KY); W - 19, at home, b. Hardbury, KY, d/o Sam Begley (coal miner, Hardbury, KY) and America Miller (housewife, Ary, KY)

Nicholas of New Castle m. Candous **Deaton** of New Castle 2/17/1943
in New Castle; H - 21, machinist, b. Avawam, KY, s/o Wes
Whitaker (farmer, Avawam, KY) and Eunice Shepherd
(housewife, Avawam, KY); W - 21, at home, b. Altro, KY, d/o
Sollie Deaton (Altro, KY) and ----- Griffin (Altro, KY)

WHITE,

Andrew B. of New Castle m. Octavia **Becker** of New Castle 6/1/1904
in New Castle; H - 27, machinist, b. New Castle, s/o Andrew H.
White (painter, New Castle) and Clara Vennard (housewife, New
Castle); W - 24, housewife, b. New Castle, d/o Henry Becker
(seaman, No. Berwick, ME) and Ellen Amazeen (housewife, New
Castle)

Kelly Norman of Winston-Salem, NC m. Vira Winifred **Cooper** of
Kittery Point, ME 9/11/1917 in New Castle; H - 26, soldier,
USA, b. Winston-Salem, NC, s/o John W. White (engineer,
Germanton, NC) and Sarah E. Tuttle (Bristol, TN); W - 23, b.
Portsmouth, d/o Fred E. Cooper (grocer, England) and Anna L.
Anderson (England)

Richard H. of New Castle m. Jan **Rathgeber** of New Castle 6/11/1981
in New Castle; H - s/o Warren M. White and Jeanette I. Talbot;
W - d/o William H. Rathgeber and Charlotte D. Flahive

Stephen O. of New Castle m. Corinne K. **Hayes** of Portsmouth
8/28/1971 in New Castle; H - b. NH, s/o Frederick S. White and
Mary M. Odiorne; W - b. OH, d/o Herman H. Hayes and Barbara
N. Oakley

Warren M. of New Castle m. Jeanette **Talbot** of New Castle
9/28/1946 in New Castle; H - 28, maritime s., b. Portsmouth, s/o
Arnold B. White (ret. c. guard, New Castle) and Louise E. Jordan
(housewife, Cape Elizabeth, ME); W - 24, nurse, b. Caribou, ME,
d/o Harlan M. Talbot (caretaker, Lewiston, ME) and Beatrice
Mitton (housewife, Caribou, ME)

William G. of New Castle m. Clara M. **Sheehan** of New Castle
1/7/1903 in Portsmouth; H - 21, engineer, b. New Castle, s/o
James W. White (New Castle) and Catherine Robinson (Isles of
Shoals); W - 25, housewife, b. Meriamchi, NB, s/o Daniel

Sheehan (Barnaby River, NB) and Catherine O'Shea (Barnaby River, NB)

WHITEHOUSE,
Donald Earl m. Estelle M. **Bauer** 7/19/1973 in Portsmouth; H - s/o Reginald E. Whitehouse and Alice C. MacDonald; W - d/o Edward Misiaszek and Nellie Green

Reginald E. m. Marcia Louise **Foss** 4/11/1959 in New Castle; H - 24, b. NH, s/o Reginald E. Whitehouse and Alice C. MacDonald; W - 20, b. NH, d/o Reginald A. Foss and Evelyn G. Cousins

Richard Edward m. Priscilla Gail **Harris** 6/2/1962 in Portsmouth; H - 23, b. Portsmouth, s/o Samuel Whitehouse and Elizabeth Morehead; W - 20, b. Portsmouth, d/o Bevuell J. Harris and Pauline Stenzel

Scott E. of New Castle m. Margaret M. **Clifford** of Portsmouth 1/12/1985 in Portsmouth; H - s/o Reginald E. Whitehouse and Marcia Foss; W - d/o John T. Clifford and Barbara McLaughlin

WHITLOCK,
Paul LeR. of New Castle m. Ethel **Turner** of New Castle 6/14/1906 in Portsmouth; H - 25, expressman, b. Harrisburg, PA, s/o M. W. Whitlock (carpenter, Castleton, VT) and Ida Radifer (housewife, Harrisburg, PA); W - 22, housewife, 2d, b. Merrimack, d/o Andrew Manson (laborer, Kittery, ME) and Hannah Bell (housewife, New Castle)

WHITNEY,
Leonard E. of Kittery, ME m. Robin R. **Moebus** of Kittery, ME 9/2/1993 in New Castle

Ricky Allen of Eliot, ME m. Debora Ethel **Pridham** of Eliot, ME 2/25/1994 in New Castle

WHITTELL,
Giles Q. S. of Pacific Palisades, CA m. Karen L. **Stirgwolt** of Pacific Palisades, CA 6/27/1996 in New Castle

WIGGIN,
Gerald L. of North Rochester m. Lena A. **Dauria** of Brooklyn, NY
9/26/1942 in New Castle; H - 21, coast artillery, b. Tuftonboro,
s/o Harry L. Wiggin (laborer, Melvin Village) and Mabel Drowne
(mill hand, Ossipee); W - 21, at home, b. Brooklyn, NY, d/o
Davie Dauria (tailor, Italy) and Mary Liaocon (housewife, Italy)

WILLERINGHOUSE,
Dudley of Hove, England m. Dorothy A. **Marvin** of Mamaroneck, NY
9/5/1936 in New Castle; H - 27, Austin motor, b. London,
England, s/o Frederick Willeringhouse (London, England) and
Minnie Lunan (at home, London, England); W - 20, at home, b.
Toronto, Canada, d/o Robert S. Marvin (life insurance, Syracuse,
NY) and Dorothy L. Cook (at home, Mexico City)

WILLETTE,
Frederick D. m. Carolyn A. **Bushey** 6/21/1969 in Greenland; H - s/o
Frederick J. Willette and Helen Perry; W - d/o John Bushey and
Lena Robbins

WILLEVER,
Craig Clayton of James Island, SC m. Melinda **LaBosquet** of New
Castle 12/24/1979 in New Castle; H - s/o Clayton I. Willever and
Lorraine Buchman; W - d/o Thomas P. LeBosquet and Joanne M.
Jameson

WILLIAMS,
Richard L. of New Castle m. Lisa E. **Olson** of New Castle 6/20/1996
in Portsmouth
William of New Castle m. Gladys M. **Huntley** of New Castle
6/15/1982 in Portsmouth; H - s/o Chester Williams and Mabel
Pridham; W - d/o John W. Austin and Lillie Webster

WILLIAMSON,

Lee E. m. Shirley A. **Pollard** 12/29/1976 in Portsmouth; H - s/o Howell D. Williamson and Emma Iacobelli; W - d/o Marvin Johnson and Anne Perfetti

WILSON,

William W. of New Castle m. Marion E. **Tarlton** of New Castle 6/30/1920 in New Castle; H - 29, laborer, b. Port Deposit, MD, s/o Hughie Wilson (mason) and Cassie McMullen (housewife, Port Deposit, MD); W - 29, bookkeeper, b. Portsmouth, d/o William M. Tarlton (st. keeper, navy yard, New Castle) and Carrie E. Hall (housewife, Portsmouth)

WINNEKE,

Leo T. of Fort Constitution m. Alice **Sharcet** of Newmarket 4/1/1920 in New Castle; H - 22, corp., USA, b. Dunlap, IA, s/o Henry Winneke and Mary Winneke; W - 18, housewife, b. Lawrence, MA, d/o George Sharcet (silk mfr., Newmarket) and Anna Lagarie (housewife, Newmarket)

WISWELL,

John Mulvey of Amherst m. Kathleen Ellen **Dewhirst** of New Castle 11/8/1980 in New Castle; H - s/o Edward B. Wiswell and Margaret F. Mulvey; W - d/o Leo Francis Shea and Ellen L. Robbins

WOLFORD,

Ronald Glenn m. Bette Lynnette **Mori** 6/3/1959 in Portsmouth; H - 19, b. OH, s/o Ralph Dana Wolford and Elva G. Lake; W - 14, b. NH, d/o Albert Mori and Hilda G. Ricker

WOOD,

Ralph T. m. Madeline A. **Kimball** 6/10/1972 in Portsmouth; H - s/o Fred L. Wood and Lizzie Thompson; W - d/o Arthur Dozois and Leah Snyder

WOODMAN,

Alfred K. of New Castle m. Mary E. **Owsley** of New Castle 7/35/1953
in New Castle; H - 57, painter, 2d, b. ME, s/o Daniel N.
Woodman (ME) and Harriet W. Kendall (ME); W - 34, at home,
2d, b. NH, d/o Andrew J. Horning (OH) and Ivalean Emery (NH)

WOODWARD,

Douglas L. of Concord m. Geraldine L. **Haywood** of New Castle
7/11/1936 in New Castle; H - 24, sanitary insp., b. Franklin, s/o
Oscar Woodward (clerk, Franklin) and Sarah Waddell (at home,
NS); W - 23, teacher, b. Portsmouth, d/o LeRoy Haywood
(machinist, New Castle) and Ellen I. Winn (at home, Brentwood)

Douglas R. of New Castle m. Beverly S. **Powell** of Hampton Falls
11/8/1986 in Hampton Falls; H - s/o Oscar H. Woodward and
Sara Waddell; W - d/o Wendell C. Swain and Ruth E. Sargent

WOODWORTH,

Dale T. m. Jean A. **Bowman** 5/16/1968 in New Castle; H - b. VT, s/o
Lyle S. Woodworth and Ruby D. Bowden; W - b. VT, d/o Arthur
I. Littlefield and Lovonia A. Nichols

Daryl Thomas m. Gail Pamela **Bowman** 1/26/1973 in New Castle; H
- s/o Dale T. Woodworth and Joyce E. Woodward; W - d/o
William H. Bowman and Jean A. Littlefield

WOZIACK,

James S. of Holyoke, MA m. Barbara H. **Johnson** of New Castle
10/15/1944 in New Castle; H - 21, sgt., USA, b. Passaic, NJ, s/o
Stanley Woziack (garage mech., Poland) and Mildred Conner
(Plattsburgh, NY); W - 17, at home, b. Portsmouth, d/o Haven
W. Johnson (machine op., York, ME) and Annie G. Goodwin
(Boston, MA)

WRIGHT,

William A. of 78 Barry St., Dorchester, MA m. Ethel O. **King** of 50
Joy St., Boston, MA 6/27/1924 in New Castle; H - 31, salesman,
b. Bangor, ME, s/o Francis S. Wright (bookkeeper, Bangor, ME)

and Maude E. White (housewife, Levant, ME); W - 37, nurse, b. Charlestown, MA, d/o Maynard E. King (farmer, East Corinth, ME) and Carrie E. Sanborn (housewife, Charlestown, MA)

YEATON,

Byron S. of New Castle m. Florence A. **White** of New Castle 11/25/1899 in Portsmouth; H - 42, shoe cutter, b. New Castle, s/o John E. Yeaton (laborer, New Castle) and Sarah A. Yeaton (deceased, New Castle); W - 31, housewife, b. New Castle, d/o Andrew H. White (painter, New Castle) and Clara S. Vennard (housewife, New Castle)

Henry S. of New Castle m. Helen L. **White** of New Castle 10/11/1899 in New Castle; H - 31, shoe operative, b. New Castle, s/o John E. Yeaton (laborer, New Castle) and Sarah A. Yeaton (deceased, Rye); W - 29, b. New Castle, d/o Sullivan H. White (seaman, New Castle) and Mary A. Oliver (housewife, New Castle)

Nathaniel B. of New Castle m. Clara S. **Glass** of New Castle 12/17/1903 in Portsmouth; H - 61, 3d, b. New Castle, s/o John Yeaton (seaman, New Castle) and Dorothy Amazeen (housewife, New Castle); W - 39, housewife, b. Madbury, d/o John D. Glass (farmer, Nottingham) and Betsey E. Lyons (housewife)

YOBLONSKY,

Richard E. m. Charlene S. **Magoon** 7/3/1965 in Portsmouth; H - 19, b. MD, s/o Edmund Yoblonsky and Mary R. Lewis; W - 19, b. NH, d/o Hollis C. Magoon and Carrie E. Proctor

YORK,

Charles T. of Lorain, OH m. Suzanne D. **Harris** of New Castle 11/26/1957 in New Castle; H - 20, US Navy, b. VA, s/o Leon H. York (VA) and Grace H. Brock (VA); W - 18, at home, b. NH, d/o Bevuell J. Harris (NH) and Pauline D. Stenzel (NH)

Raymond F. of So. Eliot, ME m. Josephine G. **Butler** of So. Eliot, ME 1/14/1918 in New Castle; H - 25, sheet metal worker, b. So. Eliot, ME, s/o J. Frank York (machinist, Wells, ME) and Emma L. Staples (So. Eliot, ME); W - 22, dressmaker, b. So. Eliot, ME, d/o Joseph Butler (teamster, Eliot, ME) and Hannah Goodwin (Eliot, ME)

YOUNG,
Charles E. of New Castle m. Gertie L. **Wells** of New Castle 10/4/1901 in New Castle; H - 25, soldier, b. Cincinnati, OH, s/o Frank E. Young (laborer) and Mary Chelsey (housewife, Cincinnati, OH); W - 25, 2d, b. New Castle, d/o Selden F. Wells (surfman, Kennebunk, ME) and Annah Amazeen (housewife, New Castle)

Charles E. of Cincinnati, OH m. Gertrude L. **Young** of New Castle 5/1/1906 in New Castle; H - 30, blacksmith, 2d, b. Cincinnati, OH, s/o Frank E. Young (manager, Cincinnati, OH) and Marie Shelby (housewife, Cincinnati, OH); W - 30, housewife, 2d, b. New Castle, d/o Selden F. Wells (captain, Kennebunkport, ME) and Anna F. Wells (housewife, New Castle)

E. Gordon of New Castle m. Marianne **Pernold** of New Castle 12/7/1995 in New Castle

ZWINGSTIEN,
Emil of Pittsfield, MA m. Mabel **Bullett** of Pittsfield, MA 8/6/1911 in New Castle; H - 21, baker, b. Pittsfield, MA, s/o James Zwingstien (barber, France) and Rose Chourt (housewife, France); W - 19, time keeper, b. Adams, MA, d/o John Bullett (janitor, NY) and Matilda Danoville (housewife, Canada)

DEATHS

ADAMS,

Mary Paige, d. 6/9/1996 in New Castle; b. 6/15/1916*

Woodbury, d. 8/29/1972 at 64 in New Castle; married; b. NH; Edward H. Adams and Florence Sanderson

ALDEN,

Clarence S., d. 3/20/1967 at 78 in Portsmouth; married; b. MA; Walter Alden and Emma Serrat

ALLEY,

Charlotte A., d. 7/7/1945 at 74/9/16 in Hampton Falls; at home; widow; b. Jonesport, ME; Amaziah Beal (ME) and Abigail Alley (ME)

George W., d. 9/18/1938 at 73/9/13 in Brentwood; fisherman; married; b. Jonesport, ME; Andrew Alley (ME) and Priscilla ----- (ME)

Madge, d. 8/31/1911 at 2/2 in New Castle; pneumonia; b. Jonesport, ME; Morris A. Alley (Jonesport, ME, USLSS) and Edith Beal (Grand Menan)

Mary E., d. 5/7/1950 at 69 in Brookline, MA; at home; married; b. Jonesport, ME; George Alley and Charlotte -----

ALLISON,

Lewis, d. 10/11/1903 at 0/2 in Portsmouth; marasmus; b. Portsmouth; Lewis Allison and Melissa Manson (New Castle)

ALMGREN,

George B., d. 11/2/1991 at 80 in Portsmouth; Kenneth Almgren and Agnes Larson

ALNAS,

Anna Louise, d. 5/3/1934 at 67/4/1 in New Castle; at home; married; b. Norway; Amund Aars (Norway) and Ingborg Aarons (Bulso, Norway)

Bertha J., d. 7/17/1923 at 40/7/25 in New Castle; at home; married; b. Norway; Peder Widdel (Norway) and Randy Hole (Norway)

Birgthe O.K., d. 9/15/1928 at 57/1/4 in Portsmouth
Karen M., d. 6/5/1928 at 84/9/11 in New Castle; at home; widow; b.
   Norway; Peter Brandel (Norway) and Olive Ulesto (Norway)
Peter A., d. 1/26/1942 at 72/7/16 in Kittery, ME; Cf. Bos'n Mate;
   widower; b. Norway; Ingbrigt Alnas (Norway) and Karen Brandel
   (Norway)

AMAZEEN,
Abby, d. 8/31/1892 at 64/4/21 in New Castle; housekeeper; married;
   b. New Castle; father and mother both b. New Castle
Adaline B., d. 1/27/1897 at 62/7/3; married; b. New Castle; Eben
   Yeaton (Rye) and Hipsabeth Meloon (New Castle)
Andrew W., d. 9/11/1916 at 61/11/6 in New Castle; watchman;
   widower; b. New Castle; Benjamin T. Amazeen (New Castle) and
   Sarah E. Frost (New Castle)
Benjamin T., d. 10/20/1898 at 87/5/12 in New Castle; Bright's
   disease; widower; b. New Castle; Ephraim Amazeen (New
   Castle) and Hannah Tarlton (New Castle)
Carrie, d. 8/3/1924 at 72/4/2 in New Castle; at home; married; b. New
   Castle; Capt. John Murray (NY) and Fillie Yeaton (New Castle)
Charles, d. 1/12/1911 at 49 in Long Island, NY; broncho pneumonia;
   Christopher Amazeen (New Castle, inventor)
Charles Benjamin, d. 3/22/1923 at 66/9/19 in New Castle; melter,
   Navy Yard foundry; married; b. New Castle; Benjamin F.
   Amazeen (New Castle) and Sarah Frost (New Castle)
Christopher, d. 8/14/1909 at 79 in Somerville, MA; apoplexy;
   inventor; married; b. New Castle; Abram Amazeen (New Castle)
Clarence, d. 11/13/1957 at 72 in Brentwood; gardener; single; b. NH;
   Granville Amazeen and Harriet Baker
Daniel, d. 1/29/1892 at 55/4 in New Castle; laborer; single; b. New
   Castle; father and mother both b. New Castle
Edward B., d. 8/16/1908 at 76 in New Castle; nephritis septic blad.;
   seaman; widower; b. New Castle; Ephraim Amazeen (New
   Castle) and Susan Vennard (New Castle)
Elizabeth C., d. 12/13/1955 at 89 in Portsmouth; at home; single; b.
   New Castle; John W. Amazeen and Mary O. Cole

Ella F., d. 7/25/1957 at 90 in Portsmouth; at home; widow; b. Isles of Shoals; John H. Robinson and Mary A. Becker

Ellen S., d. 3/4/1900 at 45 in New Castle; tuberculosis; nurse; single; b. New Castle; Benjamin T. Amazeen (New Castle) and Sarah E. Frost (New Castle)

Fred A., d. 8/3/1954 at 72 in Portsmouth; police chief; single; b. NH; Granville Amazeen and Hattie Baker

George H., d. 11/2/1937 at 76/3/16 in Brentwood; harness maker; married; b. New Castle; George W.T. Amazeen (New Castle) and Lucy C. Amazeen (New Castle)

George W.T., d. 7/10/1929 at 72/6/8 in Brentwood; retired; widower; b. New Castle; William I. Amazeen (New Castle) and Lucretia Trefethen (New Castle)

Gerard Burton, d. 2/27/1983 at 73 in New Castle; Luther Amazeen and Marianne Gleavey

Granville A.N., d. 11/24/1919 at 61/3/19 in New Castle; laborer; married; b. New Castle; Edward B. Amazeen (New Castle) and Adaline Yeaton (New Castle)

James Henry, d. 12/18/1918 at 82/5/28 in Portsmouth; married

Jesse F., d. 6/19/1899 at 42/7/11 in New Castle; chronic gastric enteritis; housewife; married; b. New Castle; Benjamin Batson (New Castle) and Martha A. Locke (New Castle)

John, d. 9/25/1904 at 89/5 in Kittery, ME; old age; pilot; b. New Castle; William Amazeen (New Castle)

John T., d. 4/7/1915 at 74/3/20 in New Castle; drowning; shoemaker; single; b. New Castle; Abram Amazeen (New Castle, seaman) and Sarah A. Tucker (Portsmouth)

John William, d. 2/23/1923 at 80/2/13 in New Castle; pilot; married; b. New Castle; John Amazeen (New Castle) and Dorothy Neal (New Castle)

Joseph, d. 3/5/1915 at 83/3/8 in New Castle; arteriosclerosis; fisherman; single; b. New Castle; Benjamin Amazeen (New Castle, fisherman) and Lydia Payne (Kittery, ME)

Joseph S., d. 7/22/1934 at 73/5/4 in New Castle; barber; married; b. New Castle; Benjamin T. Amazeen (New Castle) and Sarah Frost (New Castle)

Lizzie, d. 1/29/1947 at 81/9/24 in Portsmouth; at home; widow; b. Rye; John C. Poole (Edgecomb, ME) and Angeline E. Caswell (Rye)

Lucinda S., d. 3/5/1895 at 82; widow; b. New Castle; Thomas B. Frost (New Castle) and Sarah E. ----- (New Castle)

Lucretia, d. 2/10/1892 at 78/6 in New Castle; housewife; widow; b. Monhegan, ME; father b. New Castle and mother b. Monhegan, ME

Luther, d. 4/30/1907 at 69/4/16 in Rye; accidental drowning; fisherman; married; b. New Castle; Benjamin Amazeen (New Castle, seaman) and Lydia Paine (Kittery, ME)

Luther M., d. 8/2/1944 at 73/10; farmer, fisherman; widower; b. New Castle; Luther Amazeen (New Castle) and Maryanna Hayford (New Castle)

Lydia, d. 2/14/1892 at 81 in New Castle; housewife; widow; b. Kittery, ME; father b. New Castle and mother b. Kittery, ME

Lydia J., d. 1/24/1934 at 91/0/28 in Portsmouth; at home; single; b. New Castle; Benjamin Amazeen (New Castle) and Lydia Payne (Kittery, ME)

Marianna, d. 5/16/1922 at 79/9/12 in Groveland, MA; widow; b. New Castle; Columbus Hayford (New Castle) and Savina Martin (New Castle)

Mary Olivia, d. 1/20/1926 at 81/5/19 in New Castle; at home; widow; b. New Castle; Charles Cole (ME) and Martha Kinnear (New Castle)

Mollie, d. 4/19/1911 at 40 in New Castle; tuberculosis; housewife; married; b. England; Timothy Gleary (Ireland) and Margaret Norton (England)

Nancy A., d. 8/11/1962 at 68 in Portsmouth; married; b. Providence, RI; Hesekiah Cook and Hattie Pierce

Octavia, d. 6/23/1892 at 53/9 in New Castle; housewife; married; b. New Castle; father and mother both b. New Castle

Orville C., d. 10/2/1942 at 57/9/14 in Portsmouth; married; b. New Castle; Charles B. Amazeen (New Castle) and Jessie F. Batson (New Castle)

Raymond, d. 5/20/1985 at 83 in Portsmouth; Luther M. Amazeen and
   Mollie Gleavy
Ruth W., d. 7/24/1950 at 45 in New Castle; at home; married; b.
   Kittery, ME; John S. Tilton and Edith Kendrick
Samuel B., d. 3/2/1895 at 77; married; b. New Castle; Ephraim
   Amazeen (New Castle) and Jane Bell (New Castle)
Sarah A., d. 5/14/1895 at 90/8; widow; b. Portsmouth; Henry Tucker
   (Portsmouth)
Stephen L., d. 7/13/1919 at 65/1/0 in New Castle; laborer; single; b.
   New Castle; William J. Amazeen (New Castle) and Lucretia
   Trefethen (New Castle)
William E., d. 9/2/1929 at 58/0/8 in Plainview, NY; married;
   Christopher Amazeen (New Castle)
William G., d. 5/12/1966 at 74 in Hampton Falls; widower; b. NH;
   Granville Amazeen and Harriett Baker
Winslow A., d. 1/24/1927 at 78/8/3 in New Castle; fisherman;
   widower; b. New Castle; William J. Amazeen (New Castle) and
   Lucretia Trefethen (ME)

ANDERSON,
Karoline H., d. 11/17/1952 at 72 in Portland, ME; at home; widow; b.
   Aalesund, Norway; Henry Blindheimsvig and Karen -----
Olof, d. 9/24/1937 at 62/6/29 in New York, NY; master mariner;
   married; b. Sweden

ARMSTRONG,
Leslie R., d. 7/7/1937 at 56/9/5 in Everett, MA; teamster; single; b.
   NS; George Armstrong

ARNOLD,
son, d. 11/30/1952 at 0/0/2 in Kittery, ME; b. Kittery, ME; Thomas S.
   Arnold and Agnes J. Allanson
Marvin, d. 9/21/1929 at -- in Portsmouth
William A., d. 8/10/1939 at -- in Portsmouth

ASPEN,

Bessie Mae, d. 8/26/1989 at 61 in Brentwood; Lucius McKenzie and Gertrude Watkins

Erik S., d. 8/11/1989 at 64 in Portland, ME; Erolf A. Aspen and Borghild I. Wold

Kirt, d. 12/3/1954 at 0/0/1 in Portsmouth; b. NH; Erik S. Aspen and Bessie McKenzie

AUDIBERT,

Natalie W., d. 10/17/1975 at 85 in Dover; William Whiting and Mary Allen

AYERS,

Penelope Virginia, d. 6/30/1931 at 79/11/12 in Portsmouth

BADGER,

Frances Whidden, d. 10/7/1994 in Portsmouth; b. 10/12/1903*

Marian M., d. 10/3/1985 at 86 in New Castle; Irving Mansfield and Ella Carver

Paul C., d. 6/3/1980 at 79 in Portsmouth; Charles Badger and Catherine Hutchinson

BAKER,

Adeline C., d. 5/24/1900 at 44/3 in New Castle; pluro pneumonia; single; b. New Castle; Joshua Baker and Catherine Pridham (New Castle)

Catherine L., d. 11/21/1904 at 88/4/1 in New Castle; valvular dis. of heart; housewife; widow; b. New Castle; Nathaniel Pridham (New Castle) and Mary Mitchell (New Castle)

Charles H., d. 8/1/1917 at 63/11 in New Castle; laborer; single; b. New Castle; Joshua Baker (New Castle) and Catherine Pridham (New Castle)

Edward B., d. 9/24/1920 at 56 in New Castle; laborer; divorced; b. North Andover, MA; George Baker and ----- Woodbury

Ellen A., d. 12/30/1944 in Kittery Point, ME; at home; widow; b. Kittery Point, ME; James Call (Kittery Point, ME) and Elizabeth Parry (Kittery Point, ME)

James, d. 5/30/1917 at 68/0/13 in New Castle; fisherman; single; b. New Castle; Joshua Baker (New Castle) and Catherine Pridham (New Castle)

James H., d. 3/27/1917 at 73/8/15 in New Castle; laborer; married; b. New Castle; James Baker (New Castle) and Abbie Martin (Dover, NH)

John, d. 12/19/1902 at 56/11/11 in New Castle; pulmonary tuber.; laborer; single; b. New Castle; Joshua Baker (New Castle) and Catharine Pridham (New Castle)

William L., d. 9/2/1904 at 58 in New Castle; heart disease; single; b. New Castle; Joshua Baker (New Castle) and Catherine Pridham (New Castle)

BAKETEL,

Helen Epler, d. 2/26/1967 at 61 in Portsmouth; married; b. MA; Percy H. Epler and Helen York

Marie, d. 8/18/1980 at 85 in Portsmouth; Thomas G. Barber and Frances Patterson

BANKS,

Ina Barclay, d. 7/21/1968 at 92 in New Castle; widow; b. Canada; Charles R. Barclay and Emma Morrison

BARBER,

Clara E. Hall, d. 3/29/1904 at 48/1/15 in New Castle; cancer uterus; housewife; married; b. New Castle; William H. Hall (New Castle) and Margaret Smith (Westport, NS)

Lydia A., d. 10/26/1896 at 43/6

Thomas H., d. 9/9/1940 at 87/2/1 in New Castle; coast gd., ret.; married; b. Boston, MA; William Barber (England) and Hannah Murphy (England)

BARCLAY,
Marion R., d. 8/1/1975 at 61 in New Castle; E. Florens Revinus and
Marion Martin

BARKER,
Gladys, d. 1/16/1985 at 95 in Portsmouth; William I. Haywood and
Jennie Haven Williams
William Haywood, d. 12/24/1961 at 47 in Wells, ME; married; b.
WA; Quentin J. Barker and Gladys Haywood

BARRON,
John F., d. 9/1/1982 at 67 in New Castle; John Barron and Margaret
Marnane

BARTON,
Pamela A., d. 7/21/1993 in Portsmouth; b. 2/7/1938*

BATCHELDER,
Cyrus P., d. 7/18/1933 at 71/2/15 in Shrewsbury, MA
Lois A., d. 2/10/1901 at 40/9/26 in New Castle; pulmonary
tuberculosis; housewife; married; b. New Castle; Thomas Rand
(Rye, farmer) and Adaline Twombly (New Castle)

BATSON,
Benjamin J., d. 4/21/1915 at 65/8/8 in Boston, MA; pulmonary
odemeis; mason; widower; b. New Castle; Benjamin Batson
(New Castle, seaman) and Martha A. Locke (New Castle)
Charlotte C., d. 7/26/1905 at 65/6 in New Castle; cancer; housewife;
b. New Castle; John Tarlton (New Castle) and Mary Amazeen
(New Castle)
Elizabeth J., d. 3/17/1913 at 57/6/10 in Boston, MA; bronchitis;
married
Florence G., d. 1/14/1945 at 73/4/11 in Newmarket; at home; widow;
b. So. Boston, MA; John C. Healey (E. Candia) and Adeline Kohr
(Boston, MA)

Mary L., d. 9/23/1895 at 79/5/28; widow; b. New Castle; William
Neal (New Castle) and Eunice Locke (New Castle)

Samuel, d. 10/20/1926 at 87/11/1 in New Castle; mason; widower; b.
New Castle; Samuel Batson (New Castle) and Mary Neal (New
Castle)

Samuel Elmer, d. 6/7/1933 at 71/9/14 in New Castle; pipe fitter;
married; b. New Castle; Samuel Batson (New Castle) and
Charlotte Tarlton (New Castle)

BAYLEY,

Delia, d. 9/26/1894 at 30 in Portsmouth; single

BEAL,

Rebecca R., d. 6/6/1904 at 85/8/21 in New Castle; cerebral
hemorrhage; housewife; widow; b. New Castle; Barnabus Yeaton
(New Castle, fisherman)

BEAUREGARD,

Roger M., d. 12/26/1976 at 20 in New Castle; Marcel M. Beauregard
and Rachel Poirier

BECKER,

Charles E., d. 3/8/1926 at 93/2/8 in New Castle; mariner; widower; b.
So. Berwick, ME; Henry Becker (Berlin, Germany) and Annie
Pray (Newington)

Charles H., d. 3/13/1940 at 81/3/8 in Portsmouth; married; b. New
Castle; Charles Becker (No. Berwick, ME) and Esther M. Brown
(Kittery, ME)

Chester Amazeen, d. 8/7/1959 at 81 in Portsmouth; widower; b. NH;
Henry Becker and Ellen Amazeen

Dorothy Miller, d. 4/10/1996 in Portsmouth; b. 10/8/1901*

Elizabeth S., d. 8/24/1951 at 82 in York, ME; at home; widow; b.
New Castle; Jothan Emery and Hannah Hubley

Ellen, d. 7/26/1915 at 44/8/13 in New Castle; cancer of pelvic organs;
housework; single; b. New Castle; Henry Becker (No. Berwick,
ME, fisherman) and Ellen Amazeen (New Castle)

Ester M., d. 1/26/1918 at 81/3/20 in New Castle; married; b. Kittery, ME; William Brown (Kittery, ME) and Ester Fernald (Kittery, ME)

Floyd O., d. 7/5/1906 at 3/7/11 in Portsmouth; f. body in bronchial tubes; single; b. New Castle; Chester A. Becker (New Castle, engineer) and Martha A. Amazeen (New Castle)

Forrest, d. 9/28/1933 at 72/10/15 in Kittery, ME; shoe salesman; married; b. Kittery, ME; Charles E. Becker (So. Berwick, ME) and Esther M. Brown (Kittery, ME)

Forrest L., d. 11/11/1962 at 75 in New Castle; married; b. New Castle; Charles Becker and Leona Ricker

Henry, Capt., d. 2/21/1911 at 80/0/15 in New Castle; chronic int. nephritis; fisherman; widower; b. No. Berwick, ME; Henry Becker (Berlin, Germany) and Annie Pray (No. Berwick, ME)

Henry, d. 3/12/1924 at 62 in New Castle; caretaker; married; b. New Castle; Henry Becker (No. Berwick, ME) and Ellen Amazeen (New Castle)

Henry, d. 1/26/1981 at 74 in Portsmouth; Chester A. Becker and Martha A. Amazeen

Leona J., d. 5/28/1945 at 78/9/21 in Newton, MA; at home; widow; b. New Castle; John Ricker (Lebanon, ME) and Mary ----- (Halifax, NS)

Mabel, d. 10/22/1930 at 63/7/5 in New Castle; at home; widow; b. New Castle; Sullivan H. White (New Castle) and Mary A. Oliver (New Castle)

Martha Batson, d. 7/29/1955 at 73 in Portsmouth; housewife; married; b. New Castle; Benjamin Amazeen and Jessie Batson

Martha E., d. 9/29/1937 at -- in Portsmouth; infant; b. Portsmouth; Henry Becker (New Castle) and Dorothy Shafner (Newburyport, MA)

Pauline Trafton, d. 1/28/1966 at 93 in New Castle; widow; b. ME; Thomas C. Blaisdell and Melvina Butterfield

Walter M., d. 1/21/1984 at 68 in Portsmouth; Forrest L. Baker and Laurel Miller

William Henry, d. 10/2/1934 at 48/11/22 in New Castle; secretary; single; b. Bridgeport, CT

BEHR,

Carl, Jr., d. 1/14/1948 at 74/1/15 in New Castle; agent; married; b. Roxbury, MA; Carl Behr (Boston, MA) and Ann Zallas

Florence Emily, d. 9/27/1965 at 85 in York, ME; widow; b. MA; Samuel Spyrvee and Emily S. Hooke

BELL,

Frederick, d. 6/30/ 1931 at 85 in Portsmouth; single; b. New Castle; Hannah Leach (England)

Mary M., d. 1/18/1897 at 56/7/14; married; b. New Castle; William Hall (Kittery, ME) and Margaret Yeaton (Kittery, ME)

BELMONT,

Joseph, d. 9/25/1938 at 43/5/22 in New Castle; lineman; married; b. Portsmouth; August Belmont (Switzerland) and Elsie M. McNamara (Ireland)

BERRY,

Frances Ada, d. 7/7/1963 at 83 in Portsmouth; widow; b. NY; Charles A. Mevlart and Luqueer Lawrence

John J., d. 4/24/1925 at 66/8/21 in New Castle; physician, retired; b. Litchfield, CT; Rev. Joshua D. Berry and Jane Belden

BICKFORD,

Albert Haven, d. 12/19/1917 at 66/4 in New Castle; mason; widower; b. New Castle; Joshua Bickford (New Castle) and Maria Vennard (New Castle)

Charlotte A., d. 4/13/1909 at 67/6/3 in Portsmouth; nephritis; b. New Castle; Thedore W. Frost (New Castle) and Eliza Priest (New Castle)

Fannie, d. 2/17/1940 at 88/11/29 in Lynn, MA

Frank Jones, d. 1/9/1965 at 80 in Portsmouth; widower; b. NH; John Bickford and Charlotte Frost

Harriet N., d. 12/29/1926 at 87/4/22 in Beverly, MA; widow; b. New Castle; Thomas Tarlton (New Castle) and Mary Vennard (New Castle)

J. Mahlon, d. 10/1/1914 at 76/3/12 in Portsmouth; chronic nephritis; US Navy Yard; married; b. New Castle; Joshua Bickford (New Castle, seaman) and Maria Vennard (New Castle)

Joshua, d. 10/14/1906 at 98 in New Castle; old age; seaman; widower; b. New Castle

Lizzie T., d. 5/11/1893 at 38/1; ahahus polanlus; housewife; married; b. New Castle; John V. White (New Castle, carpenter) and Miss Trefethen (New Castle)

Maria, d. 2/24/1895 at 81; married; b. New Castle; Zaccheus Vennard (New Castle) and Annie Roberts (New Castle)

Mary A., d. 9/26/1954 at 83 in Portsmouth; housewife; married; b. MA; John Lane and Gertrude -----

Melvin W., d. 4/2/1918 at 24/2/2 in Waterville, ME; single; Walter M. Bickford (New Castle) and Etta C. White (New Castle)

Myra Fernald, d. 11/28/1924 at 83/6/29 in New Castle; milliner (retired); single; b. New Castle; John Bickford (New Castle) and Hannah Butson (New Castle)

Walter M., d. 12/4/1912 at 49 in Brentwood; cancer on neck; shoemaker; married; b. New Castle; John W. Bickford (New Castle, shoemaker) and Charlotte A. Frost (New Castle)

Winfield Clarkson, d. 1/1/1928 at 22/5/13 in Portsmouth; clerk; single; Frank Bickford (New Castle) and ----- Tobey (Kittery, ME)

Zacheris, d. 5/19/1920 at 82/7/16 in Lynn, MA; shoemaker; married; b. New Castle; Joshua Bickford (New Castle) and Maria Venard (New Castlc)

BLAISDELL,

Annie M., d. 3/3/1936 at 80/6/28 in New Castle; at home; widow; b. Belmont, MA; Lucian Rowe (NH) and ----- Roberts (NH)

Clyde V., d. 10/11/1956 at 66 in New Castle; leadingman; married; b. NH; Hosea Blaisdell and Annie M. Rowe

Florence Mildred, d. 9/14/1959 at 69 in Portsmouth; widow; b. MA; Samuel E. Batson and Florence G. Healy

BLOOM,

Harry, d. 10/30/1937 at 58/11/10 in New Castle; janitor; married; b. Brooklyn, NY; Richard Bloom (England) and Cornelia Gross (NY)

BOGER,

Alberta M., d. 1/14/1983 at 86 in Portsmouth; Cyrus M. Boger and Bertha Forester

BOHLEY,

Lawrence J., d. 8/10/1973 at 33 in New Castle; married; b. NJ; Frederick W. Bohley and Lena Rossi

BOOMA,

Scott C., d. 4/5/1954 at 70 in Salem, MA; machinist; widower; b. NH; Frank E. Booma and Martha Fields

BOOTE,

Nancy H., d. 8/25/1991 at 70 in New Castle; Arthur Howe and Janet Rogers

BOPREE,

James C., d. 6/22/1940 at 50/7/7 in Portsmouth

BOWDOIN,

Colleen Marie, d. 7/3/1959 at 24 in Biddeford, ME; married; b. ME; Timothy Sullivan and Mary D. Soucy

BOYD,

Isabelle C., d. 8/15/1957 at 86 in No. Berwick, ME; at home; married; b. PEI; John Bears and Flora McSadden

Robert John, d. 5/13/1960 at 87 in Portsmouth; widower; b. MA; John Boyd and Frances Hamilton

BOYLSTON,

Joseph, d. 11/9/1934 at 68/9/28 in Hellgate; dentist; married; b. Duxbury, MA; Benjamin Boylston (Duxbury, MA) and Huldah Sprague (Duxbury, MA)

BRACKETT,

Emma P., d. 7/16/1965 at 72 in Portsmouth; widow; b. ME; William Gilmore and Margaret Broderick

Eugene A., d. 2/27/1953 at 66 in Exeter; prop. Gro. Store; married; b. ME; Charles Brackett and Elizabeth Piper

BRAGDON,

Marion A., d. 3/13/1967 at 48 in Portsmouth; married; b. VT

BRIDLE,

Florence E., d. 8/27/1991 at 83 in Portsmouth; Wendell Van Bubar and Celia Tilley

BRISKAY,

Albert A.C., d. 2/13/1979 at 86 in New Castle; Martin Briskay and Mary Redcalls

Laurel, d. 1/29/1980 at 87 in Portsmouth; Elizah Miller and Addie Dagget

BRITTON,

Jennie, d. 7/7/1941 at 73/3/27 in North Hampton; ret. store kpr.; single; b. Scotland; John Britton (Scotland) and Catherine McLane (Scotland)

BROOKS,

Frank E., d. 9/29/1973 at 82 in Portsmouth; married; b. MA; Frank O. Brooks and Alice Grant

M. Virginia, d. 4/15/1986 at 70 in New Castle; John R. Gamester and Josephine Coffey

BROWN,

Horace Alfred, d. 10/9/1973 at 74 in Portsmouth; married; b. NH; Horace D. Brown and Mary Ellen Miner

Louise A., d. 9/27/1932 at 83/3/16 in Portsmouth; widow; b. New Castle; Joshua Bickford (New Castle) and Maria ----- (New Castle)

Olive M., d. 8/13/1952 at 66 in Portsmouth; dressmaker; single; b. Needham, MA; William H. Brown and Louisa Maiers

BRUCE,

Mildred B., d. 3/12/1987 at 85 in Portsmouth; Walter Becker and Pauline T. Blaisdell

Robert Merritt, d. 2/7/1962 at 73 in New Castle; married; b. Lempster; John W. Bruce and Louella J. Lowell

BURTON,

Robert W., d. 1/30/1977 at 69 in Portsmouth; George L. Burton and Emma Woodworth

BURZYNSKI,

Carolyn S., d. 11/27/1984 at 74 in Portsmouth; Charles Cogswell Smith and Eunice Thomas

BUTTERWORTH,

Irving, d. 3/11/1963 at 77 in Portsmouth; widower; b. MA; Robert Butterworth and Clarissa Gibbs

CABANA,

John B., d. 3/16/1986 at 82 in Portsmouth; Frederick Cabana and Eugenie Bishop

John Bishop, Jr., d. 3/29/1967 at 27 in South Vietnam; John B. Cabana and Marilda T. LeDuc

Marilda T., d. 11/28/1991 at 86 in New Castle; Alfred LeDuc and Helen Robinson

CALLAHAN,

Frances Estelle, d. 10/31/1978 at 86 in Portsmouth; John Dow and
Dorothy Yeaton

Kenneth H., d. 9/29/1972 at 72 in Portsmouth; married; b. MA;
Howard R. Callahan and Florence Thayer

Marion K., d. 9/6/1931 at 41 in Norfolk, MA

CAMMETT,

Elizabeth, d. 4/2/1954 at 49 in Concord; housewife; b. NH; John H.
Low and Lena Caswell

CAMPBELL,

Bessie S., d. 6/12/1917 at -- in Portsmouth; b. Portsmouth; Henry
Campbell and Bessie Hubley (New Castle)

Bessie S., d. 11/10/1954 at 71 in Portsmouth; housewife; widow; b.
NH; Jacob Hubley and Sarah Martin

Charles E., d. 10/9/1908 at 76/1/13 in New Castle; valvular disease
heart; watchman; widower; b. New Castle; John Campbell (VA,
lighthouse keeper) and Elizabeth Card (New Castle)

Charles R., d. 5/25/1926 at 26 in Portsmouth; electrician; married; b.
New Castle; Henry E. Campbell (New Castle) and Rose
McCanon (Ireland)

Cora A., d. 6/28/1892 at 20/7 in New Castle; single; b. New Castle;
father and mother both b. New Castle

Elizabeth Thorne, d. 3/12/1959 at 81 in Portsmouth; single; b. PA;
Robert Campbell and Elizabeth MacArthur

Ellen S., d. 2/10/1949 at 79/3/23 in Kittery, ME; widow; b. Strafford

Ethel C., d. 6/17/1893 at 27/4; pentinitus; housewife; married; b.
Frankfort, ME; Ruel Butterfield (quarryman) and Lucy Catlin
(Damariscotta, ME)

Harry N., d. 6/25/1964 at 75 in Portsmouth; widower; b. MA; Eliot B.
Campbell and ----- MacDonald

Henry E., d. 7/12/1956 at 93 in New Castle; pipefitter; married; b.
New Castle; Charles E. Campbell and Sarah Porter

Henry S., d. 10/20/1914 at 12/3/14 in New Castle; peritonitis; b.
Portsmouth; Henry E. Campbell (New Castle, engineer) and Rose
McCarron (Ireland)

John, d. 3/24/1903 at 58 in Brentwood; terminal demiti; cook;
married; b. New Castle; John Campbell (New Castle)

Katherine E., d. 1/16/1996 in New Castle; b. 6/10/1906*

Lucy G., d. 12/7/1913 at 43/3/20 in Portsmouth; cerebral hemorrhage;
single; b. New Castle; Nathaniel P. Campbell (New Castle) and
Nancy G. Pridham

Luvia E., d. 9/8/1935 at 71/6/4 in Raymond; at home; married; b.
Hatley, Canada; John Knight (England)

Margaret L., d. 1/1/1973 at 57 in Exeter; single; b. DC; Harry
Campbell

Mary Ellen, d. 11/4/1960 at 72 in New Castle; married; b. MA; Daniel
Kiley and Honorah O'Neill

Mary Louise, d. 5/16/1927 at 3/6/8 in New Castle; b. Portsmouth;
Charles R. Campbell (New Castle) and Muriel White
(Portland, ME)

Muriel Jordan, d. 9/12/1993 in Dover; b. 7/5/1906*

Nancy G., d. 1/23/1908 at 68/4/3 in Portsmouth; pneumonia; widow;
b. New Castle; John Pridham (fisherman)

Rose I., d. 11/5/1962 at 90 in New Castle; widow; b. Ireland; Patrick
McCarron

Sarah E., d. 11/21/1904 at 71/3/25 in New Castle; disease of heart;
housewife; married; b. Hardwick, VT; John Porter (New Castle)
and Marinda Palmer (Warner)

Sarah J., d. 7/10/1924 at 27/3/10 in New Castle; stenographer; single;
b. New Castle; Henry E. Campbell (New Castle) and Rose L.
McCarron (Ireland)

Walter E., d. 8/13/1923 at 18/9/21 in New Castle; at school; single; b.
New Castle; Henry E. Campbell and Rose McCarron (Ireland)

Wentworth, d. 10/24/1953 at 43 in Rye; machinist; married; b. NH;
Henry Campbell and Rose McCarron

CARD,

Agnes Weston, d. 5/20/1915 at 31/9/7 in New Castle; sarcoma; none; single; b. New Castle; Charles A. Card (New Castle, stable keeper) and Nellie A. Emerson (New Castle)

Ambrose, d. 5/15/1914 at 76/1/15 in Kittery, ME; purulent cystitis; laborer; divorced; b. New Castle; James Card (New Castle, seaman) and Hipsey Card (New Castle)

Annie S., d. 9/25/1904 at 1/2/20 in Portsmouth; cholera infantum; b. Portsmouth

Charles A., d. 1/22/1906 at 52/2/5 in New Castle; cerebral hemorrhage; stable keeper; married; b. New Castle; Joshua K. Card (New Castle, lighthouse keeper) and Dorothy A. Beal (New Castle)

Hepsibah, d. 9/24/1893 at 90/0/18; old age; widow; b. New Castle; William Neal (New Castle, seaman) and Lucretia Bell (New Castle)

James W., d. 1/19/1913 at 82/6/25 in Portsmouth; nephritis; laborer; widower; b. New Castle; James Card (New Castle, seaman)

Joshua K., d. 6/5/1911 at 88/9/6 in Newburyport, MA; uraemia poisoning; light keeper; widower; b. New Castle

Lettie L., d. 4/21/1902 at -- in Portsmouth; meningitis; Elias Card (New Castle)

Lewis D., d. 8/1/1934 at 63/0/23 in Portsmouth; steam fitter, ret.; married; b. New Castle; Ambrose Card (New Castle) and Mary Davidson (New Castle)

Nellie A., d. 3/24/1941 at 81/6/17 in New Castle; at home; widow; b. New Castle; Nathaniel Emerson (Durham) and Sarah Chesley (Durham)

CARKIN,

Walter Reno, d. 5/22/1957 at 60 in Portsmouth; rigger, Navy Yard; widower; b. MA; Frank E. Carkin and Susie Potts

CARR,

Hannah E., d. 10/21/1914 at 64 in Haverhill, MA; cerebral hemorrhage; b. New Castle; Frederick Bell (seaman) and Hannah M. Leach

CARTER,

son, d. 7/18/1899 at 0/0/1 in New Castle; exhaustion; b. New Castle; William A. Carter (soldier, US Army) and Lulu C. Hatton

CASSO,

Alberta, d. 9/15/1983 at 54 in Portsmouth; Paul Babula and Caroline Archie

CASWELL,

Anna B., d. 9/27/1893 at 87; debility of age; widow; b. Rye; Reuben Marden (Rye, farmer) and Hannah Brown (Hampton)

Emma B., d. 11/22/1927 at 57 in Portsmouth; single; Oren Caswell and Lucia Amazeen (New Castle)

Josephine H., d. 11/30/1963 at 69 in Rye; married; b. ME; Wilford Trecartin and Mabel Hawkin

CELLIS,

Hubert, d. 8/22/1925 at 77/5/28 in New Castle; banker; widower; b. Germany

CHAPMAN,

Edna M., d. 7/14/1894 at 6 in New Castle; b. Cambridgeport, MA; Orville Chapman and Priscilla Amazeen

CHEEVER,

M. Eliza, d. 5/5/1911 at 80 in Portsmouth; gastritis

CHENEY,

Ruth Louise, d. 5/21/1963 at 58 in New Castle; married; b. NH; Wallace Junkins and Emma Manent

Warren E., d. 12/24/1963 at 64 in Mt. Holly, NJ; widower; b. NH; Arthur D. Cheney and Gertrude Emery

CHILDS,
Madeline F., d. 7/9/1978 at 88 in New Castle; Bert Fellows and Edith Warren

CLARE,
Wendell P., d. 5/24/1974 at 83 at Edgewood Manor; married; b. MA; James P. Clare and Sarah Belle Richards

CLARK,
Addie Meloon, d. 4/21/1959 at 82 in York, ME; widow; b. NH; James M. Meloon and Charlotte Campbell
Ethel Fottler, d. 1/22/1963 at 72 in Portsmouth; widow; b. MA; Edward W. Vose and Elizabeth Fottler
Evelyn, d. 11/27/1960 at 80 in Brentwood; single; b. VT; Gilman Clark and Emma Marston
Helen Mildred, d. 1/21/1966 at 62 in Brookline; married; b. MA; John E. Johnson and Anna Christopherson
Ralph Everett, d. 12/11/1958 at 84; married; b. ME; John Clark and Sarah Rogers
William W., d. 5/28/1951 at 75 in Portsmouth; salesman; married; b. Medford, MA; William F. Clark and Annie G. Head

CLAY,
Mercie, d. 8/27/1961 at 66 in York, ME; widow; b. MA; Edmund C. Tarbell and Emiline Souther

COBURN,
Louise B., d. 12/19/1971 at 69 in Portsmouth; widow; b. NH; William A. Bragdon and M. Elrita Remick

213

COLE,

Martha Martin, d. 6/17/1904 at 87/8 in New Castle; old age; housewife; widow; b. New Castle; Benjamin Cornelius (New Castle) and Dorcas Amazeen (New Castle)

COLEMAN,

Catherine, d. 8/10/1897 at 68/8/29; married; b. Portsmouth; James Rand (Portsmouth) and Sarah White (New Castle)

COLLINS,

Addie S., d. 12/4/1935 at 68/3/6 in New Castle; at home; widow; b. New Castle; Mark Simpson (New Castle) and Mary Ellen Yeaton (New Castle)

Luther P., d. 11/11/1912 at -7/8 in New Castle; tuberculosis; fisherman; married; b. Kittery, ME; Robert Collins (Kittery, ME) and Martha Blake

COLLITON,

child, d. 12/8/1938 at -- in Portsmouth; b. Ox; Frank L. Colliton (Malden, MA) and Alice L. Gilligan (Holyoke, MA)

Alice L., d. 4/6/1956 at 55 in Portsmouth; housewife; married; b. MA; Michael H. Gilligan and ----- Tierney

Frank Leo, Sr., d. 12/30/1972 at 81 in New Castle; married; b. MA; Hugh Colliton and Helen Waite

CONNER,

Olivia Cook, d. 2/14/1956 at 85 in New Castle; housewife; married; b. ME; Silas Cook and Lydia Briggs

Perry Enoch, d. 6/24/1963 at 86 in New Castle; widower; b. NH; Enoch Conner and Adelaide Pease

CONOVER,

Charlotte C., d. 1/13/1991 at 85 in Portsmouth; Courtney Conover and Mae Sears

Jewel H., d. 8/15/1974 at 71 in New Castle; single; b. NJ; Courtney Conover and May Eichorn

CONRAD,

Ruth V., d. 6/10/1985 at 79 in Greenfield, MA; William Vlachos and Ruth Mitchel

CONROY,

Annie M., d. 2/21/1964 at 83 in Portsmouth; widow; b. NH; Franklin Penney and ----- Blood

COPLEY,

James Riley, d. 10/12/1968 at 78 in Chelsea, MA; married; b. KY; James Copley and Mildred Patterson

Joseph Patrick, d. 10/4/1990 at 62 in Portsmouth; James Copley and Theresa Joyce

Theresa B., d. 11/3/1977 at 83 in Portsmouth; John Joyce and Catherine Gannon

COSTELLO,

Catherine, d. 7/5/1928 at 74/10/19 in Newburyport, MA; b. Ireland

Thomas F., d. 4/9/1967 at 56 in Portsmouth; married; b. MA; Alexander Costello and Delia O'Toole

COTTON,

Fred P., d. 7/21/1902 at 21 in New Castle; Bright's disease; clerk; single; b. New Castle; William W. Cotton (Portsmouth, merchant) and Anna Moses (Portsmouth)

William W., d. 8/17/1923 at 79/10/15 in New Castle; hardware merchant; married; b. Portsmouth; Leonard Cotton (Portsmouth) and Martha Clarkson

COUSINS,

Francis Joseph, d. 2/21/1958 at 76; widower; b. NH; Francis Cousins and Mary Gallagher

Gertrude J., d. 7/12/1932 at 56/5/28 in New Castle; at home; married; b. Rye; Woodbury Jenness (Rye) and Mary Poole (Gloucester, MA)

CREED,
Maynard E., d. 10/29/1962 at 64 in Portsmouth; divorced; b. Boston, MA; Edward Creed and Anna B. MacKenzie

CROSBY,
Irene G.M.A., d. 11/16/1994 in Rye; b. 5/13/1894*

CULL,
Francis, d. 4/29/1969 at 60 in New Castle; single; b. RI; James F. Cull and Josephine B. Cramer

CULLEN,
Charles E., Sr., d. 9/6/1964 at 74 in Portsmouth; widower; b. NH; William Cullen and Catherine Flynn
Charles Thomas, d. 1/18/1987 at 66 in Portsmouth; Charles Thomas Cullen and Anna Kelliher

CUMMINS,
Anna, d. 4/15/1925 at 46 in New Castle; at home; married; b. Ireland; James Coyne (Ireland) and Mary Nash (Ireland)

CURTIS,
Benjamin F., d. 2/10/1936 at 78/5/6 in New Castle; painter; married; b. New Castle; Moses R. Curtis (New Castle) and Sarah J. Amazeen (New Castle)
Chester B., d. 6/18/1931 at 65/0/3 in St. Louis, MO; married; b. New Castle; Howard M. Curtis (New Castle) and Lucretia Bickford (New Castle)
Ellen A., d. 8/29/1948 at 91/0/10 in Portsmouth; at home; widow; b. New Castle; John V. White (New Castle) and Miriam Trefethen (New Castle)
Howard M., d. 1/9/1916 at 80/6/28 in New Castle; retired; married; b. New Castle; Thomas Curtis (New Castle) and Catherine Berry (Portsmouth)

Lucretia V., d. 4/17/1928 at 88/6/12 in Milton; at home; widow; b.
New Castle; Capt. John Vennard (New Castle) and Hannah
Batson (New Castle)

Moses Ricker, d. 7/12/1901 at 68/0/10 in New Castle; cerebral
hemorrhage; rigger; married; b. New Castle; Thomas Curtis
(New Castle) and Catherine Berry (Portsmouth)

Roy H., d. 2/8/1943 at 65/1/28 in Brentwood; ret. laborer; single; b.
Boston, MA; Charles Curtis (New Castle) and Harriet Tarlton
(New Castle)

Sarah Jane, d. 1/5/1928 at 93/6/6 in New Castle; at home; widow; b.
New Castle; William Amazeen (New Castle) and Lucretia
Trefethen (ME)

CURTISS,
Malcolm Tucke, d. 3/21/1992 at 77 in New Castle

CUSKLEY,
Mary E., d. 7/6/1938 at 66/2/7 in New Castle; at home; married; b.
Portsmouth; Leander White (New Castle) and Elizabeth Murphy
(New Castle)

CUTHBERT,
Marion C., d. 4/2/1954 at 54 in New Castle; housewife; married; b.
VA; George E. Banks and Anna Creswell

DALE,
Margaret Ann, d. 11/20/1976 at 49 in Portsmouth; Francis E. Bean
and Edna May Driscoll

Thomas Marvin, d. 6/29/1965 at 44 in Portsmouth; married; b. MA;
Charles M. Dale and Marion Marvin

DAMON,
Newcomb L., d. 9/29/1969 at 82 in Kittery, ME; married; b. MA;
Newcomb L. Damon and Amelia R. Snow

DANA,

Olive L., d. 9/16/1917 at 74/10/20 in New Castle; at home; widow; b. New Castle; William L. Neale (New Castle) and Abigail Hauch (Portsmouth)

DAVIDSON,

Florinda, d. 9/16/1958 at 92; single; b. NH; James Davidson and Mary Rand

George Harris, d. 5/--/1924 at 61 in New Castle; carpenter; widower; b. New Castle; Ralph Davidson (New Castle) and Lucretia Harris (New London, CT)

James, d. 6/1/1908 at 76 in Boston, MA; cerebral hemorrhage; seaman; widower; b. New Castle; James Davidson (England, soldier) and Ann T. ----- (New Castle)

John, d. 7/19/1934 at 73/7/17 in Portsmouth; retired mariner; single; b. New Castle; James Davidson (New Castle) and Mary Rand (Kittery, ME)

Josephine O., d. 7/7/1919 at 57/4/24 in New Castle; at home; married; b. NS; William Ord (NS) and Jane Hazelton (NS)

Lillian, d. 4/12/1968 at 83 in Deerfield; widow; b. NH; Charles Drowne and Sarah -----

Lucretia L., d. 11/5/1905 at 69/6/27 in New Castle; cerebral hemorrhage; housewife; married; b. New London; George Harris (New London) and Frances Lewis (New London)

Mary, d. 11/3/1898 at 63/2/14 in New Castle; chronic interstitial nephritis; housewife; married; b. Kittery, ME; Samuel Rand (Rye) and Sarah Dixon (Eliot, ME)

Thomas, d. 8/15/1951 at 92 in Portsmouth; fisherman; married; b. New Castle; Ralph Davidson and Lutricia Harris

DAVIS,

Harry L., d. 6/24/1940 at 72/4/5 in New Castle; bank treas.; married; Charles Davis (NH) and Betsy Wentworth (NH)

DAY,

Gordon A., d. 2/26/1936 at 29/2/9 in Portsmouth; truck driver; married; b. Essex, MA; Wallace H. Day (Essex, MA) and Bessie Haywood (Essex, MA)

DEANE,

Albert S., Jr., d. 9/27/1986 at 75 in Midland, MI

DEARBORN,

Carrie S., d. 10/28/1924 at 80/8/16 in New Castle; at home; widow; b. No. Hampton; Jeremiah Batchelder (No. Hampton) and Caroline M. Chesley (Lee)

DECKER,

Ellen, d. 8/15/1897 at 58/10/22; married; b. New Castle; John Amazeen (New Castle) and Dorothy Neal (New Castle)

DECOFF,

John W., d. 10/15/1913 at 77/11/9 in Leominster, MA; senility; married

Margaret Frances, d. 3/19/1926 at 87/2/16 in New Castle; at home; widow; b. New Castle; Capt. Elias Tarlton (New Castle) and Ann J. Yeaton (New Castle)

DECOURCY,

John Henry, III, d. 7/4/1994 in Portsmouth; b. 7/8/1906*

Ruth H., d. 4/3/1987 at 77 in Portsmouth; Joseph Hassett and Delia Casey

DEHUE,

Wilhelminia, d. 1/3/1946 at 37/4/27 in So. Eliot, ME; at home; married; b. Portland, ME; Archie Cochrane (Concord, MA) and Wilhelminia Willard (So. Portland, ME)

DELANEY,

Josephine M., d. 8/25/1912 at -- in Halifax, NS; perforation of
stomach

DENNETT,

Frank M., d. 12/12/1947 at 92/0/26 in New Castle; retired; widower;
b. Portsmouth; William H. Dennett (NH) and Mary E. Robertson
(NH)

DESJARDIN,

Amedes, d. 8/14/1929 at 48/8/12 in New Castle; shoe salesman; b.
Farnham, Canada; Ferdinand Des Jardin (Canada) and Anestasie
Pelletier (Canada)

DESMOND,

Virginia, d. 4/19/1973 at 59 in Dover; widow; b. RI; Arthur Decosta
and Elizabeth M. Daly

DICKSON,

Thomas, d. 5/12/1951 at 75 in Portsmouth; laborer; widower; b.
Scotland; William Dickson

DOANE,

Louise C., d. 4/14/1932 at 84/11/10 in Merrimac, MA; widow; b.
New Castle; Robert White (New Castle) and Elizabeth Batson
(New Castle)

DODD,

Edwin M., d. 11/3/1951 at 63 in New Castle; prof. of laws; married;
b. Providence, RI; Edwin Dodd and Ellen Teffany
Winifred H., d. 11/3/1951 at 72 in New Castle; at home; married; b.
Milwaukee, WI; Stephen D. Hyde and Lucy A. Stunn

DODGE,

Anna R., d. 8/21/1931 at 84/2/7 in Portsmouth
Eugene Rogers, d. 3/18/1929 at 82/4/8 in Kittery, ME

DOE,

Dorothy Becker, d. 1/30/1995 in New Castle

Lillian M., d. 2/20/1929 at 64/0/18 in Westborough, MA; widow; b. New Castle; Ephraim Urch (London, England) and Arabella Vennard (New Castle)

DOW,

Alice L., d. 2/3/1980 at 73 in Exeter; William H. Pridham and Jane Condon

Dorothy Meloon, d. 12/2/1927 at 57/10/21 in Portsmouth; married; b. New Castle; Nathaniel B. Yeaton (New Castle) and Louise Meloon (New Castle)

John T., d. 7/25/1942 at 72/8/17 in Portsmouth

DREW,

Josephine Inez, d. 11/20/1961 at 80 in Portsmouth; married; b. MA; Robert Aldrich and Lizzie Lang

William Garvin, d. 1/1/1968 at 89 in Portsmouth; widower; b. ME; Thomas Drew and Anna -----

DRINKER,

Pemberton Hutchinson, d. 6/21/1987 at 66 in Exeter; Henry S. Drinker and Sophie Hutchinson

DROWNE,

Charles Sawyer, d. 7/4/1935 at 77/2/12 in New Castle; retired sailmaker; widower; b. Charlestown, MA; Charles W. Drowne (Portsmouth) and Mary Ann Hall (VT)

Maude S., d. 9/11/1936 at 50/3/3 in New Castle; at home; single; b. Portsmouth; Charles S. Drown (Charlestown, MA) and Sarah Alton (Portsmouth)

DUGGER,

Brenda, d. 10/23/1976 at 14 in New Castle; Harley Dugger and Georgiana Kilgore

DUNN,

Walter K., d. 12/30/1956 at 69 in New Castle; colonel USA; married; b. VA; Beverly W. Dunn and Stella Kilshaw

DURAND,

Frances M., d. 2/13/1978 at 44 in Exeter; Gordon Young and Mary Ordiorne

DURGIN,

John, d. 12/13/1899 at 85/8/17 in Portsmouth; old age; schoolmaster; married; b. Strafford; Samuel Durgin (Strafford) and Susan Sewards (Strafford)

Louise A., d. 9/4/1902 at 78/1/2 in Portsmouth; apoplexy; housewife; widow; b. New Castle

DURKEE,

Grace, d. 2/6/1940 at 75 in Haverhill, MA; Alexander White and Sarah E. Martin

DWYER,

Ambrose R., d. 3/26/1984 at 81 in Portsmouth; John O'Dwyer and Mary Hanrahan

Nicholas J., d. 1/13/1953 at 73 in New Castle; fireman, navy yard; married; b. Ireland; Patrick Dwyer and Mary Morrissey

Sarah Agnes, d. 12/12/1966 at 82 in Bellows Falls, VT; widow; b. NH; Charles Eastman and Mary Jane Libby

EAGLETON,

Wells P., d. 9/11/1946 at 80/11/23 in New Castle; doctor; married; b. Brooklyn, NY; Thomas P. Eagleton and Mary E. Phillips (NY)

EASTLER,

William Edmund, Jr., d. 10/3/1992 at 52 in New Castle

EASTMAN,
Susan T., d. 2/2/1905 at 76/11/13 in New Castle; bronchitis, insanity; widow; b. Camden, ME; Jacob Trussell (Camden, ME) and Sarah Wood (Camden, ME)

EATON,
Elmer E., d. 3/29/1948 at 82/9/25 in Portsmouth; plumber; married; b. Wells, ME; Samuel Eaton (Wells, ME) and Mary Hatch (Wells, ME)
Susan R., d. 10/27/1952 at 88 in Portsmouth; at home; widow; b. Brunswick, ME; Capt. James Sylvester and Julia A. Raymond

EISLER,
Bela D., d. 8/10/1949 at 78 in New Castle; lawyer; married; b. NY; Maurice Eisler and Katherine Scharles

ELDERS,
daughter, d. 12/23/1911 at 6 hrs. in New Castle; b. New Castle; John H. Elders (Atlanta, GA, Sergeant, USDA) and Edith Ramsdell (Greenland)

EMERSON,
Sarah R., d. 2/10/1902 at 81/0/26 in New Castle; arteris sclerosis; housewife; widow; b. Durham; James Chesley and Sarah Reynolds

EMERY,
Elias J., d. 8/2/1927 at 61/7/21 in Danvers, MA; married; Jotham Emery (Biddeford, ME) and Hannah Hubley (NS)
Elizabeth J., d. 4/28/1954 at 85 in Portsmouth; housewife; widow; b. NH; William H. Horn and Mary A. Randall
Hannah, d. 7/22/1892 at 45/10 in New Castle; housewife; married; b. NS; father and mother both b. NS
Jonathan, d. 2/5/1913 at 74/11/7 in New Castle; pneumonia; laborer; married; b. Biddeford, ME; Jotham Emery (Biddeford, ME, laborer) and Sarah Cummines (Saco, ME)

Josephine P., d. 6/22/1937 at 65/10/11 in New Castle; at home; married; b. Stark, ME; Moses Piper (Stark, ME) and Marie Mosher (Harrison, ME)

Jotham, d. 10/20/1916 at 76/6/11 in New Castle; married; b. Biddeford, ME; Jotham Emery (Biddeford, ME) and Sarah Cummings (Saco, ME)

Julia A., d. 10/13/1895 at 70/6/1; widow; b. York, ME; William Fernald (York, ME) and Elizabeth Payne (York, ME)

Louisa S., d. 5/6/1918 at 74/8/19 in New Castle; widow; b. New Castle; Joshua Baker (New Castle) and Catherine Pridham (New Castle)

Martha E., d. 8/24/1899 at 83/7 in New Castle; peritonitis; widow; b. Portsmouth; Andrew W. Bell (Portsmouth) and Elizabeth B. Manning (Portsmouth)

Rufus J., d. 11/6/1952 at 74 in New Castle; mech. Helper; widower; b. New Castle; Jonathan Emery and Louisa Straw

ERNEST,
daughter, d. 4/19/1909 at 0/0/0 in New Castle; b. New Castle; Jetta W. Ernest (OH) and Alice L. Meloon (New Castle)

FARNSWORTH,
Maynard, d. 4/30/1944 at 50/8/20 in Kittery, ME; USCG; married; b. Jonesport, ME; Bryant Farnsworth (Jonesport, ME) and Lillian Farnsworth (Jonesport, ME)

FAY,
Roberta M., d. 9/6/1984 at 89 in Portsmouth; George G. Miller and Minnie G. Stowe

FELLOWS,
James Gilman, d. 7/31/1916 at 77/11/25 in New Castle; b. Deerfield; Jeremiah Fellows (Deerfield)

FERNALD,
Sophia L., d. 9/5/1911 at 52/4/16 in New Castle; tuberculosis and pneumonia; married; b. Manchester, MA; Capt. Thomas Hannabile (Englnad) and Mary Ayers (Manchester, MA)

FINN,
Ann Jane Theiler, d. 9/7/1994 in New Castle; b. 10/3/1925*
Mary Patricia, d. 4/26/1958 at 0/2/1; b. ME; Philip P. Finn and Ann Jane Theiler
Philip Patrick, d. 6/21/1994 in Portsmouth; b. 6/24/1918*

FLANDERS,
Clydie Mildred, d. 12/18/1914 at 40/8/22 in New Castle; disease of spleen; school teacher; single; b. New Castle; Stephen H. Flanders (Alton, stone cutter) and Mary Locke (New Castle)
Mary K., d. 10/2/1903 at 52/0/7 in Pembroke; apoplexy; housewife; married; b. New Castle; John Locke (New Castle, farmer) and Sarah Trefethen (New Castle)
Roy P., d. 3/1/1943 at 55/7/20 in Portsmouth; chief, fire dept.; widower; b. New Castle; Simeon C. Flanders (Suncook) and Sarah Jane Yeaton (New Castle)
Sarah Jane, d. 8/22/1931 at 77/3/21 in New Castle; at home; widow; b. New Castle; William J. Yeaton (New Castle) and Miriam Amazeen (New Castle)
Simeon C., d. 8/9/1912 at --/3/19 in New Castle; cirrhosis of liver; married; b. Alton; Dyer Flanders (Alton) and Serene G. Dudley (Alton)

FLETCHER,
daughter, d. 12/24/1964 at 0/0/0 in Portsmouth; b. NH; Royce Fletcher and Eleanor Marvin

FLYNN,
Elizabeth, d. 4/13/1901 at 28/8 in New Castle; diabetes; housewife; married; Angus McDonald (England) and Elizabeth ----- (England)

James W., d. 5/15/1892 at 68/1 in New Castle; shoemaker; widower

William L., d. 1/21/1922 at 71/10/15 in New Castle; shipfitter; widower; b. New Castle; James Flynn and Martha Yeaton

FOURNIER,

Nellie C., d. 12/20/1953 at 77 in Eliot, ME; seamstress; divorced; b. NH; Eli Sherman and Barbara A. Clark

FOWLER,

David E., d. 1/18/1940 at 51/6/6 in Medford, MA; electrician; married; b. Waltham, MA; Josiah Fowler (St. John, NB) and Emma L. Bourne (Charlestown, MA)

FREE,

son, d. 4/6/1916 at 0/0/0 in New Castle; b. New Castle; Vern Free (Williamsport, PA) and Cora M. Collins (New Castle)

Harry Verne, d. 1/22/1915 at 0/0/21 in New Castle; premature birth; b. New Castle; Verne Free (PA, soldier) and Cora M. Collins (New Castle)

FRENCH,

Geraldine M., d. 5/15/1949 at 17 in Alton; com. laundry; single; b. Laconia; W. F. French (Columbia, ME) and Isabel I. Bunker (Gaze, VT)

Sonia Adelaie, d. 11/10/1957 at 31 in Portsmouth; at home; married; b. NY; Erolf Aspen and Borghild Wald

FROBISHER,

Margaret R., d. 2/12/1978 at 80 in Portsmouth; George W. Bryan and Sarah Urry

Ralph S., d. 8/7/1969 at 70 in Portsmouth; married; b. NJ; Joseph E. Frobisher and Emma Ferris

FROST,

Addie M., d. 10/28/1927 at 74/8/30 in Medford, MA; retired; b. New Castle; Abram Bell (New Castle) and Mary Hall (New Castle)

Susan M., d. 3/19/1926 at 80/11/21 in Pepperell, MA
Theodore W., d. 1/19/1905 at 69/10 in Portsmouth; strangulated
hernia; widower; b. New Castle; Theodore W. Frost

GARLAND,
Elizabeth W., d. 12/11/1936 at 76/5/11 in Haverhill, MA; Leander
Garland (New Castle) and Ann L. Yeaton (New Castle)
Leander, d. 10/2/1902 at 72/0/6 in Haverhill, MA; apoplexy;
carpenter; married; b. New Castle

GARVIN,
Clarence, d. 3/9/1928 at 65 in Boston, MA; b. Acton, ME; John
Garvin (New Castle) and Ann White (Acton, ME)
Elizabeth May, d. 12/25/1929 at 59/7/24 in Salem, MA; milliner;
single; b. Acton, ME; John A. Garvin (Acton, ME) and Ann B.
White (New Castle)
John, d. 10/30/1904 at 79 in Danvers, MA; arteria selerians gan.

GAVIN,
Celia T., d. 3/11/1990 at 82 in Portsmouth; Chester Williams and
Mabel Pridham

GEANOULIS,
Anne Fox, d. 11/8/1993 in Exeter; b. 6/1/1928*

GEKAS,
Sophia, d. 2/7/1988 at 90 in Portsmouth; George Angelicas and Maria
-----

GERRIER,
Arthur J., d. 10/15/1990 at 35 in Portsmouth; Arthur J. Gerrier, Sr.
and Barbara McDonald

GETMAN,
James H., d. 2/7/1978 at 32 in New Castle; John Getman and
Geraldine Gelen

GFROERER,

Alice, d. 7/19/1975 at 67 in Portsmouth; Arthur M. Farrand and Helen
Pennell

Rudolph, d. 11/24/1977 at 81 in Milton, MA; Daniel Gfroerer and
Emily Kammler

GILBRIDE,

Alice, d. 8/8/1896 at 1/6

GILES,

Charles H., d. 11/23/1925 at 92/11/26 in New Castle; teamster,
retired; married; b. Lawrence, MA; Daniel Giles (Barrington) and
Alvira Willey (Durham)

Martha A.H., d. 12/12/1925 at 90/1/4 in New Castle; at home; widow;
b. Portsmouth; Thomas Haywood (London, England) and
Abagail Berry (ME)

GILKEY,

Jean Neal, d. 3/13/1962 at 82 in North Hampton; widow; b.
Philadelphia, PA; Robert Campbell and Elizabeth MacArthur

GILL,

Elizabeth W.R., d. 10/23/1945 at 27/5/1 in Portsmouth; at home;
married; b. W. Medford, MA; Frank H. Remick (Kittery, ME)
and Myrtis Becker (New Castle)

GILLIAM,

Claude C., d. 8/3/1918 at 28/1/12 in New Castle; inspector; married;
b. Yale, VA; Joseph L. Gilliam (Yale, VA)

GILLIS,

Isaac, d. 1/21/1929 at 77/5/12 in Rye; retired; widower; b. St. John,
NB

GLASSMEYER,

Elizabeth Fellows, d. 9/6/1982 at 67 in New Castle; James W. Fellows and Marion Floyd

GLIDDEN,

Earl W., d. 10/17/1982 at 70 in Portsmouth; James W. Glidden and Haddie Davis

Gary Earl, d. 9/20/1962 at 19 in Anchorage, AK; single; b. Portsmouth; Earl W. Glidden and Norma Reed

GLOVER,

Albert M., d. 8/15/1938 at 75/1/4 in New Castle; real est. dlr.; widower; b. Brooklyn, NY; Austin H. Glover (Danbury, CT) and Fanny Betts (Derby, CT)

GOODEY,

Martha E., d. 9/17/1935 at 84/2/20 in New Castle; at home; widow; b. Boston, MA; William Kohr (Philadelphia, PA) and Martha Linton (Boston, MA)

GOODWIN,

Charles R., d. 11/29/1931 at 77/1/21 in Portsmouth; ret. rigger; married; b. NS; ----- Goodwin (NS) and Nancy ----- (NS)

Williamena, d. 12/4/1957 at 84 in Portsmouth; at home; widow; b. NS; Dan MacKinnon and Ann Bain

GORDON,

Helen R., d. 4/23/1983 at 64 in Portsmouth; John Berner and Helen Wiseman

GRADY,

James Bizzell, d. 3/10/1972 at 62 in Kittery, ME; married; b. NC; James Bizzel Grady and Florence Herring

GRANT,

Sara Louise, d. 11/24/1990 at 81 in Portsmouth; Willard Emerson Grant and May McDuffee

GRAY,

Agnes McNamara, d. 11/25/1972 at 67 in Portsmouth; married; b. MA; Thomas McNamara and Mary Jennings

Frederick S., d. 8/23/1982 at 79 in Portsmouth; Charles W. Gray and Sarah Roberts

Horace W., d. 12/10/1945 at 86/4/22 in New Castle; meat cutter; widower; b. Portsmouth; William H. Gray (Portsmouth) and Ellen Leach (Portsmouth)

Kathleen B., d. 9/21/1985 at 78 in Portsmouth; John Berry and Frances Meylert

Walter S., d. 7/30/1981 at 80 in Portsmouth; Edwin W. Gray and Pearl Seavey

GREEN,

Annie M., d. 6/23/1919 at 79/11/16 in Lynn, MA

Ephraim, d. 10/17/1895 at 83/7/3; widower; b. Greenland; John Green (Rye) and ----- Nutter (Portsmouth)

Louis Lawrence, d. 7/19/1973 at 92 in New Castle; widower; b. NH; Ephraim Green and Leah Felleman

Mary Kinnear, d. 3/2/1895 at 78/6; married; b. New Castle; Benjamin White (New Castle) and Elizabeth Martin

Robert White, d. 4/5/1909 at 69/10/15 in New Castle; angina pectoris; married; b. New Castle; Ephriam Green (Greenland) and Mary Kinnear (New Castle)

Virginia T., d. 8/7/1950 at 68 in New Castle; at home; married; b. Boston, MA; John A. Tanner and Caroline Littlefield

GREENBERG,

Henry, d. 3/6/1993 in Portsmouth; b. 7/6/1905*

Mary T., d. 10/16/1967 at 59 in Portsmouth; married; b. MA; Michael Toomey and Catherine McCarthy

GREENE,

Edith M., d. 6/18/1951 at 79 in New London; at home; widow; b.
  Quebec; James Mills and Eliza Hume

Fred P., d. 1/3/1938 at 68/7/18 in New Castle; clerical work; married;
  b. New Castle; Robert Greene (New Castle) and Annie A.
  Lerman (Portsmouth)

Sarah T., d. 1/16/1917 at 85/10/11 in Boston, MA; widow; b. So.
  Berwick, ME; William A. Tompson (So. Berwick, ME) and Anna
  M. Adams

GREER,

Frances, d. 10/17/1950 at 43 in Portsmouth; at home; single; Franklin
  H. Greer and Gertrude L. Flint

GRENIER,

Sarah, d. 2/22/1948 at 26/2 in Portland, ME; married; b. New Castle;
  Stephen Wargo and Jessie Meloon (New Castle)

GRIER,

Gertrude L., d. 10/9/1949 at 73 in New Castle; at home; widow; b.
  Andover, MA; John H. Flint and Frances A. Tyer

GRIFFIN,

Arnold Henry, d. 4/14/1961 at 48 in New Castle; married; b. NH;
  William Griffin and C. Adeline Hughes

Dorothea D., d. 5/18/1985 at 72 in Portsmouth; Clarence Drew and
  Stella Grace

GRIGG,

Annie R., d. 1/15/1949 at 56 in Portsmouth; housekeeper; widow; b.
  New Castle; Jacob Hubley (Spry Harbor, NS) and Sarah Martin
  (New Castle)

Robert I., d. 9/19/1947 at 78/11/3 in Concord; RR foreman; married;
  b. PEI; Edward B. Grigg and Eleanor Ramsay (PEI)

GROGAN,

David R., d. 1/21/1902 at 64/1 in Ponce Park, FL; apoplexy; seaman; married; David Grogan (Eastport, ME) and Lucy Holbrook (New Castle)

Herbert L., d. 1/6/1946 at 81/6/15 in New Castle; retired; married; b. New Castle; David R. Grogan (New Castle) and Lydia Bickford (New Castle)

Lydia A., d. 11/27/1925 at 88/3/12 in New Castle; at home; widow; b. New Castle; Joseph Bickford (New Castle) and Mary Amazeen (New Castle)

Mary E., d. 3/19/1948 at 77/0/8 in Portsmouth; single; b. New Castle; David Grogan (Portsmouth) and Lydia Bickford (New Castle)

GROSSE,

Patricia, d. 8/29/1979 at 32 in New Castle; Joseph Cronin

GROTON,

Miriam E., d. 8/6/1997 in New Castle; b. 12/5/1920*

Robert E., d. 12/26/1949 at 62 in York, ME; married; b. Augusta, ME

Ruth E., d. 10/23/1981 at 89 in Portsmouth; Winfield Gray and Evelyn Trafton

GROVER,

Rogers D., d. 1/12/1988 at 77 in New Castle; Charles Grover and Frances Dimmoch

GUEX-WALKER,

Marc Francois, d. 5/1/1986 at 19 in New Castle; Henry Guex and Wendy Walker

GUPTILL,

Ellen H., d. 4/6/1977 at 78 in Portsmouth; George H. Hoitt and Lura M. Sleeper

Eva Mahala, d. 6/12/1961 at 67 in No. Hampton; married; b. MA; George Manson and Lillian Furbish

Mary Davis, d. 4/19/1931 at 70/11/4 in Springfield, MA; housewife; widow; b. Lubec, ME; Harman Davis (Lubec, ME) and Sophia Dinsmore (Lubec, ME)

William B., d. 4/9/1928 at 72/2/24 in W. Springfield, MA; ret. C.G. surfman; b. Lubec, ME; Oliver Guptill (Lubec, ME) and Lizzie Myers (Lubec, ME)

William Benjamin, d. 3/22/1962 at 72 in Portsmouth; married; b. Charlestown, MA; William Guptill and Mary Davis

GUSNOLD,
Samuel K., d. 8/3/1903 at 59 in New Castle; dilatation heart; merchant; married; b. Whitehall, NY; Isaac Gusnold and Eliza G.H. -----

HAINES,
Charles Siders, d. 8/17/1926 at 66/11/27 in New Castle; real estate; married; b. Bradys Bend, PA; John Hatch Haines (Portsmouth) and Jane McCleary (OH)

HALL,
child, d. 1/1/1916 at 0/0/13 in Portsmouth

Abbie N., d. 1/12/1914 at 75/7/17 in Boston, MA; intestinal obstruction; married; b. New Castle; George O. Neal (New Castle, mariner) and Abigail Ordiorn (Rye)

Andrew J., d. 9/19/1931 at 91/2/15 in Laconia; b. New Castle; William Hall (Rye) and Margaret ----- (New Castle)

Annie M., d. 4/3/1911 at 48/1/25 in New Castle; chronic int. nephritis; single; b. New Castle; John Hall (New Castle, pilot) and Annie M. Linscott (Somersworth)

Benjamin H., d. 3/30/1905 at 66/5/15 in Dover; heart disease; shoemaker; single; b. New Castle; William Hall (fisherman) and Margaret Hall

Clara A., d. 1/26/1913 at 85/2 in New Castle; arteris sclerosis; widow; b. Readfield, ME; James Magrath (Natick, MA) and Clarrissa Coy (Augusta, ME)

Clara M., d. 2/18/1917 at 52/5/3 in Everett, MA; married

Emma, d. 3/15/1918 at 78/8/19 in Cambridge, MA; widow

Ephraim A., d. 12/3/1907 at 79/11/2 in New Castle; cancer of stomach; seaman; married; b. New Castle; William Hall (Berwick, ME, seaman) and Margaret Yeaton (New Castle)

Frank, d. 2/1/1943 at 85/3/11 in Portsmouth; fisherman; widower; b. New Castle; William Hall (New Castle) and Margaret Smith (NS)

George Bell, d. 2/15/1931 at 78/4/29 in New Castle; Coast Guard ret.; married; b. New Castle; John Q. Adams Hall (New Castle) and Maria Linscott (Great Falls, ME)

Gerald E., d. 10/16/1949 at 34 in Eliot, ME

John L., d. 1/15/1917 at 91/11 in New Castle; retired; widower; b. New Castle; William Hall (Berwick, ME) and Margaret Yeaton (New Castle)

Julia M., d. 1/15/1937 at 85 in New Castle; at home; widow; b. Duxbury, MA; William Turner (MA) and Deborah Sampson (MA)

Margaret S., d. 2/1/1905 at 84/8/25 in New Castle; pneumonia; widow; b. NS; George Smith and Sophia Morrill

Oren L., d. 11/14/1917 at 61 in New Castle; fisherman; b. New Castle; John L. Hall (New Castle) and Ann M. Linscott (Great Falls)

Sarah L., d. 5/22/1941 at 80/10/22 in New Castle; at home; single; b. New Castle; William Hall (New Castle) and Margaret Smith (NS)

Stacy, d. 2/24/1929 at 92/7/26 in Eliot, ME; retired; widower; b. New Castle; William Hall and Margaret Yeaton (New Castle)

Stacy B., d. 12/4/1947 at 79/5/11 in Eliot, ME; machinist; married; b. New Castle; Stacy Hall (New Castle) and Abbie Neal (New Castle)

Stacy William, d. 9/7/1962 at 45 in Portsmouth; married; b. Portsmouth; Gerald O. Hall and Helen E. Bonin

William H., d. 9/12/1901 at 78/0/2 in New Castle; cerebral hemorrhage; rigger; married; b. New Castle; William Hall (Kittery, ME) and Margaret Yeaton (New Castle)

Winfred Lincoln, d. 12/22/1963 at 76 in Portsmouth; widower; b. MA; George B. Hall and Julia -----

HAMER,
George F., Jr., d. 2/19/1983 at 82 in Portsmouth; George F. Hamer, Sr. and Alice Meyers

HANCOCK,
Marcia M., d. 2/1/1912 at -- in New Castle; suicide by poison; housewife; married; b. Washington, DC

HANSCOM,
Delia H., d. 5/1/1922 at 75/5/9 in New Castle; at home; married; b. Salem, MA; Israel Norwood (Gloucester, MA) and Lucretia Yeaton (New Castle)
Delphine, d. 4/7/1892 at 57/9 in New Castle; housewife; married; b. New Castle; father and mother both b. New Castle
Justin F., d. 2/1/1893 at 25/0/9; phthisis pulmonalis; clerk; married; b. New Castle; A. W. Hanscom (Eliot, ME, carpenter) and Fannie E. Beal (New Castle)
Mary B., d. 2/16/1912 at --/7/11 in New Castle; mitral regurgitation; housewife; married; b. New Castle; James Neal (New Castle, shoemaker) and Lucy A. Green (New Castle)
Mary Theresa, d. 1/15/1968 at 86 in Portsmouth; widow; b. NH; ----- Cragen

HAPNER,
Mary A., d. 5/27/1961 at 68 in Portsmouth; married; b. NH; John L. Tredick and Julia A. Ford

HARDING,
Albert, d. 12/2/1914 at 50 in Portland, ME; fracture base of skull
Frances, d. 5/6/1911 at 74/4 in Somerville, MA; heart disease
Frances A., d. 4/18/1929 at 78/6/12 in New Castle; married; b. New Castle; Robert F. White (New Castle) and Abagail Patch (New Castle)

235

Silas H., d. 5/27/1937 at 86/2/20 in Portsmouth; dis. com.; widower;
b. Chatham, MA; Silas H. Harding (Chatham, MA) and Clarissa
Eldredge (Chatham, MA)

William, d. 4/5/1905 at 68 in Somerville, MA; valvular disease; b.
New Castle

HARDY,
Richard, d. 2/2/1938 at 50/5/3 in Natick, MA; stationary eng.;
married; b. Portsmouth; Walter Hardy (Concord) and Jennie L.
Randall (Isles of Shoals)

HARRIS,
Bevuell James, d. 2/8/1996 in Portsmouth; b. 4/15/1918*

Catherine Nugent, d. 6/13/1961 at 71 in New Castle; widow; b.
Newfoundland; Michael Nugent and Mary Keough

Joseph Thomas, d. 3/29/1955 at 73 in New Castle; machinist ret.;
married; b. Springfield, MO; William Harris and Frances Paine

Woodrow Wilson, d. 2/17/1920 at 0/4/18 in New Castle; b. New
Castle; Joseph T. Harris (Springfield, MO) and Katherine Harris
(St. John's, NF)

HART,
Florence A., d. 10/24/1908 at 56/0/22 in Portsmouth; heart disease

HARTE,
Neil A., Jr., d. 12/16-17/1982 at 40 in New Castle; Neil A. Harte, Sr.
and Ann Sullivan

HARTSHORN,
Benjamin M., d. 8/14/1964 at 72 in Portsmouth; married; b. MA;
Martin B. Hartshorn and Minnie Murray

HASSETT,
Delia Elizabeth, d. 11/20/1960 at 92 in Portsmouth; widow; b. KY;
Patrick Casey and Margaret Burke

HAWES,

Mary P., d. 9/15/1911 at 49 in Worcester, MA; tuberculosis; widow; b. NS

HAY,

Arline Jessie, d. 12/16/1904 at 0/3/16 in New Castle; tuberculosis; b. New Castle; Thomas Hay (Morristown, NJ) and Lizzie Meloon (New Castle)

Elizabeth S., d. 3/30/1905 at 20/0/16 in New Castle; pulmonary tuberculosis; housewife; married; b. New Castle; Amory J. Meloon (New Castle, carpenter) and Sarah E. Yeaton (New Castle)

HAYDEN,

Mildred Y., d. 5/8/1989 at 87 in Portsmouth; Harry S. Yeaton and Helen L. White

Walter C., d. 3/2/1985 at 87 in Portsmouth; Walter R. Hayden and Grace Ireland

HAYES,

Barbara M., d. 6/2/1992 at 86 in Portsmouth

Edith M., d. 2/21/1953 at 72 in Portsmouth; housewife; widow; b. NH; Andrew Torr and Emma York

Frank, d. 4/18/1917 at 60/9/10 in Boston, MA

Fred F., d. 2/27/1944 at 69/9/13 in New Castle; master mech.; married; b. Chicago, IL; John Hayes (Great Falls) and Mary Ann Paul (York, ME)

Ralph Ring, d. 8/21/1971 at 76 in Kittery, ME; married; b. MA; Fred Hayes and Alice Harmon

Stanley B., d. 12/17/1977 at 75 in Portsmouth; Kenneth F. Hayes and Bernice Prime

HAYFORD,

Fannie Shaw, d. 2/14/1927 at 82/7/7 in Portsmouth; single

Harriet A., d. 9/14/1926 at 77/10 in Nottingham

HAYWOOD,

Dollie F., d. 1/13/1922 at 72/4/13 in New Castle; at home; widow; b. New Castle; Benjamin Amazeen (New Castle) and Sarah Frost (New Castle)

Ellen Ida, d. 4/29/1957 at 65 in Portsmouth; at home; married; b. NH; Wilbur O. Winn and Estelle Henderson

Jennie Haven, d. 1/5/1962 at 94 in Portsmouth; widow; b. New Castle; Frances A. White and Albert Williams

Thomas, d. 2/24/1900 at 65/2/21 in New Castle; pneumonia; retired; married; b. Portsmouth; Thomas Haywood (London, England) and Abagail Burleigh (ME)

William I., d. 11/24/1945 at 80/5/10 in New Castle; supply dept.; married; b. New Castle; Thomas Haywood (Portsmouth) and Hattie Batson (New Castle)

HEALEY,

Mary Veronica, d. 4/5/1969 at 60 in New Castle; married; b. MA; Thomas Mullen, Sr. and Nora Leary

HENDERSON,

Ralph A., d. 11/4/1975 at 62 in Portsmouth; Arthur G. Henderson and Sybil McKenzie

HENESSEY,

Agnes V., d. 5/9/1957 at 80 in Portsmouth; supt. hosp.; single; b. PA; Philip Henessy and Ellen Dumphey

HENLEY,

son, d. 5/1/1902 at 0/0/1 in New Castle; premature birth; C. D. Henley (Washington, DC, laborer) and Bertha Manson (New Castle)

HENRICH,

George Victor, d. 6/22/1959 at 59 in New Castle; married; b. MA; Fred Henrich and Barbara Thieringer

HENSON,

Florence L., d. 10/30/1988 at 68 in Bradenton, FL; George Guptill and Eva Manson

HERSEY,

Perley David, d. 4/16/1968 at 80 in New Castle; widower; b. NH; Francis Hersey and Mary McDonald

HILL,

Arthur Dehon, Jr., d. 7/16/1968 at 58 in Portsmouth; married; b. MA; Arthur Dehon Hill and Henriette McLean

Sally E., d. 3/13/1977 at 66 in Portsmouth; John Fultz

HILLS,

Lois A., d. 6/11/1924 at 83/8/6 in New Castle; at home; single; b. Portsmouth; Charles W. Hills and Lois Smith

Mary E., d. 2/25/1920 at 73/3/19 in Boston, MA; single; b. Portsmouth; Elias W. Hills (Franklin, MA) and Lois Smith (New Gloucester, ME)

HOGAN,

Ronald B., d. 7/3/1982 at 42 in New Castle; William Hogan and Mary Wilson

HOLBROOK,

Almira E., d. 12/17/1902 at 85/4/28 in Portland, ME; senility; widow

Elias T., d. 2/5/1894 at 85 in Peak's Island, ME; married; b. New Castle

Evelyn L., d. 10/4/1917 at 68/0/4 in So. Portland, ME; at home; married; b. Portsmouth; Samuel Clark and Abigail Foster

John B., d. 3/12/1902 at 59/2/12 in Portland, ME; disease of liver; seaman; married; b. New Castle; Elias Holbrook and Almira Coggins (Brier Island)

Sarah A., d. 5/5/1905 at 60/1/23 in Peaks Island, ME; cancer of stomach

William T., d. 11/3/1927 at 83/9/16 in Portland, ME; retired; Elias T. Holbrook (NH) and Almyra Coggins (NS)

HOLDEN,
John C., d. 9/9/1936 at 93/11/4 in New Castle; sea captain; widower; b. NS; Charles Holden (England) and Ellen White (Scotland)

HORNER,
Robert S., d. 6/28/1987 at 85 in Portsmouth; Thomas J. Horner and Florence Boardman
Virginia Vennard, d. 9/24/1993 in New Castle; b. 9/30/1902*

HORNING,
Andrew J., d. 6/23/1932 at 53/6/4 in Portsmouth; b. Melville, OH
Andrew J., Jr., d. 10/25/1916 at 1/4/20 in New Castle; b. Portsmouth; Andrew J. Horning (Melville, OH) and Ivalean W. Emery (New Castle)
Elise Florence, d. 8/20/1909 at 0/1/13 in New Castle; marasmus; b. New Castle; Anrdew J. Horning (Melville, OH) and Ivalean Emery (Bx)
Esther F., d. 10/7/1914 at 0/9/11 in New Castle; cholera infantum; b. New Castle; Andrew J. Horning (OH, engineer) and Ivelean Emery (New Castle)
Harold L., d. 6/10/1944 at 43/1/22 in Lowell, MA; foundry; divorced; b. New Castle; Andrew J. Horning (Melville, OH) and Ivalean Emery (New Castle)
Phyllis W., d. 7/10/1920 at 0/2/25 in New Castle; b. Portsmouth; Andrew J. Horning (Melville, OH) and Ivaleau W. Emery (Wx)

HOWE,
Annie Isabelle, d. 10/7/1930 at 61/8/13 in New Castle; at home; married; b. East Boston, MA; John DeCoff (NH) and Margaret Tarlton (New Castle)
Charles E., d. 12/12/1955 at 88 in York, ME; carpenter, ret.; widower; b. Leominster, MA

HOYT,

Margery, d. 12/7/1985 at 80 in Portsmouth; Eugene Hoyt and Hannah Hayes

HUBBARD,

Lloyd F.,d . 2/19/1949 at 39/1/2 in New Castle; melter; married; b. Wells, ME; Deland Hubbard and Ella Goodwin

HUBLEY,

Benjamin B., d. 11/11/1901 at 58/3 in New Castle; apoplexy; seaman; single; b. NS; Jacob Hubley (NS, farmer) and Lizzie Winnouth (NS)

Lorin E., d. 2/4/1929 at 68 in Pittsfield, MA; retired; married; b. New Castle; Jacob Hubley (NS) and Sarah F. Martin (New Castle)

Pauline O.S., d. 10/18/1906 at 58/6/9 in Portsmouth; pulmonary tuberculosis

Sarah Frances, d. 3/29/1926 at 86/0/4 in Portsmouth; at home; widow; b. New Castle; John Martin (New Castle) and Olive Pridham (New Castle)

Sophie C., d. 3/24/1933 at 69/5/27 in Pittsfield, MA; housewife; married; b. Sweden; Gustav Hanson (Sweden)

HULSHOF,

Frank A., d. 9/17/1974 at 84 in Portsmouth; married; b. NY; John Hulshof and Sophie Nagel

Gretchen A., d. 4/22/1990 at 98 in Portsmouth; Valentine Aloysius Hett and Anna Lord

HUTCHINS,

Myrtis, d. 10/13/1908 at 6/10 in Portsmouth; diphtheria; b. Portsmouth; Elmer Hutchins (ME, seaman) and May Simpson (New Castle)

HUTCHINSON,

Arthur W., d. 10/17/1975 at 56 in Manchester; Alvin Hutchinson and Katherine Daley

IRWIN,

Elizabeth B., d. 8/7/1977 at 79 in Exeter; Conrad C. Born and Mary Echardt

JACKSON,

Doris W., d. 7/16/1894 at 0/4 in New Castle; b. Portsmouth; Harrie W. W. Jackson and Helen F. Peck

Eva B., d. 8/20/1934 at 54/7/3 in Portsmouth; at home; married; b. New Castle; Granville Amazeen (New Castle) and Harriet Baker (New Castle)

JAMES,

Osary, Jr., d. 4/15/1946 at 0/0/0 in Portsmouth; b. Portsmouth; Osary James (FL) and Rita M. Masse (Lowell, MA)

JENKINS,

Bertha Louise, d. 1/10/1958 at 66; married; b. NH; August Hett and Mary Bennett

JENNESS,

Eleanor O., d. 5/3/1965 at 74 in G. B., MD; widow; b. ME; Henry L. Molton and Sarah D. Goodwin

Forrest L., d. 4/6/1965 at 70 in New Castle; married; b. NH; Alvado Jenness and Enrina M. Brown

JOHNSON,

daughter, d. 3/3/1921 at 0/0/1 in New Castle; b. New Castle; Olgia Johnson (KY) and Mayant Walsh (Ireland)

Annie Grace, b. 2/10/1942 at 44/8/11 in Portsmouth; at home; married; b. Boston, MA; Charles R. Goodwin (NS) and Wilhelminia McKinnon (NS)

JONES,

Beverly J., d. 6/10/1989 at 66 in Portsmouth; Cecil E. Tarleton and Lulu E. Guptill

Dorothy B., d. 3/12/1977 at 72 in Portsmouth; Chester A. Becker and Martha A. Amazeen

Harold Lewis, d. 3/8/1964 at 67 in Portsmouth; married; b. NH; Frank Jones and Lizzie Chase

Jeffrey Robert, d. 4/20/1969 at 21 in Newmarket; single; b. NH; Robert S. Jones and Beverly Tarlton

Mary Hite, d. 7/19/1930 at 28/1/7 in New Castle; housewife; divorced; b. Huntington, WV; William Francis Hite (WV) and Anna Clarinda Ensign (Huntington, WV)

JOYCE,

Clarence E., d. 11/5/1948 at 34/5/9 in Kittery, ME; US Army; married; b. Coal City, IN; Clifford Joyce (Coal City, IN)

KANADA,

Genevieve C., d. 12/23/1951 at 54 in New Castle; nurse chiroprac.; married; b. Manchester; James Butler and Belle Lougee

KELLENBECK,

Lillie F., d. 5/28/1941 at 63/4/3 in Portsmouth; at home; widow; b. Portsmouth; John E. Beasley (England) and Julia ----- (Ireland)

KELLNER,

Harold N., d. 10/23/1983 at 47 in Portsmouth; Abraham Kellner and Kay Tannenbaum

KENNEDY,

Carol B., d. 11/14/1997 in Portsmouth; b. 7/7/1915 in Unionville, CT; Raymond K. Brooks, Sr. and Mildred -----

Robert J., d. 8/27/1987 at 73 in Portsmouth; Robert A. Kennedy and Ethel Stevens

KIMBALL,

Charles M., d. 9/18/1903 at 0/3/10 in New Castle; marasmus; b. New Castle; Charles M. Kimball (Chelsea, MA) and Florence E. Seavey (Rockland, ME)

George H., d. 5/16/1988 at 75 in Rye; Daniel Kimball and Clara N. Dodge

Ivory G., d. 12/1/1988 at 74 in Manchester; Guy Kimball and Laura

-----

KINCH,

Pamela Jane, d. 4/4/1955 at 0/0/2 in York, ME; b. York, ME; Ralph W. Kinch and Pauline C. Dow

KING,

Frank A., d. 9/30/1950 at 67 in New Castle; carpenter; single; b. Raynham, MA; Asa F. King and Maria Wilbur

Irene B., d. 9/14/1973 at 78 in Portland, ME; widow; b. RI; Herbert Brackett and Josephine Piper

Izette Neal, d. 5/15/1912 at --/6/18 in Kittery, ME; apoplexy; housewife; married; b. New Castle; John Amazeen (New Castle, pilot) and ----- Neal (New Castle)

Mary A., d. 7/27/1983 at 64 in New Castle; Herbert O. Little and Viola Stacey

Ruth Esther, d. 5/10/1912 at --/5/5 in New Castle; convulsions; b. Fort Warren, MA; Humphrey King (Grove Castle, IN) and Delia Eblin (Chillicothe, OH)

KINNEAR,

Benjamin, d. 1/23/1901 at 82/6/5 in New Castle; internal obstruction; seaman; married; b. New Castle; Benjamin Kinnear (New Castle, seaman) and Dorcas Neal (New Castle)

Cordelia C., d. 10/8/1904 at 84 in New Castle; debility of age; housewife; widow; b. Salem, ME; Albert Hayford (Hartford, ME) and Deborah Bonney (Plymouth, MA)

Louis E., d. 12/22/1926 at 75 in Boston, MA; carpenter; widower; b. New Castle

Susan E., d. 11/11/1916 at 64/7/2 in Boston, MA; married

KIRBY,

George H., d. 8/11/1935 at 60/6/2 in New Castle; physician; married;
b. Goldsboro, NC; George L. Kirby (Sampson Co., NC) and
Mary C. Green (Goldsboro, NC)

KIRKPATRICK,

Katherine, d. 12/12/1944 at 68/0/3 in New Castle; housewife; widow;
b. Portsmouth; George Scott (Ireland) and Annie Coreovau
(Portsmouth)
Robert J., d. 6/12/1943 at 74/6/25 in New Castle; retired; married; b.
New York, NY; Archibald Kirkpatrick (Scotland) and Ellen Kane
(Scotland)

KITCHEN,

John R., d. 8/17/1950 at 52 in New Castle; painter; married; b.
England; John R. Kitchen

KITCHING,

N. H., d. 6/11/1949 at 46 in Portsmouth; phys. Director; married; b.
Sanford, ME; John F. Kitching and Ethel Murdock

KIZAK,

Thomas M., d. 12/26/1976 at 22 in New Castle; Thomas Kizak and
Ceceilia Kupiec

KLAUSSEN,

Bjarne, d. 4/25/1981 at 89 in Portsmouth; Karl J. Klaussen and
Martha Schilling
Emily Hooker, d. 1/2/1978 at 79 in New Castle; Albert H. Hooker and
Ambolena Jones

KLINE,

Kenneth Lee, d. 4/9/1995 in Portsmouth; b. 1/19/1925*

KLOTZ,

Virginia Helen, d. 10/17/1995 in New Castle; b. 8/21/1937*

KNOX,

Virgie M., d. 6/22/1946 at 65/8/24 in New Castle; chambermaid; single; b. Garland, ME; Mason Knox (Exeter, ME) and Mary Hughes (Garland, ME)

KYDD,

Ann, d. 2/20/1948 at 60 in Orlando, FL; widow; John Tredick and Julia Ford

David E., d. 7/7/1944 at 53/7/26 in New Castle; ship fitter; married; b. New Haven, CT; David E. Kydd (Scotland) and ----- Wright (Scotland)

KYRIOS,

James S., d. 12/9/1988 at 77 in New Castle; Emanuel Kyrios and Anna Serdis

LADD,

George Edward, d. 11/21/1918 at 21/3/19 in New Castle; soldier; single; b. W. Schuyler Falls, NY

LADOPOULOS,

Efststhia, d. 3/2/1980 at 75 in Portsmouth; Athanasie Lolos and Jean Lolos

LAHAN,

Margaret, d. 9/4/1911 at 0/11/20 in New Castle; diphtheria; b. Boston, MA; John R. Lahan (Troy, NY, soldier) and Emily A. Linsmane (So. Boston, MA)

LAMBERT,

Thomas Douglas, d. 9/27/1996 in New Castle; b. 9/16/1932*

LAMSON,

Caroline T., d. 6/27/1966 at 86 in Portsmouth; single; b. DC; Franklin S. Lamson and Anne Mathes

LANE,

Marion Peale, d. 6/21/1966 at 75 in Portsmouth; widow; b. PA;
Algernon Peale and Martha Davis

LAROSE,

Elsie V., d. 11/2/1939 at 50/2/30 in New Castle; at home; widow; b.
York, ME; Fred Norton (York, ME) and Mary Kimball (York,
ME)

Harold J., d. 2/9/1981 at 64 in Portsmouth; Harry LaRose and Elsie V.
Norton

Henry R., d. 5/31/1922 at 32/6/17 in New Castle; electrician; married;
b. Warwick, NY; Joseph A. LaRose and Lydia Taylor

LASKOWSKI,

Henrietta, d. 6/1/1970 at 72 in Exeter; married; b. VT; Henry Miles
and Louisa Boule

LAWRENCE,

Agnes May, d. 6/9/1972 at 90 in Portsmouth; widow; b. VT; Charles
Palmer and Mary Hill

Harley B., d. 4/8/1958 at 74; married; b. VT; Silas Lawrence and
Lucretia Bingham

LEAR,

Fannie A., d. 3/24/1900 at 67/2/5 in New Castle; chronic Bright's
disease; single; b. New Castle; Nathaniel Lear (New Castle) and
Mary White (New Castle)

Nathan W., d. 1/14/1912 at --/3/3 in Portsmouth; chronic nephritis; b.
New Castle

LEARNARD,

Rose B., d. 9/12/1977 at 90 in New Castle; Robert C. Chase and
Jeanette Begg

LEE,
Lloyd Alfred, d. 7/26/1968 at 59 in New Castle; single; b. NH; James
P. Lee and Florence Johnson

LEGNARD,
Ethel M., d. 3/30/1988 at 98 in Portsmouth; Robert Horn and
Catherine Moren

LENTZ,
Bessie Ann, d. 10/25/1932 at 53/7/3 in New Castle; at home; married;
b. Shepardstown, WV; Daniel Hurley (WV) and ----- Licklider
(WV)

LESCROART,
Julie M., d. 5/30/1980 at 22 in New Castle; Eugene Lescroart and
Thelda Corrillo

LESHER,
Everett P., d. 8/10/1912 at -- in Piscataqua River; drowning accident;
USMC; single

LEWIS,
Borghild I., d. 3/23/1986 at 84 in Portsmouth; ----- Wold and Karen
-----
Chris, d. 5/30/1969 at 84 in Hampton; married; b. Greece

LIBBEY,
Adeline J., d. 6/5/1951 at 82 in Boston, MA; at home; single; b. Eliot,
ME; George Libby and Frances Tarlton
Frances A.C., d. 6/11/1938 at 93/4/8 in Boston, MA; b. New Castle;
Henry Farlton (New Castle) and Adeline C. Yeaton (New Castle)

LIBBY,
Addie, d. 5/20/1919 at 85 in Brentwood
Orlando, d. 2/1/1898 at 28/3/0 in Epping; phthisis; burial permit

LINCOLN,

Sally H., d. 10/24/1977 at 38 in New Castle; George Hume and Louise Manley

LITTLEFIELD,

Addie F., d. 7/21/1900 at 40/0/29 in New Castle; acute melancholia; housewife; married; b. New Castle; William C. White (New Castle) and Abbie A. Martin (New Castle)

Isabelle J., d. 6/3/1907 at 0/11 in Portsmouth; syncope; b. Portsmouth; O. C. Littlefield (Oquinquit, ME, seaman) and Susan Trussell (New Castle)

James S., d. 6/23/1930 at 70 in Kittery, ME

Kenneth Harlan, d. 1/16/1935 at 6/5/22 in Portsmouth

Mildred Althea, d. 12/23/1926 at -- in Kittery, ME

Oliver C., d. 10/8/1942 at 77/7/14 in Kittery, ME; sea captain; married; b. Oqunquit, ME; Samuel C. Littlefield (Ogunquit, ME) and Almada Welch (Wells, ME)

Oliver M., d. 6/17/1937 at 49/7/2 in Portsmouth; painter; married; b. New Castle; Oliver C. Littlefield (Ogunquit, ME) and Susan Trussell (New Castle)

Susie F., d. 5/24/1944 at 74/6/28 in Kittery, ME; housewife; widow; b. New Castle; Gilbert A. Trussell (Camden, ME) and Sarah C. Becker (Isles of Shoals)

LLEWELLYN,

Stanley Dunlap, d. 7/15/1994 in New Castle

LOCKE,

George V., d. 5/22/1894 at 80 in New Castle; b. New Castle; Jonathan Locke and Dorothy Vennard

Ida, d. 12/26/1929 at 74/11/25 in Portsmouth; single; b. New Castle; John Locke (New Castle) and Sarah Trefethen (New Castle)

John, d. 5/17/1899 at 76 in New Castle; heart disease; farmer; married; b. New Castle; Jonathan Locke (New Castle) and Mary Vennard (New Castle)

Sarah H., d. 7/13/1912 at --/10 in New Castle; altuward; housewife; widow; b. New Castle; William Trefethen (New Castle) and Mary White (New Castle)

LOCKHART,
Richard S., d. 7/24/1983 at 56 in New Castle; Hubert Lockhart and Emily Buckout

LOCKWOOD,
Helen J., d. 7/20/1957 at 73 in New Castle; housewife; widow; b. MA; George Johnson and Maria Stearns

LOVELL,
Dorothy Alberta, d. 3/31/1995 in New Castle; b. 7/19/1911*
Stewart Foster, d. 1/3/1996 in Portsmouth; b. 5/26/1907*

LUSSEY,
George T., d. 6/1/1943 at 37/3/9 in New Castle; private, Army; single; b. Washington, DC; Helen M. -----

MACDANIEL,
Charles William, d. 11/27/1931 at 78/6/22 in New Castle; toolmaker, ret.; widower; b. So. Berwick, ME; Charles MacDaniel and Sarah M. Frost

MACDONALD,
John L., d. 11/11/1972 at 81 in New Castle; married; b. ME; John W. MacDonald and Mary Maher
Pauline S., d. 9/7/1991 at 99 in Rye; Fred W. Severance and Annie O. Smart

MACLAREN,
A. G., d. 12/11/1957 at 86 in Brentwood; married; b. NY

MACRELLI,
Cimbro A., d. 2/23/1984 at 94 in Portsmouth; Michele Macrelli and
   Nerina Moroni

MAGOON,
Burton C., d. 11/7/1934 at 49/6/21 in New Castle; carpenter; married;
   b. Danville, VT; Joseph Magoon and Emma Magoon
Nellie Geneva, d. 11/6/1965 at 90 in Portsmouth; widow; b. NH; John
   C. Poole and Evangeline Caswell

MANSFIELD,
Ella E., d. 3/8/1966 at 92 in Portsmouth; widow; b. ME; Benjamin F.
   Carver and Abbie Bagley

MANSON,
Andrew, d. 10/14/1918 at 65/8/14 in New Castle; moulder; widower;
   b. Kittery, ME; Ivory Manson (Eliot, ME) and Mary Duncan
   (Eliot, ME)
Hannah C., d. 1/17/1912 at --/9/24 in New Castle; cancer of stomach;
   housewife; married; b. New Castle; Abram Bell (New Castle) and
   Mary Hall (New Castle)

MARCHAND,
Andree, d. 4/28/1971 at 56 in New York; widow; b. France; Marcel
   Marchand and Laurence Carrere

MARCHANT,
John, d. 12/18/1972 at 71 in Portsmouth; married; b. Scotland; -----
   Marchant

MARCONI,
Hugo, d. 10/30/1980 at 75 in New Castle; Vincenzo Marconi and
   Emma Yates

MARDEN,
Emily L., d. 5/2/1920 at 74/8/9 in New Castle; widow; b. Canada; George B. Smith (Scotland) and Sophia Mowell (Canada)

MARGESON,
Miriam, d. 3/8/1987 at 79 in Portsmouth; Jabez King and Fannie Kearley
Richman S., d. 3/1/1972 at 69 in Boston, MA; married; b. NH; Robert C. Margeson and Abbie Beane

MARPLE,
son, d. 8/2/1971 at 0/0/0 in Portsmouth; b. NH; Jeffrey Marple and Sylvia Hoffman
Irene Forman, d. 10/4/1982 at 76 in New Castle; Paris R. Forman and Jennie Zimmerman

MARSTON,
Mary Daley, d. 3/22/1968 at 74 in Portsmouth; widow; b. NH; Michael Daley and Margaret McCool

MARTIN,
Chandler, d. 5/10/1904 at 86/9/27 in New Castle; senile dementia; married; b. New Castle; John Martin (New Castle) and Martha Cornelius (New Castle)
Harriet N., d. 7/1/1917 at 90/9/6 in New Castle; widow; b. New Castle; Zaccheus Vennard (New Castle) and Ann Vennard (New Castle)
John Edward, d. 6/30/1962 at 24 in New Castle; single; b. Iron Mountain, MI; Melvin Martin and Elva E. Cassell
John Q.A., d. 1/14/1892 at 36/1 in New Castle; painter; married; b. New Castle; father and mother both b. New Castle
Margaret Mary, d. 9/22/1973 at 82 in Portsmouth; widow; b. MA; James Scanlon and Celia McCarron
Mary E., d. 1/4/1908 at 83/9/11 in New Castle; pneumonia; widow; b. New Castle; Benjamin Kinnear (New Castle) and Dorcas Amazeen (New Castle)

Myra Bickford, d. 3/16/1933 at 72/2/4 in New Castle; at home; widow; b. New Castle; Benjamin J. Batson and Martha Ann Locke (NH)

Ralph K., d. 3/22/1896 at 46/3/7

MARVIN,

Cora I.W., d. 10/5/1951 at 75 in Portsmouth; at home; married; b. Lynn, MA; James W. Wheeler and Isabella Rand

Edward S., d. 8/11/1956 at 49 in Boston, MA; design eng'r; married; b. NH; William Marvin and Susan Bent

Eliza Salter, d. 1/7/1932 at 85/6/29 in New Castle; at home; widow; b. Portsmouth; Edward N. Anderson (MA) and Martha S.H. Rand (Rye)

Marie H., d. 12/22/1978 at 73 in Portsmouth; Daniel J. Hussey and Mary Fitzgerald

Oliver B., d. 9/9/1978 at 78 in Portsmouth; Oliver B. Marvin and Cora I. Wheeler

Oliver Bell, d. 8/14/1968 at 88 in Brentwood; widower; b. NH; William Marvin and Eliza S. Anderson

Phillip E., d. 2/23/1947 at 45/0/24 in Providence, RI; civil eng.; divorced; b. New Castle; Oliver B. Marvin (Portsmouth) and Cora I. Wheeler (Lynn, MA)

Robert, d. 5/27/1958 at 55; single; b. NH; William E. Marvin and Susan R. Bent

Ruth A., d. 2/18/1938 at 67/10/26 in New Castle; at home; single; b. Portsmouth; William Marvin (Portsmouth) and Eliza S. Anderson (Portsmouth)

Thomas E.O., d. 4/9/1919 at 81/3/22 in Boston, MA; widower

William, d. 11/7/1919 at 79/3/1 in New Castle; retired; b. Portsmouth; William Marvin (New Castle) and Martha B. Amazeen (New Castle)

William E., d. 9/28/1938 at 66/8/27 in Portsmouth; lawyer; married; b. Portsmouth; William Marvin (Portsmouth) and Eliza Anderson (Portsmouth)

William E., II, d. 8/15/1990 at 53 in New Castle; Edward Sheafe Marvin and Eleanor Jordan

Winthrop L., d. 2/3/1926 at 62/8/18 in New York, NY; publisher; married; b. New Castle; Thomas E.O. Marvin (Portsmouth) and Ann Lippitt

MASON,
Ella E., d. 12/14/1891 at 23/4/1 in New Castle; housekeeper; married; b. NS; father and mother both b. NS

MATHEWS,
Edward R., d. 10/18/1957 at 83 in Portsmouth; Broker NY Stock Exch.; married; b. PA; Ed. J. Mathews and Armanda Knox
Mabel Priscilla, d. 7/5/1924 at 24/5/17 in New Castle; at home; married; b. Portsmouth; Fred G. Locke (Portsmouth) and Fannie Martin (NS)

MAXAM,
David, d. 7/4/1980 at 33 in New Castle; Bernard C. Maxam and Agnes Bleau
Ida May, d. 1/15/1968 at 90 in Portsmouth; widow; b. NH; John C. Poole and Angeline E. Caswell

MAXIM,
Welcome, d. 2/19/1920 at 44/1/19 in Concord; married

MAYO,
Dana H. Nickerson, d. 11/11/1959 at 68 in New Castle; married; b. MA; William B. Mayo and Susan H. Dana
Ethel Marie, d. 7/29/1971 at 72 in Portsmouth; widow; b. MA; Hazen B. Chapman and Jessie -----

McARTHUR,
Mary, d. 5/16/1947 at 88/4/23 in New Castle; at home; widow; b. Scotland; Robert Cunningham (Scotland) and Elizabeth ----- (Scotland)

McCAFFERY,
Thomas F., d. 3/8/1962 at 73 in New Castle; widower; b. Portsmouth; John McCaffery and Alice Linchey

McCARRON,
Frances E., d. 4/23/1989 at 73 in Portsmouth; Harry L. Edwards and Lottie F. Mitchell

McCARTHY,
Louis Blalock, d. 7/12/1960 at 63 in New Castle; married; b. MA; Louis McCarthy and Theodosia Blalock

McCULLOUGH,
James A., d. 8/26/1971 at 45 in New Castle; married; b. MA; Frank W. McCullough and Pauline Day

McDONALD,
James, d. --/1908 at 30 at sea; unknown cause; seaman; b. Moncton, NB; John R. McDonald (New Glasgow, NS, stone cutter) and Helen Hall (Yarmouth, NS)

McDONOUGH,
Marion, d. 9/27/1962 at 83 in Portsmouth; widow; b. Somerville, MA; Isaac Phillips and Harriet Weeks
Richard P., d. 6/29/1971 at 69 in Chelsea, MA; married; b. NH; Richard D. McDonough and Marion Phillips

McKONE,
Bernard, d. 9/10/1897 at 38; single

MEIER,
Sophie, d. 8/14/1965 at 79 in New Castle; widow; b. NJ; Anton Germann and Mary Ploepfe

MELOON,
Abram C., d. 12/29/1896 at 62/5/29 in Chelsea, MA

Alfred, d. 9/20/1981 at 77 in Portsmouth; George B. Meloon and Julia H. Healey

Alfred M., d. 9/15/1909 at 57/4/9 in New Castle; chronic interstitial nephritis; married; b. New Castle; Alfred A. Meloon (New Castle) and Doretha Yeaton (New Castle)

Alpharetta P., d. 3/10/1918 at 55 in Portsmouth

Amory J., d. 1/3/1904 at 47/3/11 in New Castle; phthisis pulmonalis; carpenter; married; b. New Castle; James M. Meloon (New Castle, joiner) and Charlotte O. Campbell (New Castle)

Amory Jewett, d. 2/23/1955 at 72 in Portsmouth; elec. engin.; divorced; b. New Castle; Amory J. Meloon and Sarah Yeaton

Arline L., d. 1/24/1898 at 0/7/0 in New Castle; convulsions; b. New Castle; Armory J. Meloon (New Castle, carpenter) and Sadie Yeaton (New Castle)

Charles M., d. 10/13/1897 at 17/0/13; single; b. New Castle; James M. Meloon (New Castle) and Charlotte Campbell (New Castle)

Charlotte C., d. 7/17/1915 at 80/6/18 in New Castle; senility; none; widow; b. New Castle; John M. Campbell (Norfolk, VA, light keeper) and Elizabeth Card (New Castle)

Claire Campbell, d. 12/23/1972 at 74 in Portsmouth; widow; b. NH; Joseph Schurman and Annie Badger

Dorothy C., d. 1/8/1895 at 73/4; widow; b. New Castle; Barnabas Yeaton (New Castle) and Philadelphia Jenkins (Kittery, ME)

Elizabeth J., d. 6/4/1909 at 74/9/24 in Rochester

Everett Scott, d. 2/8/1970 at 77 in Portsmouth; single; b. NH; Amory Meloon and Sarah S. Yeaton

Frank H., d. 1/4/1937 at 74/9/21 in Portsmouth; furn. dealer; b. New Castle; William A. Meloon (New Castle) and Mary Beal (New Castle)

Frank H., d. 5/3/1942 at 60/1/2 in Weymouth, MA; b. Portsmouth

George B., d. 1/5/1922 at 41/9/11 in New Castle; expressman; married; b. New Castle; Alfred M. Meloon (New Castle) and Susan Yeaton (New Castle)

George L., d. 11/25/1908 at 43/10/3 in Portsmouth; pneumonia; married; b. New Castle; William A. Meloon

Henry, d. 3/10/1895 at --; single; b. New Castle; Amory J. Meloon
(New Castle) and Sarah Yeaton (New Castle)

Ina P., d. 10/11/1946 at 74/5/25 in Concord; housewife; b. Greenville,
TN; William Putnam (NH) and Jane Dodge (Greenville, TN)

Ira H., d. 5/24/1945 at 38/2/19 in Laconia; foreman mach.; married; b.
Portsmouth; George Meloon (New Castle) and Mary Seaver
(Harrisville)

Ivan L., d. 11/9/1949 at 87/5/2 in NY; retired; widower; James M.
Meloon and Charlotte Campbell

James M., d. 7/19/1906 at 16/4/24 in New Castle; phthisis
pulmonalis; single; b. New Castle; Amory J. Meloon (New
Castle, carpenter) and Sarah Yeaton (New Castle)

James M., d. 7/17/1912 at --/11/7 in New Castle; valvular disease of
heart; married; b. New Castle; William A. Meloon (New Castle)
and Mary Lear (New Castle)

Jessie F., d. 11/30/1918 at 43/4/18 in Portsmouth; married

Julia H., d. 5/31/1944 at 62/11/8 in New Castle; housewife; widow; b.
Cork, Ireland; Jeremiah Healey (Ireland) and Margaret Leary
(Ireland)

Louise, d. 12/26/1921 at 68/5 in New Castle; at home; widow; b. New
Castle; Rufus A. Yeaton (New Castle) and Louise A. Amazeen
(New Castle)

Mary Elizabeth, d. 2/21/1931 at 61/5/10 in No. Conway

Mary L., d. 11/27/1908 at 36/10/14 in Kittery, ME; intestinal hem.,
tuberculosis; married

Mildred J., d. 2/1/1981 at 75 in Branford, CT; George L. Meloon and
Mary E. Seaver

Rita S., d. 1/15/1965 at 78 in Concord; widow; b. CT; Harry Schofield
and Anna Forrester

Samuel R., d. 11/30/1905 at 76/5/13 in Portsmouth; chronic
myocarditis

Sarah E., d. 12/22/1905 at 80/4/9 in New Castle; widow; b. New
Castle; John Amazeen (New Castle) and Elizabeth Quint (New
Castle)

Sarah S., d. 10/10/1935 at 75/6/28 in New Castle; at home; widow; b. New Castle; Henry Yeaton (New Castle) and Hannah Amazeen (New Castle)

Seddie C., d. 8/4/1900 at 26/5/12 in New Castle; abdominal abscesses; single; b. New Castle; James M. Meloon (New Castle) and Charlotte O. Campbell (New Castle)

William D., d. 12/7/1980 at 72 in New Castle; George B. Meloon and Julia H. Healey

William T., d. 7/30/1913 at 64/10/30 in New Castle; fracture of skull; expressman; married; b. New Castle; Alfred A. Meloon (New Castle, laborer) and Dorothy Yeaton (New Castle)

Willis Grant, d. 2/18/1935 at 67/11/26 in Portsmouth; Eliot RR supt., ret.; married; b. New Castle; James M. Meloon (New Castle) and Charlotte Campbell (New Castle)

MILLER,

Artie, d. 2/22/1908 at 21/5 in Portsmouth; general septic; married; b. Merrimac, MA; Andrew Manson (Kittery, ME, laborer) and Hannah Bell (New Castle)

Ivery Bell, d. 11/30/1904 at 0/0/5 in New Castle; spasms; laborer (sic); b. New Castle; Daniel F. Miller (England) and Arta Manson (Merrimac, MA)

Normal O., d. 9/1/1985 at 85 in Portsmouth; Otto Miller and Lizzie Mae Caswell

MILLS,

Richard F., d. 9/2/1948 at 20/1/25 in New Castle; US Navy; single; b. Wassena, IA; John Mills

MITCHELL,

Bertha P., d. 12/30/1963 at 86 in Portsmouth; widow; b. NH; George Pierce and Laura Armour

Illene, d. 7/7/1957 at 61 in New Castle; sch. Teacher; single; b. IN; Dr. E. E. Mitchell and Anna M. Adamson

MOORE,

Edwin E., d. 8/5/1907 at 40 in New Castle; heart disease; hotel clerk; married; ----- Patch

MORAN,

Anna M., d. 5/12/1978 at 79 in Portsmouth; Edmund Martineau

William Gerard, d. 5/5/1967 at 70 in New Castle; married; b. MA; Michael E. Moran and Christine McLaughlin

MORDEN,

Elizabeth N., d. 9/22/1989 at 46 in New Castle; Wendell Sweet and Eleanor Keith

MORGAN,

Francis Xavier, d. 7/23/1996 in New Castle; b. 10/30/1925*

James, d. 10/8/1892 at 78 in Brentwood; seaman; single; b. New Castle

MORI,

Albert E., d. 12/6/1951 at 51 in Portsmouth; maint. man; married; b. Italy; Anthony Mori

Hilda Graham, d. 2/13/1996 in Dover; b. 9/6/1905*

MORRILL,

Harris, d. 1/26/1963 at 67 in Portsmouth; widower; b. NH; Harris I. Morrill and Nettie Chandler

Nella Mina, d. 6/10/1958 at 30; married; b. ME; Abner Foss and Martha Alley

MORRISON,

Charles C., d. 10/10/1937 at 54/9 in Dover

MORTENSON,

Leo W., d. 6/5/2966 at 64 in Portsmouth; married; b. NY; Andrew Mortenson and Mary M. Brennan

MORTON,

Helen M., d. 8/20/1961 at 80 in No. Hampton; widow; b. MA; Hezekiah Cook and Hattie E. Pierce

MOSES,

Caroline D., d. 7/12/1903 at 84 in New Castle; old age; housewife; widow; b. Portsmouth

John W., d. 5/12/1903 at 90/1/26 in New Castle; old age; married; b. Portsmouth; Benjamin Moses (Portsmouth) and ----- Coleman (Portsmouth)

Wallace N., d. 10/20/1992 at 78 in Portsmouth

MOULTON,

Florence G., d. 5/4/1934 at 69/10 in Somerville, MA; housewife; widow; b. New Castle; Luther A. Amazeen (New Castle) and Marianna Hayford (New Castle)

MULLAVEY,

Wayne J.E., d. 4/22/1981 at 58 in Exeter; J. Fred Mullavey and J. C. Gould

MUNRO,

Oscar C., d. 5/2/1979 at 78 in Hampton; Eben Munro and Sarah McKay

MURDOCK,

Alberta C., d. 9/1/1930 at 61/1/4 in New Castle; at home; widow; b. Pittsburgh, PA; George W. McCallam (Wheeling, WV) and Sally Blackmore (Pittsburgh, PA)

MURRAY,

stillborn son, d. 6/1/1904 at 0/0/0 in New Castle; b. New Castle; William E. Murray (Allen, TX, army officer) and Annie E. Calhone (SC)

Phila, d. 2/25/1907 at 74/2/27 in New Castle; apoplexy; widow; b. New Castle; Joseph B. Yeaton (New Castle) and Caroline Beals (New Castle)

NASH,
Mae, d. 4/7/1970 at 73 in Portsmouth; single; b. England

NEAL,
Abbie F., d. 12/27/1899 at 68 in Concord; exhaustion; housewife; widow; b. New Castle; John Tarlton (New Castle)

Addie L., d. 9/20/1913 at 51/10/29 in Boston, MA; tumor of the hypoplysis; married; b. New Castle; Alexander Amazeen (New Castle, seaman) and Octava Amazeen (New Castle)

Annie V., d. 2/7/1954 at 90 in Portsmouth; single; b. NH; William Neal and Sarah Vennard

Eliza Jane, d. 9/24/1897 at 69/9/5; married; b. New Castle; James Randall (Rye) and Dorothy Vennard (New Castle)

John W., d. 1/18/1899 at 73 in New Castle; heart disease; fisherman; married; b. New Castle; George O. Neal (New Castle) and Abigail Odiorne (Rye)

Joseph W., d. 1/16/1899 at 84/5/18 in Boston, MA; old age; carpenter; widower; b. New Castle

Martha A., d. 8/3/1893 at 70/1/8; cancer and paralysis; housewife; married; b. New Castle; Nathan Lear (New Castle, seaman) and Mary White (New Castle)

Robert, d. 2/2/1895 at 79/3/22; widower; b. New Castle; William Neal (New Castle) and Abigail Miller (Dunbarton)

Robert W., d. 2/8/1900 at 79/3/8 in New Castle; pneumonia; laborer; widower; b. New Castle; George O. Neal (New Castle) and Abagail Odiorne (Rye)

Sarah Abbie, d. 3/23/1924 at 101/6/2 in New Castle; at home; widow; b. New Castle; Zacheus Vennard (New Castle) and Ann Neal (New Castle)

William, d. 9/19/1895 at 78/8/3; married; b. New Castle; William Neal (New Castle) and Abigail Miller (Dunbarton)

NELSON,

James Howard, d. 1/10/1968 at 53 in Portsmouth; married; b. ME; John H. Nelson and Nellie Turner

NEWALL,

Minerva, d. 9/18/1984 at 99 in Portsmouth; Samuel Burpee Dodge and Susan Bowlby

NEWBERY,

Rev. A., d. 8/17/1937 at 46/1/6 in New Castle; clergyman; married; b. New York, NY; Alfred D. Newbery (NY) and Lillian Stephens (NY)

NICKELL,

Robert E., d. 6/15/1996 in New Castle

NILES,

Edward Glover, d. 8/27/1908 at 49/2/12 in New Castle; acritis stenosis; artist; married; b. Cambridge, MA; Stephen R. Niles (Portland, ME) and Minnie Whittacre (Charleston, WV)

Emily Mary, d. 4/1/1912 at -- in New Castle; hematemeris; widow; b. London, England; William Wilkes (England)

NORRIS,

Emerson S., d. 12/8/1988 at 77 in New Castle; Walter H. Norris and Effie L. Shapleigh

NOSEWORTHY,

James M., d. 3/19/1938 at -- in Portsmouth; laborer; b. Portsmouth; Randall Noseworthy (Newfoundland) and Elsie K. Littlefield (Portsmouth)

NOYES,

Alice May, d. 12/24/1959 at 72 in New Castle; Fabius W. Robinson and Annie L. Card

Fred R., d. 6/25/1934 at 50/3/24 in Portsmouth; painter; married; b. Winsor, ME; Cyrus Noyes and Susan Watson (ME)

Gary Fletcher, d. 4/2/1954 at 2 in Stratham; b. NH; David C. Noyes and Elizabeth Fletcher

George W., d. 1/19/1986 at 92 in Portsmouth; Samuel Noyes and Emma Aldrich

Mary Elizabeth, d. 3/5/1978 at 76 in Portsmouth; William Messinger and Florence Ure

NUTTING,

Walter G., d. 10/18/1936 at 34/9/27 in New Castle; machinist; married; b. Canada; Charles D. Nutting (Naples, ME) and Minnie Bellows (Brookfield, MA)

O'ROURKE,

Helen, d. 11/29/1963 at 73 in Portsmouth; widow; b. ME; Thomas L. Cleaves and Arabine Sylvester

ODIORNE,

Chester Earle, d. 11/15/1955 at 73 in Eliot, ME; engineer, ret.; widower; b. New Castle; Frank P. Odiorne and Lavina Murray

Ellen R., d. 3/18/1936 at 51/8/20 in Newburyport, MA; at home; married; b. Pleasantville, NY; Jacob Richards (NS) and Sophia Sarty (NS)

Frank P., d. 8/17/1944 at 91/5/25 in Rye; carpenter; widower; b. Rye; Charles B. Odiorne (Rye) and Mary Odiorne (Rye)

John E., d. 8/2/1914 at 75/1/13 in Tilton; cerebral embolism

John Frank, d. 6/4/1930 at 0/0/0 in Portsmouth; b. Portsmouth

Lavina D., d. 12/16/1906 at 0/1/6 in Rye; convulsions; b. Rye; Chester A. Odiorne (New Castle, fireman)

Lavina T., d. 12/3/1912 at --/7/3 in Portsmouth; pneumonia; housewife; married; b. New Castle; John Murray (Capt., USA) and Phila Yeaton

OGLES,

Gertrude Maude, d. 4/24/1921 at 21/9/29 in New Castle; housewife; married; b. Portsmouth; Fabrius Robinson (Kittery, ME) and Annie L. Card (New Castle)

OLIVER,

Nellie, d. 5/28/1935 at 67/7/20 in Newburyport, MA; at home; widow; b. Ireland; Thomas Costello (Ireland) and Catherine Gorman (Ireland)

Robert, d. 7/29/1929 at 86/10/8 in New Castle; retired; married; b. New Castle; Benjamin Oliver (New Castle) and Abagail Jacobs (at sea)

Usula, d. 12/20/1894 at 51 in New Castle; married; b. Mauch Chunk, PA; George McIntosh

OLSEN,

Frank Raymond, d. 10/22/1970 at 34 in New Castle; married; b. ME; Wilbur R. Olsen and Marjorie Bean

OSBORN,

Elmer E., d. 1/30/1947 at 54/7/20 in Framingham, MA; machine op.; married; b. Rassales, PA; Byron Osborn (Byron, NY) and Nettie Adams (Churchville, NY)

Harriet J., d. 5/25/1992 at 83 in Portsmouth

OSBORNE,

Bert Calvin, d. 9/29/1960 at 79 in New Castle; married; b. ME; Addison Osborne and Nancy L. Towle

OSGOOD,

Warren Truesdell, d. 4/12/1975 at 90 in No. Hampton; Warren A. Osgood and Eudora Truesdell

OUELLETTE,

David F., d. 8/22/1958 at 62; divorced; b. NB; Alfred Ouellette and Arthimisi St. Pierre

PAGE,

Hubert, d. 11/19/1917 at 19 in New Castle; soldier; single; b. KY

Lois T.G., d. 11/2/1997 in Exeter; b. 2/24/1918; Louis L. Green and Virginia Tanner

William F., d. 8/1/1941 at 53/7/10 in New Castle; tel. installer; married; b. Portsmouth; Walter H. Page (Manchester) and Georgiana Church (Farmington)

William L., d. 8/24/1969 at 54 in New Castle; married; b. MA; Laurence B. Page and Marion Peale

PAINE,

Sarah M., d. 7/25/1903 at 0/0/1 in New Castle; b. New Castle; Joseph S. Paine (Mt. Vernon, KY) and Edith M. Simpson (New Castle)

PALMER,

Beatrice L., d. 11/13/1989 at 83 in Portsmouth; Anthony T. Norman and Rachel J. McDaniel

Sadie M., d. 3/10/1970 at 86 in Portsmouth; married; b. Canada; William Gesner and Sophie -----

Sidney Edward, d. 7/19/1971 at 96 in York, ME; widower; b. England; John Palmer and Helen P. Briggs

PARKER,

Sherman M., d. 5/3/1920 at 20/7/22 in Boston, MA; surfman, US; married; b. Lubec, ME; Alonzo W. Parker (Steuben, ME) and Mary E. Wallace (Lubec, ME)

PARTLOW,

Elizabeth Alice, d. 10/9/1958 at 56; married; b. England; Robert T. Duxbury and Elizabeth Maden

PATTEN,

George A., d. 4/23/1989 at 66 in New Castle; Karl L. Patten and Margaret George

PATTERSON,

George T., d. 8/21/1918 at 46/4/28 in Fort Constitution; Colonel, USA; single; b. No. Platte, NE; Thomas E. Patterson (Belfast, Ireland) and May Marvis (PA)

Minnie Hubley, d. 4/29/1958 at 84; widow; b. NS; John Hubley and Maria Crouse

William Q., d. 2/15/1939 at 73/7/10 in Portsmouth; electrician; married; b. ME; Joshua Patterson (ME) and Abigail Quimby (Old Orchard, ME)

PECUNIES,

Emma C., d. 4/13/1965 at 62 in Kittery, ME; widow; b. MA; Arthur Henderson and Sybil McKenzie

PENDLETON,

Lewis E., d. 12/26/1936 at 63/5/14 in Portsmouth; caretaker; married; b. Syracuse, NY; Edmund Pendleton (NY) and Ida Smith (NY)

Mabel F., d. 2/14/1948 at 71/4/14 in Portsmouth; at home; widow; b. New Castle; Jacob Hubley (NS) and Sarah Martin (New Castle)

PERKINS,

Hannah, d. 11/25/1902 at 64/10/27 in Portsmouth; gangrene of intestines; housewife; widow; b. New Castle; Stillman Tarlton (New Castle) and Laura Priest (New Castle)

PERONI,

Barbara Jean, d. 8/16/1971 at 17 in New Castle; single; b. MA; Patrick J. Peroni and Nancy Dutton

PETTIGREW,

Helen G., d. 11/16/1988 at 75 in Portsmouth; Alvin Rowbotham and Nellie Belmont

PETTIMAN,

Osborne E., d. 1/18/1938 at 38/2/11 between New Castle and Portsmouth; elec., Navy Yard; single; b. Chelsea, MA; Osborne E. Pettiman (England) and Sarah C. Noch (New Castle)

PETTMAN,

Sarah, d. 4/4/1945 at 78 in Chelsea, MA; widow; Ephraim Urch (England) and Arabella Vennard (New Castle)

PHINNEY,

Ella Mina, d. 5/26/1958 at 82; widow; b. VT; Napoleon Lupien and Phomina Rowe

PICANCO,

Sarah E., d. 6/6/1933 at 88/8/1 in Melrose, MA; at home; widow; b. New Castle; Capt. Robert White (New Castle) and Elizabeth Batson (New Castle)

PICKETT,

Charles Waldo, d. 3/28/1960 at 75 in New Castle; married; b. NH; William P. Pickett and Addie Randall

David W., d. 2/3/1993 in New Castle

Gertrude Ella, d. 1/21/1984 at 83 in Portsmouth; Aldoph Maertins and Elizabeth Schied

PICOTT,

Clifford O., d. 9/24/1939 at 56/7/24 in New Castle; pipefitter, N. Yd.; widower; b. Rollinsford; Orin Picott (Kittery, ME) and Medisa Paul (Eliot, ME)

PIERCE,

Blanche Edna, d. 3/9/1969 at 67 in Portsmouth; married; b. ME; David Daley and Alberta Westcott

Elmer William, d. 5/26/1972 at 81 in Portsmouth; widower; b. ME; William E. Pierce and Lillian M. -----

Silas W., d. 4/21/1952 at 58 in Portsmouth; gen. Manager; married; b. MA; Vincent R. Pierce and Annie L. Marlin

PIKE,

Alfreda M., d. 11/1/1968 at 83 in Portsmouth; widow; b. NH; Charles
Pearson and Ellen T. McCarthy

H. Doris Mae, d. 1/23/1971 at 54 in Portsmouth; divorced; b. NH;
Frank Patterson and Eva Higgins

John S., d. 2/19/1939 at 77 in New Castle; farm foreman; single; b.
Goshen; Sullivan Pike and Ellen -----

PINGREE,

Elinor H., d. 7/9/1977 at 60 in Portsmouth; Karl W. Hanscom and
Mary Craigin

PITTS,

Virginia Frances, d. 7/19/1994 in Portsmouth; b. 8/24/1907*

PLUMER,

Elizabeth G., d. 2/6/1993 in New Castle; b. 2/13/1901*

Herbert E., d. 6/11/1987 at 86 in Portsmouth; Herbert E. Plumer and
Alice Southworth

POLINI,

Terry, d. 2/22/1967 at 23 in Concord; single; b. NH; Urbano Polini
and Marion Polini

POOLE,

Alice G., d. 2/8/1925 at 38/10/7 in New Castle; at home; married; b.
Manchester; Wilbur O. Winn (Tuftonboro) and Estella
Henderson (Staten Island, NY)

Angeline Esther, d. 4/5/1925 at 81/11/7 in New Castle; at home;
widow; b. Rye; Richard G. Caswell (Rye) and Annie B. Marden
(Rye)

Eleanor M., d. 11/29/1947 at 32/8/21 in Portsmouth; at home; single;
b. Portsmouth; Wayne D. Poole (New Castle) and Alice G. Winn
(Manchester, ME)

Kendrick W., d. 7/5/1971 at 58 in New Castle; married; b. NH; Wayne
D. Poole and Alice Winn

Richard E., d. 4/24/1951 at 87 in Portsmouth; harness maker; widower; b. Rye; John W. Poole and Angeline Caswell

Vincent W., d. 12/23/1970 at 53 in New Castle; married; b. NH; Wayne Poole and Alice Winn

Wayne Darlington, Sr., d. 7/7/1958 at 75; widower; b. NH; Richard E. Poole and Pearl White

Wayne Densmore, d. 3/2/1959 at 48 in Portsmouth; married; b. NH; Wayne D. Poole and Alice Winn

POWERS,

Russell B., d. 9/17/1970 at 62 in New Castle; divorced; b. NH

PREBLE,

Clara M., d. 4/22/1898 at 9/0/0 in Boston, MA; general peritonitis; Rufus A. Preble (New Castle, clerk); burial permit

Katherine B., d. 4/8/1921 at 80/7/22 in New Castle; at home; widow; b. New Castle; Benjamin Yeaton (VT) and Mary J. Yeaton (New Castle)

Rufus A., d. 1/11/1896 at 77/10/19

PRIDHAM,

son, d. 9/24/1946 at 0/0/0 in Portsmouth; b. Portsmouth; Stanley Pridham (New Castle) and Jeanne Cochrane (Boston, MA)

Anna B., d. 3/19/1941 at 69/10/21 in Concord; at home; widow; b. Ireland; John Bates (Ireland)

Douglas C., d. 1/4/1971 at 57 in Portsmouth; married; b. NH; Elmer Pridham and Ethel Poole

Elmer Sherman, d. 12/23/1958 at 79; widower; b. NH; John R. Pridham and Mary C. Ruee

Ethel O., d. 9/20/1943 at 64/1/29 in New Castle; housewife; married; d/o John C. Poole (Edgecomb, ME) and Angeline E. Caswell (Rye)

Isaac, d. 12/17/1955 at 85 in Concord; mason work; widower; b. New Castle; John R. Pridham and Mary C. Ruee

James W., d. 11/19/1946 at 71/0/6 in Portsmouth; road agent; married; b. New Castle; John R. Pridham (New Castle) and Mary C. Ruee (Eliot, ME)

John R., d. 8/11/1918 at 69 in New Castle; fisherman; married; b. New Castle; John R. Pridham (New Castle) and Ruth A. Fish (Marblehead, MA)

John W., d. 5/5/1936 at 63/1/21 in New York, NY; coast guard; married; b. New Castle; John R. Pridham (New Castle) and Mary Ruee (Eliot, ME)

Lena, d. 2/4/1940 at 66/1/16 in New Castle; at home; married; b. Isles of Shoals; Edward Caswell (Rye) and Lucy Hartz (Cambridge, MA)

Mary Arlene, d. 5/9/1973 at 56 in New Castle; widow; b. NH; Francis J. Cousins and Gertrude Jenness

Mary C., d. 12/21/1933 at 86/6/9 in New Castle; at home; widow; b. Eliot, ME; Thomas Ruee (Salem, MA) and Mary A. Leighton (ME)

Nancy Claire, d. 6/14/1930 at 0/0/0 in New Castle; b. New Castle; Gordon L. Pridham (New Castle) and Viola Watson Noyes (Coopers Mills, ME)

PRIESTLEY,

Hector, d. 10/14/1947 at 75/7/19 in Portsmouth; retired; widower; b. Leicester, England; ----- Priestley (England)

PROHASKA,

son, d. 6/5/1918 at 0/0/0 in New Castle; b. New Castle; Charles F. Prohaska, Jr. (Boston, MA) and Ida M. Murray (Newfoundland)

child, d. 8/10/1950 at 0/0/0 in Portsmouth; Ira F. Prohaska and Thelma French

Charles F., d. 4/8/1943 at 83/5/28 in New Castle; carpenter; married; b. Bohemia

Charles F., d. 10/28/1944 at 61/6/23 in New Castle; contractor; married; b. Chelsea, MA; Charles F. Prohaska (Bohemia) and Sadie Card (New Castle)

Charles Francis, 3d, d. 8/16/1926 at 0/0/18 in Portsmouth; b.
Portsmouth; Charles F. Prohaska, Jr. (Chelsea, MA) and Ida
Murray (Newfoundland)

Elizabeth B., d. 10/30/1953 at 86 in Portsmouth; at home; widow; b.
Scotland; ----- Britton

Ida M., d. 10/6/1954 at 70 in Portsmouth; prac. nurse; widow; b.
Newfoundland; John Murray and Patience Earl

Maude Emma, d. 8/12/1971 at 78 in Portsmouth; married; b. VT;
Burgess Metcalf and Nellie Merritt

Roy J., d. 9/16/1971 at 82 in Portsmouth; widower; b. MA; Charles F.
Prohaska and Sadie Card

Sadie, d. 10/4/1907 at -- in New Castle; stillborn; b. New Castle;
Charles F. Prohaska (Boston, MA) and Ida Murray
(Newfoundland)

PUSH,

Conrad, d. 5/26/1912 at --/9 in New Castle; angeni pectoris; barber;
widower; b. Germany

Henrietta E., d. 2/10/1909 at 60/5/26 in New Castle; cancer of liver;
married; b. New Castle; Willard P. Meloon (New Castle) and
Sarah Amazeen (New Castle)

QUIRIN,

John H., d. 12/23/1971 at 74 in Portsmouth; married; b. MA; William
Quirin and Grace Vandermart

Louise W., d. 3/2/1976 at 79 in Portsmouth; George Warren and Mary
Palmer

William Edward, d. 6/27/1960 at 87 in Portsmouth; widower; b. MA;
Jacques Quirin and Freda Haskell

QUIRK,

Mary Theresa, d. 7/25/1990 at 60 in New Castle; John Moran and
Laura Morin

RAND,

Edwin D., Capt., d. 4/27/1925 at 81/11/22 in New Castle; machinist, retired; b. Rye; David Rand (Rye) and Mary S. Yeaton (Rye)

Eliza A., d. 4/21/1911 at 69/7/12 in New Castle; angeni pectoris; widow; b. New Castle; James W. Wheeler (VT) and Mary Brown (ME)

Elizabeth T.C., d. 9/29/1926 at 77/11/15 in New Castle; at home; widow; b. New Castle; Albert H. White (New Castle) and Frances C. Yeaton (Portland, ME)

Horace B., d. 3/28/1892 at 24/10 in New York; laborer; single; b. New Castle; father b. Rye and mother b. New Castle

Norman E., d. 7/2/1973 at 79 in New Castle; married; b. NH; Albert Rand and Winifred Yeaton

Philip Sylvester, d. 5/5/1965 at 67 in New Castle; widower; b. ME; William G. Rand and Sophie Sylvester

Thomas, d. 4/17/1896 at 69/8

Veranus C., d. 10/13/1897 at 69/9/1; married; b. Kittery, ME; Samuel Rand (Rye) and Sarah Dixon (Eliot, ME)

RANDALL,

Angeline M., d. 1/22/1916 at 87/4/17 in New Castle; widow; b. St. Margaret Bay, NS; Jacob Hubley (NS) and Elizabeth Winott (NS)

Ann E., d. 11/11/1936 at 73/8/24 in New Castle; at home; widow; b. Raymond; Hazen Currier (Raymond) and Eliza A. Carlton (Candia)

George W., d. 4/15/1930 at 75/9/1 in New Castle; painter; married; b. New Castle; Zaccheus Randall (New Castle) and Angeline Hubley (NS)

Martha Frances, d. 2/9/1958 at 74; married; b. NH; Frank H. Greenough and Maude Goodrich

Oliver V., d. 8/27/1906 at 67/11/23 in New Castle; carcinoma of stomach; fisherman; single; b. New Castle; James Randall (New Castle, laborer) and Dorothy Vennard (New Castle)

Zacheus J.V., d. 1/9/1901 at 77/10/27 in New Castle; paranoia; seaman; married; b. New Castle; James Randall (New Castle, seaman) and Dorothy Vennard (New Castle)

Zacheus J.V., d. 3/9/1929 at 71 in Portsmouth; retired; single; b. New Castle; Zacheus Randall (New Castle) and Angelina Hubley (NS)

REDFIELD,
Leon James, d. 4/22/1959 at 44 in Portsmouth; married; b. NH; Amaziah Redfield and Mary Ducy

REED,
Alvin C., d. 1/29/1912 at --/3/8 in Portsmouth; tuberculosis; married

Frances A., d. 4/29/1901 at 0/1/20 in Portsmouth; convulsions; b. Portsmouth; Alvin Reed and Jane Hubley (New Castle)

REGAN,
Mary J., d. 4/26/1974 at 70 in New Castle; single; b. NH; Jeremiah Regan and Jane Cronin

REMICK,
Frank H., d. 7/13/1951 at 65 in New Castle; engineer; married; b. Kittery, ME; Frank Remick and Fannie Adams

Frank Harley, d. 6/4/1916 at -- in Portsmouth; F. Harley Remick and Mertys W. Becker (New Castle)

Myrtis Becker, d. 12/28/1961 at 71 in Portsmouth; widow; b. NH; Forest Becker and Elizabeth Emery

REYNOLDS,
Arthur Edgar, d. 10/16/1961 at 79 in Portsmouth; married; b. MA; Edward P. Reynolds and Emily Arnold

RHOADES,
Alice L., d. 9/26/1971 at 96 in Kingston; widow; b. MA; Leonard B. Nichols and Anna Severance

RHODES,
Ethel W., d. 1/9/1952 at 56 in Portsmouth; school tchr.; married; b.
   Farmington; Frank Kenney and Sybil Bryant

RICHARDSON,
C. R., d. 11/29/1949 at 43 in Asheboro, NC; chauffeur; married; b.
   NH

RICKER,
Annette M., d. 1/15/1947 at 28/5/21 in New Castle; govt. typist;
   single; b. New Castle; George B. Ricker (New Castle) and Sadie
   E. Waite (New Castle)
Charles F., d. 1/26/1948 at 65 in Salem, MA; retired; widower; b.
   Lynn, MA; Benjamin Ricker (ME) and Ida Peckham (ME)
Charles H., d. 3/10/1925 at 22/0/6 in Portland, ME; motor machinist;
   single; b. New Castle; George B. Ricker (New Castle) and Sadie
   Estelle White (New Castle)
Esther J., d. 4/30/1926 at 68/1/15 in Portsmouth; at home; widow; b.
   New Castle; John Pridham (New Castle) and Mary Ann Fish
George Benjamin, d. 10/27/1929 at 53/3/20 in New Castle;
   boatswain, USCG; married; b. New Castle; Samuel H. Ricker
   (New Castle) and Esther J. Pridham (New Castle)
Lyndon H., II, d. 6/6/1949 at 0/0/2 in Portsmouth; b. Portsmouth; L.
   H. Ricker (New Castle) and Louise Gaudreault (So. Berwick,
   ME)
Lyndon Harding, d. 7/26/1990 at 79 in Portsmouth; George Benjamin
   Ricker and Sadie Estelle White
Melissa, d. 12/20/1968 at -- in Portsmouth; George B. Ricker and
   Susanne E. Bernard
Nancy G., d. 9/18/1898 at 0/3/27 in Portsmouth; cholera infantum;
   burial permit
Sadie Estelle, d. 10/1/1966 at 93 in Portsmouth; widow; b. NH;
   Charles H. White and Sarah F. Randall

RIFFE,

Michael C., d. 10/31/1997 in Portsmouth; b. 9/3/1933 in Anderson, IN; B. Franklin Riffe and Marcella Sweeney

RIKER,

Ruth Anna, d. 1/5/1992 at 82 in Portsmouth

RIORDAN,

William O'Brien, d. 8/17/1978 at 22 in New Castle; Richard J. Riordan and Jean Warady

ROBERTS,

Amelia, d. 9/13/1914 at 56/0/10 in New Castle; cancer; married; b. Swampscott, MA; Robert McCullon and Ruth Smith (Orleans, MA)

C. Francis N., d. 3/9/1971 at 79 in Portsmouth; married; b. MA; Nathaniel Roberts and Phoebe Newhook

ROBINSON,

Annie L., d. 10/18/1942 at 81/7/4 in New Castle; housewife; widow; b. New Castle; James Card (New Castle) and Mary Tarlton (New Castle)

Charles Henry, d. 4/4/1933 at 63/5/2 in New Castle; laborer; single; b. Isles of Shoals; John H. Robinson (Isles of Shoals) and Mary A. Becker (New Castle)

Douglas P., d. 5/11/1905 at 0/7 in New Castle; membraneous croup; b. New Castle; J. Blake Robinson (ME, time keeper) and L. Gertrude Palmer (ME)

Ernest F., d. 2/9/1969 at 80 in Kittery, ME; married; b. NH; Fabius W. Robinson and Annie Card

Fabius W., d. 11/1/1925 at 69/8/26 in New Castle; fisherman; married; b. Kittery, ME; John H. Robinson (New Castle) and Mary Ann Becker (New Castle)

Flora, d. 9/2/1936 at 77/11/17 in New Castle; at home; widow; b. Hornell, NY; John Foster (NY) and Mary Olive Allen (NY)

John W., d. 4/27/1926 at 68/11/9 in Portsmouth; retired; widower; b.
    Isles of Shoals; John H. Robinson (Portsmouth) and Mary Becker
Marie Annie, d. 12/9/1918 at 92/6/15 in Portsmouth; widow
Myra Estelle Redington, d. 7/27/1914 at 55/11/20 in New Castle;
    cancer; nurse; married; b. Perry, ME; John Redington (NS) and
    Elmira G. Trott (ME)

ROCHE,

Helen E., d. 11/27/1991 at 53 in New Castle; William Lanagan and
    Florence Butts
James Francis, d. 3/19/1993 in Portsmouth; b. 10/24/1921*

ROSS,

Fred Daniel, d. 9/23/1955 at 62 in New Castle; traffic mgr.; married;
    b. Everett, MA; James J. Ross and Mary E. MacInnes

ROTH,

Alice Louise, d. 4/26/1955 at 86 in New Castle; housewife; widow; b.
    New Castle; John W. Amazeen and M. Olivia Cole
George P., d. 1/16/1946 at 77/7/29 in W. Newbury, MA; married; b.
    W. Newbury, MA; George P. Roth and Regina Rodenburg
    (Heidelburg)

ROWE,

Frederick, d. 2/2/1979 at 72 in Portsmouth; Edward Rowe and
    Margaret Wallace

ROWLAND,

Benjamin A., d. 6/21/1992 at 81 in Portsmouth; Benjamin H. Rowland
    and Mary A. Smith

ROY,

Cheryl P., d. 10/21/1976 at 20 in Portsmouth; Thomas L. Roy and
    Patricia M. Tergesen
Louis J., Jr., d. 8/28/1991 at 34 in New Castle; Louis J. Roy, Sr. and
    Eleanor W. Dempster

RUEE,

Thomas, d. 9/29/1891 at 84/9/26 in New Castle; widower; b. Salem, MA; father and mother both b. Salem, MA

RUGGLES,

Carter K., d. 11/12/1981 at 77 in Portsmouth; Walter G. Ruggles and Juliette Carter

RYLANDER,

Mira Neal, d. 8/27/1967 at 69 in Portsmouth; married; b. MA; John P.C. Neal and Addie Amazeen

Thor Albin, d. 5/14/1969 at 70 in Portsmouth; widower; b. MA; Albin Rylander and Mina Anderson

SABER,

William, d. 7/5/1971 at 59 in Gosport Harbor; married; b. MA; Peter Saber and Ethel Hill

SANBORN,

Eleanor Anderson, d. 6/23/1960 at 51 in Portsmouth; widow; b. ME; Olaf Anderson and K. Blindheimsvieg

SANDLER,

Jennie, d. 6/9/1987 at 86 in Brentwood; Jacob Shafron and Rachel -----

SARGENT,

Ellen L., d. 1/6/1955 at 85 in Wenonah, NJ; housewife; widow; b. New Castle; Ephriam Urch and Arabelle -----

Philip H., d. 3/26/1903 at 6 in Philadelphia, PA; appendicitis; b. Philadelphia, PA; Redford Sargent (Kittery, ME, inspector) and Ellen Urch (New Castle)

Redford A., d. 9/7/1905 at 0/0/2 in NJ; convulsions; b. NJ; Redford A. Sargent (Kittery, ME) and Ellen L. Urch (New Castle)

SAWYER,
Ida M., d. 8/25/1907 at 0/3 in Rye; cholera infantum; b. New Castle; Daniel Sawyer (Jonesport, ME, surfman) and Carrie Smith (St. John, NB)

SCAMMON,
Clarence I., d. 2/17/1982 at 80 in Portsmouth; James E. Scammon and Mary Picard
Irving H., d. 5/22/1970 at 61 in New Castle; married; b. ME; Walter A. Scammon and Elizabeth Hirst
Jessie Schurman, d. 3/5/1996 in Portsmouth; b. 10/6/1901*

SCANLON,
Esther Louise, d. 1/22/1933 at 45/7 in New Castle; housewife; widow; b. York, ME; Albert Kimball (York, ME) and Lydia Plaisted (York, ME)

SCHAFFER,
Mary T., d. 8/9/1991 at 94 in New Castle; Edmund C. Tarbell and Emmeline A. Souther

SCHIOT,
Theodore, d. 9/27/1930 at 1/5/14 in Boston, MA; b. Portsmouth; Theodore Schiot (Newport, RI) and Pauline Martenson (Portsmouth)

SCHURMAN,
Annie F.T., d. 11/8/1961 at 85 in Portsmouth; widow; b. NH; David Badger and Nancy Campbell
Joseph L., d. 4/11/1940 at 72/0/26 in Portsmouth; insurance agent; married; b. Rawden, NS; Solomon A. Schurman (Canada) and Clara J. Mason (NS)
Joseph Leonard, Jr., d. 3/28/1996 in Portsmouth; b. 12/20/1909*

SCOTT,

Katherine G., d. 12/14/1964 at 84 in Portsmouth; widow; b. VT; Michael H. Gilligan and Eleanor Tierney

Lee A., d. 9/26/1950 at 64 in New Castle; machinist; married; b. Warren; George Scott and Carrie Mason

SEARS,

Louise H., d. 9/22/1912 at -- in Piscataqua River; drowning - suicidal; housewife; married; b. Cleveland, OH; William Halliday (England) and Emma Mason (England)

SEYBOLT,

Carolyn B., d. 4/23/1997 in Portsmouth; b. 5/15/1902 in Newington; Daniel W. Badger and Edith Whidden

John Edward, d. 5/12/1972 at 70 in Portsmouth; married; b. NY; Edward Seybolt and Clara D. Stout

SHAFNER,

Elizabeth L., d. 10/9/1952 at 86 in New Castle; at home; widow; b. Newburyport, MA; Richard Libby and Sarah H. Pearson

SHAPLEIGH,

Waldron E., d. 5/4/1964 at 53 in Portsmouth; married; b. ME; Edson Shapleigh and Bessie Shapleigh

SHATTUCK,

Martha I. Boger, d. 2/7/1959 at 63 in New Castle; widow; b. WV; Dr. Cyrus M. Boger and Bertha Forrester

SHAW,

Eliza J., d. 8/10/1895 at 66/7/15; married; b. Boston, MA; William Wright (Boston, MA)

SHEEHAN,

Thomas Leo, d. 8/31/1992 at 86 in Portsmouth

SHERMAN,

Mary E., d. 3/2/1920 at 93/2/6 in Portsmouth

SHULER,

Katherine, d. 2/22/1918 at 30/8 in New Castle; married; b. Boston, MA; John O'Malley (Ireland)

SIAS,

Walter P., d. 10/4/1945 at 72/1/4 in Concord; salesman; married; b. Boston, MA; Joseph B. Sias and Abbie O. Mcfadden (Bath, ME)

SIMPSON,

George A., d. 7/18/1946 at 72/2/29 in New Castle; USCG; married; b. New Castle; Mark Simpson and Mary E. Yeaton (New Castle)

Mary Ellen, d. 3/22/1925 at 76/9/23 in New Castle; at home; widow; b. New Castle; John R. Yeaton (New Castle) and Mary F. Tredick (New Castle)

Sarah E., d. 12/7/1964 at 83 in Kittery, ME; widow; b. MA; Thomas Haywood and Dolly Frost

SKAROUPKA,

Ljubica, d. 1/4/1981 at 83 in Portsmouth; Guro Jezic and Antonia Mesaros

SKIDMORE,

Kathleen E., d. 9/28/1959 at 1 in New Durham; b. NH; Sheridan Skidmore and Shirley Lankford

Mary Agnes, d. 10/11/1968 at 63 in Portsmouth; married; b. NH; Nicholas Dwyer and Sadie Eastman

SLAWSON,

Loretta H., d. 10/13/1980 at 82 in New Castle; Joseph Hassett and Delia Casey

SLOCOMB,

Mary K., d. 7/21/1969 at 71 in New Castle; widow; b. ME; Charles Montgomery and Bridget E. Cotter

SMALL,

Edward F., d. 3/7/1916 at 68 in Portsmouth; married

Elizabeth, d. 10/25/1916 at 77/4/10 in Portsmouth; widow

SMART,

Ann W., d. 7/9/1939 at 72/6 in Boston, MA; at home; single; b. New Castle; William H. Smart (Concord) and Helen Henderson (Claremont)

SMITH,

George, d. 8/16/1945 at 31/6/28 in New Castle; janitor; married; b. Scotland; George Smith (Scotland) and Margaret McKenzie (Scotland)

Jessie F., d. 12/21/1926 at 63/0/29 in Portsmouth; at home; married; b. Maitland, NS; Capt. William White (NS) and Elizabeth White

John O., d. 4/16/1950 at 88 in New Castle; gardener; widower; b. New Castle; James Smith and Mary O. Obrey

Mary Olive, d. 4/3/1902 at 78 in New Castle; disease of bladder; housewife; widow; b. New Castle; John Obrey and Mary Pridham (New Castle)

SNYDER,

Jean Phyllis, d. 11/17/1996 in Portsmouth; b. 2/14/1926*

William Lewis, d. 3/27/1996 in Portsmouth; b. 3/23/1924*

SOLES,

Eugene P., d. 5/1/1995 in Portsmouth; b. 6/10/1916*

SOMERBY,

Edna Louise, d. 11/20/1993 in Portsmouth; b. 6/16/1913*

SOULE,

Pearl D., d. 5/15/1937 at 73/3/7 in New Castle; married; b. New
Castle; James R. White (New Castle) and Katherine Buchanan
(New Castle)

SOUTER,

William Norwood, d. 11/24/1935 at 73/1/13 in New Castle; physician,
oculist; married; b. Berryville, VA; Henderson Souter (VA) and
Minerva Davidson (VA)

SOUTHER,

Harrison A., d. 9/18/1939 at 76/0/23 in New Castle; veterinary;
widower; b. So. Boston, MA; Harrison P. Souther (Quincy, MA)
and Mercy Smith (New Bedford, MA)

SPAULDING,

Judson A., d. 9/22/1982 at 64 in Portsmouth; Albert Spaulding and
Vivian Harris

SPEAR,

Berenice D., d. 11/19/1926 at 57/4/3 in Portsmouth; accountant;
widow; b. New Castle; William Trefethen (New Castle) and
Izette Neal (New Castle)

SPILLER,

Jay Roy, d. 2/21/1920 at 43/5/6 in New Castle; N.Y. employee;
married; b. Concord; John J. Spiller and Lucy Carter (Concord)

SPINNEY,

Paschal M., d. 7/2/1917 at 67/1 in Portsmouth; married

STALEY,

John Bridgford, d. 3/13/1972 at 86 in Portsmouth; married; b. NY;
Bowen Staley and Elizabeth Jones

STANDISH,

Myles, d. 7/5/1962 at 64 in Portsmouth; married; b. Anson, ME; Fred
    D. Standish and Josie Piper

STARKEY,

Gladys G., d. 4/18/1981 at 89 in Portsmouth; Edgar F. Gilkey and
    Rosalie St. Thomas

STARR,

George A., d. 8/23/1953 at 69 in Concord; mechanic; widower; b.
    MA; John Starr and Elizabeth Parsons

Helen P., d. 10/31/1950 at 66 in New Castle; at home; married; b.
    Henniker; Charles H. Peasley and Annette Jones

STEIN,

Fred, d. 6/1/1977 at 27 in New Castle; Merril Stein and Leona Berg

STENZEL,

Herman, d. 11/11/1933 at 68/11/23 in New Castle; weaver; widower;
    b. Germany; ----- Stenzel (Germany)

STEVENS,

Robert Gordon, Jr., d. 11/20/1993 in New Castle

STEWART,

Constance, d. 12/18/1933 at 57/11/27 in New Castle; at home;
    married; b. Liverpool, England; Frederick Broadhead (England)
    and Mary Morris (Wales)

Jeremy P., d. 7/9/1991 at 21 in Portsmouth

Robert K., d. 1/8/1982 at 66 in Portsmouth; Robert A. Stewart and
    Adeline G. Simmons

STOCKMAN,

Arch E., d. 9/22/1913 ar 34/0/8 at Ft. Constitution; acute alcohol
    poisoning; soldier; single; b. Arkansas

STOWE,
Winnefred Grace, d. 9/15/1912 at -- in Portsmouth; premature birth;
    b. Portsmouth

STRINGHAM,
Edward B., III, d. 4/4/1992 at 64 in Portsmouth

STUART,
Ethel Urch, d. 6/10/1966 at 83 in Lowell, MA; widow; b. NH;
    Ephriam Urch and Arabella -----
Kenneth A., d. 8/7/1948 at 65/2/4 in Lowell, MA; married

SULLIVAN,
Bernadette M., d. 6/9/1989 at 79 in New Castle; Morris McGary and
    Catherine Devitt
James B., d. 3/24/1987 at 81 in New Castle; James B. Sullivan and
    Catherine Coughlin

SVENDSEN,
Gustav, d. 7/4/1956 at 85 in Manchester; machinist; married; b.
    Norway

SWEET,
Eleanor K., d. 8/24/1992 at 82 in New Castle

SWEETSER,
Harriette S., d. 8/21/1954 at 45 in New Castle; at home; married; b.
    NH; Harold Stewart and Constance Broadhead
Jane W., d. 6/9/1977 at 58 in Portsmouth; Newton Wood and
    Margaret Twaits

SYLVESTER,
James E., d. 3/25/1945 at 66/3/25 in Portsmouth; ship fitter; married;
    b. Quincy, MA; James Sylvester (Brunswick, ME) and Julia
    Raymond (Brunswick, ME)

TABBUTT,

Arlene R., d. 8/10/1949 at 41 in New Castle; housewife; married; b. New Castle; Benjamin Ricker (New Castle) and Sadie White (New Castle)

Clifford Colon, d. 7/3/1980 at 81 in Addison, ME; Eugene Tabbutt and Viola Naughton

Richard C., d. 12/3/1990 at 55 in Portsmouth; Clifford C. Tabbutt and Arlene Ricker

TALBOT,

Beatrice B., d. 1/21/1974 at 72 at Edgewood Manor; married; b. ME; Henry S. Milton and Jeannette Gammon

Harlan M., d. 9/27/1985 at 84 in Portsmouth; William M. Talbot and Inez Maxwell

William W., d. 1/11/1957 at 80 in Portsmouth; pharmacist; widower; b. ME; Archie Lee Talbot and Nina V. Adams

TARBELL,

Edmund A., d. 10/7/1954 at 56 in Boston, MA; retired; married; b. NH; Edmund Tarbell and Emeline Souther

Edmund C., d. 8/1/1938 at 76/3/6 in New Castle; artist; married; b. W. Groton, MA; Edmund W. Tarbell (Groton, MA) and Mary Fernald (Groton, MA)

Emeline A., d. 9/22/1947 at 82/5/12 in Portsmouth; at home; widow; b. So. Boston, MA; Harrison P. Souther (New Bedford, MA) and Mercy Smith (New Bedford, MA)

TARLTON,

Ann E., d. 4/18/1896 at 89/2/4

C. S. P., d. 4/30/1911 at 69 in Brentwood; arteris sclerosis; stone mason; single; b. New Castle; Stillman Tarlton (New Castle, seaman) and Laura Priest (New Castle)

Carrie E., d. 3/25/1945 at 84/1/7 in No. Hampton; at home; widow; b. Isles of Shoals; John C. Poole (Edgecomb, ME) and Angeline E. Caswell (Rye)

Carrie E., d. 10/21/1955 at 73 in Eliot, ME; housewife; widow; b. Portsmouth; Robert Hall and Elizabeth -----

Charles C., d. 10/5/1920 at 57/5/17 in New Castle; helper; widower; b. New Castle; Boardman Tarlton (New Castle) and Eliza Jane Frost (New Castle)

Elias, d. 5/21/1939 at 82/4/23 in Portsmouth; ret. USS Serv.; married; b. New Castle; Elias Tarlton (New Castle) and Mary Ann Batson (New Castle)

Elias C., d. 3/13/1950 at 56 in New Castle; US Navy Yard; married; b. New Castle; Elias Tarlton and Carrie E. Poole

Elizabeth Tredick C., d. 12/20/1927 at 80/10/20 in Boston, MA; single; b. New Castle; Henry Tarlton (New Castle) and Adeline Yeaton (New Castle)

Harriet, d. 11/25/1901 at 54 in Brentwood; pneumonia; housewife; married; b. New Castle; William H. Franklin (New Castle) and Maria S. White (New Castle)

Jane P., d. 3/18/1903 at 54/9/7 in Portsmouth; cancer; single; b. New Castle; Thomas J. Tarlton (New Castle, merchant) and Pauline Priest (New Castle)

Mary A., d. 12/1/1898 at 62 in New Castle; diabetes; housewife; married; b. New Castle; Samuel Batson (New Castle) and Mary Neal (New Castle)

Mary Adaline, d. 4/18/1908 at 85/8/28 in New Castle; old age; widow; b. New Castle; Edward Yeaton (New Castle) and Elizabeth Chase (Rye)

Mary Louise, d. 12/23/1918 at 46/9/12 in New Castle; at home; married; b. New Castle; Jonathan Emery (Biddeford, ME) and Louisa S. Baker (New Castle)

Nathan B.F., d. 1/3/1892 at 54/5 in New Castle; carpenter; widower; b. New Castle; father and mother both b. New Castle

Pauline Priest, d. 1/2/1899 at 80/7/26 in New Castle; pneumonia; housewife; widow; b. New Castle; Nathan Priest (Nottingham) and Jane Vennard (New Castle)

Thaddeus, d. 7/31/1905 at 72/11/11 in New Castle; cancer; widower; b. New Castle; John A. Tarlton (New Castle) and Annie E. Vennard (New Castle)

William Marvin, d. 5/14/1933 at 64/11/14 in Newington

THEILER,
Annie M., d. 10/5/1994 in Portsmouth; b. 8/1/1896*

THOMITS,
Albert R., d. 11/23/1990 at 68 in Portsmouth; Frank Thomits and
Greta Randall
Myrtle M., d. 9/1/1989 at 62 in New Castle; Joseph Harris and
Katherine Nugent

THOMPSON,
E. M., d. 7/29/1948 at 74/0/7 in North Hampton; at home; widow; b.
York, ME; Charles Johnson and Ida Adams

THURBER,
Roger Bliss, d. 5/30/1961 at 55 in New Castle; married; b. MA;
Clinton D. Thurber and Winifred Russell

TILTON,
John P., d. 2/18/1927 at 42 on NY, NH & H RR en route; married; b.
Lewiston, ME; John Tilton

TOWNER,
Edith B., d. 1/22/1951 at 79 in Portsmouth; at home; widow; b. New
Castle; Rufus Yeaton and Louise Amazeen

TREDICK,
Dorothy, d. 12/16/1894 at 81 in New Castle; married; b. New Castle;
Jonathan Locke and Dorothy Vennard
Henry, d. 8/26/1896 at 85/6

TREFETHEN,
Apollonia, d. 11/18/1942 at 66/4/21 in New Castle; housewife;
widow; b. Galicia, Austria; Ignacy Oczko (Austria) and Urszuha
Knaczyk (Austria)

Dorothy, d. 7/15/1902 at 72/0/6 in New Castle; heart disease; housewife; widow; b. New Castle; James Randall (Rye, seaman) and Dorothy Vennard (New Castle)

Ella E., d. 3/30/1902 at 46/7/20 in Exeter; apoplexy; housewife; widow; b. New Castle; Abram Trefethen (New Castle) and Frances Deverson (Portsmouth)

Frances E., d. 9/2/1893 at 33/6/4; phthisis pulmonalis; housewife; married; b. Portsmouth; Joseph Rogers (Portsmouth, printer) and Eliza Berry (Kittery, ME)

George O., d. 12/11/1895 at 39/2/5; married; b. New Castle; William Trefethen (New Castle) and Izette Neal (New Castle)

Hannah, d. 4/9/1936 at 62/2/21 in Brentwood

Helena W., d. 6/3/1931 at 74/8/4 in Portsmouth; single; b. New Castle; Dorothy Randall (New Castle)

Hope G., d. 3/17/1940 at 87/2/13 in New Castle; at home; single; b. Newington; John I. Trefethen (Rye) and Elizabeth R. Mason (Rye)

Judson, d. 5/17/1938 at 74/4/19 in Concord; laborer; married; b. New Castle; William Trefethen (New Castle) and Izette Neal (New Castle)

Lewis H., d. 2/7/1920 at 55/2/2 in Concord; painter (retired); single; b. New Castle; William Trefethen

Margaret A., d. 4/1/1906 at 84/0/7 in Somerville, MA; bronchitis

Maude H., d. 12/10/1956 at 82 in New Castle; school teacher; single; b. New Castle; William Trefethen and Izette Neal

Ordway H., d. 3/17/1895 at 0/9/3; b. New Castle; Judson Trefethen (New Castle) and Apollonio Oczko (Galacia, Austria)

William, d. 4/8/1896 at 63/3

William D., d. 10/1/1919 at 69/0/20 in Brentwood; laborer; single; b. New Castle; Abram Trefethen (New Castle) and Frances Deverson (Portsmouth)

TREMBLAY,
David Walker, d. 4/26/1993 in New Castle

Joseph L.E., d. 5/1/1963 at 27 in New Castle; single; b. NH; Arthur Tremblay and Emelda Bouchard

TRIPP,

Leslie Raymond, d. 5/27/1959 at 60 in Portsmouth; married; b. MA; Arthur G. Tripp and Ida May Stratton

TRUSSELL,

Gilbert A., d. 8/12/1940 at 78/6/29 in New Castle; fisherman, ret.; single; b. New Castle; Gilbert Trussell (Camden, ME) and Sarah A. Becker (Isles of Shoals)

Gilbert M., d. 9/9/1909 at 77/7/24 in New Castle; intersticial nephritis; married; b. Camden, ME; Jacob Trussell (Camden, ME) and Sarah Derry (Camden, ME)

Sarah C., d. 11/20/1917 at 76/5/23 in New Castle; at home; widow; b. Isles of Shoals; Henry Becker (Germany) and Annie Pray (North Berwick, ME)

TUCKER,

Willard, d. 10/9/1918 at 24/6 at Fort Constitution; soldier; married; b. Willimantic, CT; Amelia Tucker (Dover, NH)

TURNER,

Deborah, d. 11/26/1895 at 83/11/18; widow; b. Duxbury, MA; Noah Simmons (Duxbury, MA) and Abby Sampson (Duxbury, MA)

Mildred R., d. 2/13/1980 at 58 in New Castle; William Roberge and Etta May Pierce

TWITCHELL,

Ruth R., d. 3/18/1970 at 72 in Portsmouth; married; b. NH; Frank M. Dennett and Annie Carroll

UNDERHILL,

Catherine, d. 7/29/1937 at 66/8/13 in New Castle; at home; single; b. Brooklyn, NY; Samuel R. Underhill (NY) and Mary A. Woodhull (NJ)

URCH,

Arabella, d. 8/7/1916 at 81/5/10 in New Castle; widow; b. New Castle; George Vennard (New Castle) and Abigail Frost (New Castle)

Ephraim, d. 9/17/1915 at 76/5/4 in Portsmouth; arteris scherosis; painter; married; b. England

Ephriam, d. 1/1/1944 at 71 in Danvers, MA; Ephriam Urch (England) and Arabella Vennard (New Castle)

VENNARD,

Abigail, d. 9/1/1891 at 82/2/20 in New Castle; housekeeper; married; b. Dover; father and mother both b. New Castle

Dorothy N., d. 12/13/1903 at 91/3/2 in Portsmouth; apoplexy; single; b. New Castle

Eliton Gillis, d. 8/29/1969 at 59 in Portsmouth; married; b. NH; Harry W. Vennard and Ethel Gillis

George, d. 1/6/1902 at 94/10/26 in New Castle; old age; widower; b. New Castle; George Vennard (New Castle) and Dorothy Bell (New Castle)

Hannah F., d. 5/31/1895 at 88/10/15; widow; b. New Castle; Samuel Batson (New Castle) and Annie Fernald (New Castle)

VILES,

Elizabeth F., d. 9/21/1975 at 82 in New Castle; Bert J. Fellows and Edith Warren

WAINSCOTT,

Denise M., d. 2/28/1983 at 64 in Portsmouth; Francois-Marie Margry and Elise M. Brobet

William H., d. 11/10/1980 at 63 in Portsmouth; William F. Wainscott and Lily A. McDonnell

WALKER,

Lena Dean, d. 3/29/1901 at 36/4/15 in New Castle; valv. disease of heart; housewife; married; b. Vanceburg, KY; Richard Stout (Vanceburg, KY, lumber dealer) and Mary Dean (Carrollton, KY)

WARGO,

Jessie, d. 5/10/1949 at 44/2/16 in Newtown, CT; housewife; married;
b. New Castle; Amory J. Meloon (New Castle) and Seddie S.
Yeaton (New Castle)

WARREN,

George H., d. 5/27/1954 at 93 in New Castle; lawyer; widower; b.
MA; Lafayette Warren and Mary Barnard

Mary B., d. 2/1/1969 at 67 in Portsmouth; single; b. NH; George H.
Warren and Mary Palmer

Mary H., d. 4/6/1952 at 87 in New Castle; at home; married; b.
Groton, MA; Moses Palmer and Martha Eaton

WEBB,

Ella Lillian, d. 9/8/1964 at 75 in Portsmouth; widow; b. MA; Thomas
H. Berry and Sadie F. Hilton

George, d. 10/24/1959 at 82 in Brentwood; married; b. MA; George
Webb and Minnie Fisher

Lawrence Downing, d. 7/6/1968 at 78 in New Castle; married; b. MA;
Eli L. Webb and Suzan B. Brown

Thomas H., d. 5/24/1979 at 63 in New Castle; George L. Webb and
Ella Berry

WEBSTER,

Charles, d. 9/4/1908 at 2 hrs. in New Castle; premature birth; b.
Portsmouth; Ora Cook (ME)

WELCH,

Charlotte M., d. 9/30/1980 at 66 in Portsmouth; Henry E. Campbell
and Rose McCarron

James M., d. 9/22-23/1983 at 16 in New Castle; Francis E. Welch and
Marguerite Conner

WELLS,

Anna M., d. 1/18/1933 at 77/6/26 in New Castle; at home; widow; b. New Castle; Edward B. Amazeen (New Castle) and Adaline B. Yeaton (New Castle)

Selden F., d. 7/3/1920 at 64/10/9 in New Castle; coast guard; married; b. Kennebunkport, ME; Selden F. Wells (Kennebunkport, ME) and Hulda Thompson (Kennebunkport, ME)

WESTERFELD,

Edward H., d. 6/6/1993 in Portsmouth; b. 6/2/1903*

WHALEN,

Michael J., d. 5/14/1979 at 82 in Portsmouth; Edward Whalen and Alice Clohessy

WHEELER,

George W., d. 9/30/1906 at 63 in Togus, ME; cerebral hemorrhage; James W. Wheeler (VT) and Louisa Brown (Wakefield)

Isabelle Rand, d. 3/17/1918 at 74/11/12 in Portsmouth; divorced

James W., d. 4/3/1906 at 71/2/3 in New Castle; ulcer of stomach; gov. boatman; married; b. New Castle; James W. Wheeler (VT) and Louisa Brown (Wakefield)

Selma H., d. 9/4/1915 at 40/11/10 in Portsmouth; paresis; clerk; married; b. Lynn, MA; James W. Wheeler (New Castle, shoemaker) and Isabelle ----- (ME)

WHITE,

Abby A., d. 8/1/1899 at 79 in Boston, MA; dysentery; housewife; widow; b. New Castle; Edward Martin (New Castle) and Phebe Tuttle (Dover)

Abigail S., d. 7/2/1907 at 81/1/26 in New Castle; arteris sclerosis; widow; b. Kittery, ME

Adeline B., d. 10/13/1900 at 86 in New Castle; debility from old age; widow; b. New Castle; William White (New Castle) and Sarah Curtis (Kittery, ME)

Albert H., d. 3/15/1902 at 78/4 in New Castle; cerebral hemorrhage; laborer; married; b. New Castle; Robert White (New Castle) and Elizabeth Batson (New Castle)

Albert S., d. 7/3/1929 at 72/6/8 in Portsmouth; retired; widower; b. New Castle; George S. White (New Castle)

Andrew Belle, d. 1/15/1955 at 78 in Portsmouth; machinist; married; b. New Castle; Andrew H. White and Clara Vennard

Andrew H., d. 4/29/1916 at 73/6/21 in New Castle; painter; widower; b. New Castle; Isaac White (New Castle) and Rebekah Tredick (New Castle)

Anna B., d. 5/3/1986 at 80 in New Castle; Andrew B. White and Octavia Becker

Arnold Bernard, d. 3/28/1975 at 89 in New Castle; Llander White and Elizabeth Murphy

Arthur Franklin, d. 10/8/1963 at 83 in New Castle; widower; b. ME; Franklin White and Clara Mallon

Barbara Adelaide, d. 7/3/1918 at 92/8/1 in Concord; widow; b. NS; Jacob Hubley (NS) and Elizabeth Winott (NS)

Benjamin F., d. 7/11/1892 at 71/6 in Brentwood; carpenter; widower; b. New Castle; father and mother both b. New Castle

Bert, d. 4/28/1937 at 69/2/5 in New Castle; shoe stitcher; single; b. New Castle; Charles H. White (New Castle) and Sarah F. Randall (New Castle)

Bertha F., d. 7/25/1978 at 77 in Dover; Benjamin Farrow and Bertha Heap

Catherine H., d. 8/31/1912 at --/8/9 in New Castle; cancer of liver; housewife; married; b. New Castle; Duncan Buchanan (Scotland) and Elizabeth Quint (Scotland)

Charles H., d. 5/3/1893 at 60/10/20; pneumonia; fisherman; married; b. New Castle; Robert White (New Castle, fisherman) and Elizabeth Batson (New Castle)

Charles Haven, d. 3/19/1918 at 54/10/23 in New Castle; shoemaker; divorced; b. New Castle; Charles H. White (New Castle) and Sarah F. Randall (New Castle)

Charles W., d. 8/29/1909 at 81/9/19 in New Castle; arteris sclerosis; widower; b. New Castle; Charles W. White (Baltimore, MD) and Mary A. Vennard (New Castle)

Charlotte Campbell, d. 10/18/1958 at 89; widow; b. NH; James M. Meloon and Charlotte Campbell

Clara Seymour, d. 5/9/1914 at 68/10/16 in New Castle; senile dementia; housework; married; b. New Castle; George Vennard (New Castle, farmer) and Abigail Frost (New Castle)

Clarence M., d. 9/28/1930 at 68/10/28 in New Castle; marine pipe fitter; married; b. New Castle; James White (New Castle) and Catherine Buchanan (New Castle)

Eliza J., d. 3/12/1919 at 85/2/11 in Portsmouth; b. New Castle; Nathan White (New Castle) and Elizabeth ----- (New Castle)

Elizabeth, d. 4/12/1926 at 84 in Brentwood

Elizabeth J., d. 10/17/1917 at 60 in New Castle; at home; widow; b. Boston, MA; Michael Murphy

Ellen, d. 5/11/1891 at -- in Portsmouth; housekeeper; married; b. NS; father and mother both b. NS

Ellison, d. 3/12/1931 at 85 in Brentwood; b. New Castle; Thomas B. White (New Castle) and Julia Staples (Eliot, ME)

Faustina W., d. 2/11/1908 at 49/1/20 in Portsmouth; cerebral hemorrhage; b. New Castle; James White (New Castle, laborer) and Kate Buchanan

Frances A.C., d. 2/7/1905 at 80/6/4 in New Castle; pneumonia; widow; b. New Castle; Edward T. Yeaton (New Castle) and Elizabeth Chase (Rye)

Frances E.S., d. 6/28/1908 at 85/9 in New Castle; cerebral hemorrhage; married; b. New Castle; William Kinnear (New Castle) and Mary Martin (New Castle)

George S., d. 5/23/1901 at 78/5/9 in New Castle; cerebral hemorrhage; shoemaker; married; b. New Castle; Benjamin White (New Castle) and Elizabeth Martin (New Castle)

Harry H., d. 6/25/1931 at 44/8/7 in Portsmouth; Charles White (New Castle) and Susie French (Portsmouth)

Herman, d. 12/10/1927 at 62/0/29 in New Castle; supt. electrician; married; b. New Castle; Charles H. White (New Castle) and Sarah Randall (New Castle)

James, d. 12/18/1912 at --/5/10 in New Castle; arterio sclerosis; laborer; widower; b. New Castle; Thomas White (New Castle, fisherman) and Julia Staples (Eliot, ME)

James W., d. 11/26/1931 at 76/2/10 in New Castle; cement tester; married; b. New Castle; Charles H. White (New Castle) and Sarah F. Randall (New Castle)

John Vennard, d. 7/19/1915 at 89/6/3 in New Castle; arteris scherosis; carpenter; widower; b. New Castle; Charles W. White (Baltimore, MD, none) and Mary A. Vennard (New Castle)

Joseph, d. 6/21/1919 at 76 in Portsmouth; fisherman; single; b. New Castle; Thomas White (New Castle) and Julia Staples (Eliot, ME)

Julia, d. 1/27/1914 at 77 in Concord; lobar pneumonia; housework; single; b. New Castle; Thomas White (New Castle, mariner) and Julia Staples (Eliot, ME)

Katie E., d. 9/9/1932 at 73/10/16 in New Castle; at home; widow; b. Isles of Shoals; John H. Robinson (Isles of Shoals) and Mary Ann Becker (New Castle)

Leander, d. 7/16/1915 at 71/6/5 in New Castle; diabetes gangrene; US lt. keeper; married; b. New Castle; Thomas B. White (New Castle, seaman) and Julia Staples (Eliot, ME)

Louise E., d. 9/30/1952 at 63 in Portsmouth; at home; married; b. Cape Elizabeth, ME; Edgar Jordan and Marion Stevenson

Margarett A., d. 7/26/1918 at 79/7/26 in Portsmouth; single; b. NS; Nathan White (New Castle) and Elizabeth White (New Castle)

Mary A., d. 5/1/1919 at 80/9/27 in Portsmouth; widow

Mary Adelaide, d. 2/10/1929 at 90/7/7 in Newburyport, MA; widow; b. New Castle; William C. Yeaton (New Castle) and Maria Yeaton (New Castle)

Nathan, d. 5/22/1921 at 82 in Concord; widower; b. New Castle; Thomas B. White (New Castle) and Julia Staples (Eliot, ME)

Nellie M., d. 11/6/1947 at 64/3/2 in New Castle; at home; married; b. Bath, ME; Joseph W. Sullivan (NS) and Jane Killam (NS)

Octavia, d. 5/20/1962 at 82 in Portsmouth; widow; b. New Castle; Henry Becker and Ellen Amazeen

Percy H., d. 9/1/1947 at 66/0/28 in Portsmouth; shoe worker; widower; b. New Castle; Charles H. White (New Castle) and Susan French (Portsmouth)

Percy Wilson, d. 2/19/1971 at 69 in Dover; married; b. ME; Arthur White and Nellie Sullivan

Rebecca R.W., d. 5/7/1901 at 72/1/11 in New Castle; cerebral hemorrhage; housewife; married; b. Newmarket; Joseph Watson (Newmarket) and Mary Dearborn (Newmarket)

Richard G., d. 5/15/1949 at 26 in Alton; aero. mech.; single; b. New Castle; Arnold B. White (New Castle) and Louise E. Jordan (Cape Elizabeth, ME)

Robert F., d. 4/18/1902 at 76/6/16 in New Castle; heart disease; seaman; married; b. New Castle; Robert White (New Castle) and Elizabeth Batson (New Castle)

Sarah Evelyn, d. 9/16/1942 at 77/0/14 in North Hampton; at home; widow; b. York, ME; Rufus Emery (Springvale, ME) and Julianne Fernald (York, ME)

Sarah F., d. 2/23/1919 at 86/3/21 in New Castle; widow; b. New Castle; James Randall (New Castle) and Dorothy Vennard (New Castle)

Stillman H., d. 1/3/1922 at 64 in New Castle; fisherman; single; b. New Castle; Thomas White (New Castle) and Georgina Tarlton (New Castle)

Sullivan H., d. 2/18/1905 at 65/0/6 in New Castle; heart disease; married; b. New Castle; Robert White (New Castle) and Elizabeth Batson (New Castle)

Temperance, d. 5/23/1907 at 74/2/6 in New Castle; cancer; divorced; b. New Castle; Abram Amazeen (New Castle, seaman) and Sarah Tucker (Portsmouth)

Theresa W., d. 2/2/1939 at 85/8/23 in New Castle; at home; single; b. New Castle; John V. White (New Castle) and Mariam Trefethen (New Castle)

Warren Mahlon, d. 2/20/1976 at 58 in Portsmouth; Arnold B. White and Louise Jordan

Webster T., d. 2/23/1920 at 49/6/21 in Portsmouth; laborer; single; b. New Castle; George O. White (New Castle) and Temperance White (New Castle)

William G., d. 6/4/1947 at 65/8/25 in New Castle; chief eng.; married; b. New Castle; James W. White (New Castle) and Katie E. Robinson (Isles of Shoals)

WHITEHOUSE,

Alice Chamberlin, d. 3/29/1995 in Portsmouth; b. 2/29/1908*

Charles Edwin, d. 12/1/1926 at 85/9/9 in Portsmouth; widower

Edwin E., d. 12/30/1951 at 84 in Portsmouth; barber; married; b. New Castle; Charles E. Whitehouse and Dorcas Cole

Etta Blanche, d. 1/15/1960 at 91 in Portsmouth; widow; b. ME; Thomas D. Seawards and Lucinda Lewis

WHITEMAN,

Leslie William, d. 6/1/1958 at 3/4/23; b. FL; Elmer E. Whiteman and Patricia M. Barbour

WHITLOCK,

Walter LeRoy, d. 12/15/1909 at 2/10/15 in New Castle; membraneous croup; b. New Castle; Paul Whitlock (Harrisburg, PA) and Ethel Manson (Merrimac, MA)

WHITTEMORE,

Ruth A., d. 5/3/1911 at 90/1/20 in Portsmouth; pneumonia

WILLIAMS,

Bessie, d. 6/8/1970 at 88 in Brentwood; widow; b. NH; Charles White and Susie W. French

Chester, d. 9/15/1957 at 83 in Kittery, ME; USA ret.; married; b. PA; William Williams and Phoebe Warner

Clarence O., d. 12/9/1917 at 48/10/20 in Newark, OH; shoecutter; single; b. New Castle; Augustus Williams and Fannie A. White (New Castle)

Gladys Austin, d. 4/25/1996 in New Castle; b. 4/8/1918*

Mabel M., d. 1/10/1980 at 92 in Portsmouth; John Pridham and Marie Larue

WITHAM,

Charles Edward, d. 5/13/1958 at 82; widower; b. ME; James E. Witham

Gardner D., d. 7/9/1955 at 70 in New Castle; metal shop; married; b. Madison; Moses H. Witham and Edith Sanborn

WITHINGTON,

Gertrude, d. 3/22/1966 at 90 in Kittery, ME; widow; b. NH; William W. Cotton and Anna Moses

Henry S., d. 5/15/1945 at 71/5/18 in New Castle; accountant; married; b. Jamaica Plain, MA; Henry Withington (Brookline, MA) and Clara E. Lincoln (Jamaica Plain, MA)

WOOD,

Myrtle Olive, d. 2/19/1969 at 71 in Portsmouth; married; b. ME; William J. Manson and Gertrude Grover

Ralph Thompson, d. 5/22/1980 at 89 in Portsmouth; Fred L. Wood and Lizzie Thompson

WOODMAN,

Alfred King, d. 2/8/1966 at 69 in Portsmouth; married; b. ME; Daniel N. Woodman and Hattie W. Kendall

Mary Earlene, d. 1/17/1990 at 70 in Portsmouth; Andrew Horning and Ivalou Emery

WOODS,

William A.H., d. 10/30/1945 at 37/0/17 in Portsmouth; machinist; married; b. Woburn, MA; William H. Woods (Bath, ME) and Mary Haywood (Woburn, MA)

WOODSUM,

Frances D., d. 12/10/1903 at 0/4/6 in Boston, MA; pneumonia

WOODWARD,

Geraldine H., d. 4/24/1984 at 71 in New Castle; LeRoy W. Haywood and Ellen I. Winn

WORDEN,

Ellen L., d. 5/1/1946 at 65/1/8 in Portsmouth; at home; widow; b. New Castle; James Card (New Castle) and Mary Tarlton (New Castle)

Frances, d. 7/8/1908 at 11/1/1 in Portsmouth; diphtheria

Nelson Ellsworth, d. 3/14/1959 at 46 in Portsmouth; single; b. NH; William F. Worden and Ellen Card

William Frederick, d. 12/22/1959 at 60 in Portsmouth; divorced; b. NH; William F. Worden and Ellen Card

WRENSCH,

Frances B., d. 10/26/1977 at 90 in Miami, FL; Harry F. Backus and Ada M. Dustan

WRIGHT,

Alice E., d. 7/17/1997 in Portsmouth; b. 3/16/1916 in West Roxbury, MA; Marcus Hulbig and Lydia Alice Willey

Marion P., d. 12/18/1953 at 84 in Portsmouth; housewife; married; b. NH; John Bickford and Charlotte Frost

Matie Cannon, d. 9/20/1960 at 71 in York, ME; married; b. NY; William Baker and Attilla Pratt

YEATON,

Alexis A., d. 2/19/1897 at 46/7; single

Ambrose, d. 7/7/1912 at --/1/27 in New Castle; apoplexy; single; b. New Castle; John Yeaton (New Castle) and Dorothy Amazeen (New Castle)

Byron S., d. 8/27/1945 at 86/8/25 in Portsmouth; sheet m. worker; widower; b. New Castle; John E. Yeaton (New Castle) and Sarah E. Yeaton

Eben, d. 4/8/1911 at 73/4/4 in New Castle; apoplexy; seaman; single;
b. New Castle; Eben Yeaton (New Castle, seaman) and
Hephzibah Meloon (New Castle)

Edward P., d. 1/17/1913 at 62/5 in Raymond; arteris sclerosis;
railroading; b. New Castle; Nathaniel Yeaton (New Castle,
seaman) and Susan R. Coggin (West Port, NS)

Florence A., d. 6/20/1928 at 59/9/19 in New Castle; at home; married;
b. New Castle; Andrew H. White (New Castle) and Clara S.
Vennard (New Castle)

Harry S., d. 10/2/1944 at 76/7/12 in Portsmouth; joiner, vet.; married;
b. New Castle; John E. Yeaton (New Castle) and Sarah E. Yeaton
(Rye)

Helen Louise, d. 5/3/1957 at 87 in New Castle; at home; widow; b.
NH; Sullivan H. White and Mary Oliver

John E., d. 6/6/1922 at 88/11/14 in State Hospital; laborer; widower;
b. New Castle; Benjamin Yeaton (New Castle) and Mary J.
Yeaton (New Castle)

John W., d. 10/20/1916 at 78/10/16 in Kittery, ME; single

Louisa M., d. 9/12/1902 at 54/7/12 in New Castle; carcinoma of
intestines; housewife; married; b. New Castle; Alfred Meloon
(New Castle) and Dorothy Yeaton (New Castle)

Maria, d. 12/20/1898 at 86/11/8 in Haverhill, MA; infirmities of age;
burial permit

Marriam, d. 3/30/1911 at 78/7/10 in New Castle; pneumonia;
housekeeper; married; b. New Castle; William J. Amazeen (New
Castle, seaman) and Lucretia Trefethen (Kittery, ME)

Mary Jane, d. 4/19/1897 at 83/6/8; widow; b. New Castle; Isaac
Yeaton (New Castle) and Jane Mitchell (Kittery, ME)

Nathaniel, d. 3/2/1907 at 85/1/12 in Wakefield, MA; acute nephritis;
seaman; married

Nathaniel B., d. 12/29/1926 at 84/6/20 in Concord; fisherman;
widower; b. New Castle; Henry Yeaton (NH)

Rufus A., d. 7/17/1911 at 78/9/8 in New Castle; pneumonia; laborer;
widower; b. New Castle; Philip Yeaton (New Castle) and
Elizabeth Berry (Rye)

Sarah A., d. 3/4/1899 at 68/6/24 in New Castle; cerebral hemorrhage; housewife; married; b. Rye; Hopley Yeaton (Rye) and Lydia S. Foye (New Castle)

Susan R., d. 10/6/1912 at --/65/6 in Raymond; asthenia; widow

William Joseph, d. 5/16/1914 at 85/11/9 in New Castle; apoplexy; laborer; widower; b. New Castle; John Yeaton (New Castle) and Dorothy Amazeen (New Castle)

YOCUM,

Patricia L., d. 8/10/1975 at 82 in Brentwood; Patrick Lally and Ann Byrne

YORK,

Marie C-L., d. 8/25/1997 in New Castle; b. 5/26/1949 in Hopkinton, MA; George F. York and Joyce Emma Mary Allen

YOUNG,

G. L., d. 10/24/1949 at 73/2/28 in Portsmouth; widow; b. New Castle; Sheldon F. Wells (Cincinnati, OH) and Anna W. Amazeen (New Castle)

Heritage Books by Richard P. Roberts:

Alton, New Hampshire Vital Records, 1890–1997

Barnstead, New Hampshire Vital Records, 1887–2000

Barrington, New Hampshire Vital Records

Dover, New Hampshire Death Records, 1887–1937

Gilmanton, New Hampshire Vital Records, 1887–2001

Marriage Records of Dover, New Hampshire, 1835–1909

Marriage Records of Dover, New Hampshire, 1910–1937

Milton, New Hampshire Vital Records, 1888–1999

Moultonborough, New Hampshire Vital Records

New Castle, New Hampshire Vital Records, 1891–1997

New Hampshire Name Changes, 1768–1923

New Hampshire Name Changes, 1923–1947

Ossipee, New Hampshire Vital Records, 1887–2001

Rochester, New Hampshire Death Records, 1887–1951

Vital Records of Durham, New Hampshire, 1887–2002

Vital Records of Effingham and Freedom, New Hampshire, 1888–2001

Vital Records of Farmington, New Hampshire, 1887–1938

Vital Records of Lyme and Dorchester, New Hampshire, 1887–2004

Vital Records of New Durham and Middleton, New Hampshire, 1887–1998

Vital Records of North Berwick, Maine, 1892–2002

Vital Records of Orford and Piermont, New Hampshire, 1887–2004

Vital Records of Pittsburg, New Hampshire, 1904–2008

Vital Records of Sandwich, New Hampshire, 1887–2007

Vital Records of Tamworth and Albany, New Hampshire, 1887–2003

Vital Records of Tuftonboro and Brookfield, New Hampshire, 1888–2005

Vital Records of Wakefield, New Hampshire, 1887–1998

Vital Records of Warren, New Hampshire, 1887–2005

Wolfeboro, New Hampshire Vital Records, 1887–1999